TEACHING ENGLISH LANGUAGE LEARNERS IN MAINSTREAM CLASSES

MARGERY HERTZBERG

CONTRIBUTIONS BY JANET FREEMAN

PETAA
PRIMARY ENGLISH TEACHING
ASSOCIATION AUSTRALIA

First published 2012
Primary English Teaching Association Australia (PETAA)
Laura St, Newtown, NSW 2042, Australia
PO Box 3106, Marrickville Metro, NSW 2204
Tel: (02) 8020 3900
Fax: (02) 8020 3933
Email: info@petaa.edu.au
Website: www.petaa.edu.au

ISBN: 978-1-875622-85-6

National Library of Australia Cataloguing-in-Publication entry
   Author: Hertzberg, Margery, 1956-
   Title: Teaching English language learners in mainstream classes /
   Margery Hertzberg ; contributor, Janet Freeman.
   ISBN: 9781875622856 (pbk.)
   Notes: Includes bibliographical references and index.
   Subjects: English language--Studing and teaching--Foreign speakers.
   Mainstreaming in education.

Copyright © Primary English Teaching Association Australia (PETAA) 2012

Cover and internal design by Nice Stuff
Illustrations by Nice Stuff
Edited by Fiona Sim
Indexed by Fiona Sim
Project management by Rema Gnanadickam
Printed in Australia by Ligare Pty Ltd

Copying for educational purposes

The Australian *Copyright Act 1968* allows a maximum of one chapter or 10 per cent of this book, whichever is greater, to be copied by any educational institution for its educational purposes, provided that the educational institution (or the body that administers it) has given a remuneration notice to Copyright Agency Limited (CAL) under the Act.
For details of the CAL licence for educational institutions, contact CAL, Level 15, 233 Castlereagh Street, Sydney, NSW 2000, Australia, Tel: (02) 9394 7600, Fax: (02) 9394 7601, email: info@copyright.com.au

Copying for other purposes

Except as permitted under the Act, for example fair dealing for the purposes of study, research, criticism or review, no part of this book may be reproduced in any form or by any means without the prior written permission of the publisher.

This book has been printed on paper using fibre supplied from plantation or sustainably managed forests.

Dedication

For my children, Sarah and Mark Sproule; my father Mark Hertzberg and in memory of my mother Nancy Keesing (Hertzberg). In their different ways, they have helped me understand more about language learning and use.

Acknowledgements

Many people are involved in the production of a book and I wish to acknowledge the various ways people have assisted, and express my gratitude for their generosity of time and expertise.

Much of this book draws on research from the Fair Go Project which is a research partnership between the School of Education, University of Western Sydney and the NSW Department of Education and Communities' Priority Schools Programs. I wish to thank the academics and teachers who have been my fellow co-researchers. This dedicated team is committed to improving social and academic outcomes in the poorest of schools.

My thanks to Janet Freeman* for her contribution as the author of Chapter 6: Focus on writing, and our frequent chats on ELL matters.

I acknowledge the many dedicated and voluntary hours that the skilful PETAA publishing committee gives to reviewing PETAA publications in general, and the time that it gave to this book in particular. I thank them, the PETAA staff, the editor Fiona Sim and the designer Elizabeth Douglass. Thank you also to Valerie Martin for her review and edits of many drafts.

Numerous other people also read and debated drafts and I express my sincere gratitude to: Robert Jackson, John Hughes, Geoff Munns, Kerrie Reid, Joanne Rossbridge, Kim Self, Alyson Simpson, Margaret Turnbull and Annalies van Westenbrugge.

Thank you to Rebecca Hillis, who welcomed me into her classroom and collected many of the work samples and photos in this book. This book would not have been possible without Rebecca's support or the generous assistance of the following people, who also provided work samples and/or photos: Sue Barrett, Caterina Batieri, Diane Bojdak, Jacqueline Brewer, Maria Carbone, Kathryn Cleary, Georgia Constanti, Mark Diamond, Gurjeet Garewal, Kirsty Gillgren, Wendy Morrison, Nada Nona, Monica Palmer, Stacey Parker, Tiffany Parker, Kerrie Reid, Kate Russell, Helen West, Nicole Wade, Lauri Wilson, and all the students from the various schools around Australia and in particular Lansvale Public School.

---

* Janet Freeman is currently an ESL/Multicultural consultant for the NSW Department of Education & Communities. Janet is also a part-time lecturer in the Faculty of Education and Social Work at the University of Sydney, where she is enrolled as a PhD student. She is researching academic language development in English language learning classrooms.

CONTENTS

	Preface	1
ONE	Language learning and language use	5
TWO	Who are our English language learners?	11
THREE	Pedagogical conditions for learning a language	29
FOUR	Focus on oracy	48
FIVE	Focus on reading	76
SIX	Focus on writing (written by Janet Freeman)	108
SEVEN	Role to communicate: Learning English through drama	133
	Conclusion	171
	References	176
	Index	183

PREFACE

The purpose of this book is to assist mainstream teachers who may have minimal or no specialist assistance to cater for the English language learning needs of their students across all subject areas. Depending on a student's background, it can take about seven to ten years to become proficient in academic English, and so early English learning intervention programs alone are not sufficient. Furthermore, the English demands in all subject areas mean that all teachers in all grades need to be equipped to plan appropriately for these learners. Planning appropriately means providing an *English language learning* program that will meet the diverse language needs of all English language learners. This book will assist you to cater for the increasing academic language demands students will face at school, focusing on students in the middle years of schooling who have been learning English for two or more years.

In Australian primary schools, a mainstream teacher is a teacher who teaches the same class in most curriculum areas for most of the day. In such a situation, planning for the needs of a child with minimal English can be daunting. Below is a letter from a parent to his child's mainstream teacher. The eleven-year-old boy referred to in this letter had recently arrived in Australia and had little English. He was truanting because he did not like school.

Dear …

Thank you for your letter. I didn't know that my son doesn't attend the lessons. I had a very serious conversation with my son. I'm sure that he'll attend all lessons after that. The reasons why my son didn't attend the lesson, as he told me. He has only two lessons a week special English. All the rest of the time he has nothing to do except lessons on the mathematics. He is rather shy and afraid to speak to other boys because he knows English very badly. That is also the reason that he feels very dull attending all other lessons. I hope that he would benefit greatly if he has more lessons in the special English. If he miss a lecture in the future, please send me a letter because neither I nor my wife has possibility check attending the lessons by our son.

Yours sincerely …

The maths lessons the parent referred to focused on algorithms. The teacher was at a loss for what to do. Actually the statements in the letter are not entirely accurate. The child did participate in creative arts and PE and the teacher did attempt to include him in other maths, English, science and social studies activities, but it is fair to say with little success and/or knowledge about the need to teach English in all subject areas, and by implication how to teach English. The child was justified in feeling unhappy. The teacher was me! I subsequently established a very good relationship with the parents and they were most supportive. In fact, the child was a gifted mathematician and by the end of the year was teaching one of the maths groups the concept of equivalent fractions. I also had a really supportive principal (Mr Bevin Wilson) who in my first year of teaching was able to attain special funding for me to attend a six-week intensive course on teaching English Language Learners (ELLs). Since then I have completed further studies to extend my understanding of the ways in which mainstream teachers can support English Language (EL) learners.

Schools in Australia are diverse both in the numbers of EL learners and the multiplicity of cultural and linguistic backgrounds of their students. With some exceptions, the number of students who have been learning English for two years or more is greater in most schools than the number of students beginning to learn English. As will be explained in subsequent chapters, students who have been learning English for two to five years may use English proficiently in familiar and casual social situations (sometimes referred to as 'playground English' or 'conversational English') but still need ELL support in order to attain proficiency in academic language. That is the focus of this book. The book's paramount aim is to provide mainstream teachers with strategies to engage and enhance the *academic English proficiency* of students who have been learning English for two or more years.

Acronyms

At the time of writing, EAL/D (English as an Additional Language or Dialect) is the term used in the Australian Curriculum (www.acara.edu.au/curriculum/eald_teacher_resource/eald_teacher_resource.html), replacing the still commonly used term ESL (English as a Second Language). EAL/D is used because it acknowledges the students in our schools who may already speak (and possibly read and write) in two or more languages and/or dialects.

EAL/D suggests an additive function and implicitly validates that the person does have an existing language(s) and/or dialect(s). The word additional acknowledges this wealth of linguistic ability as an asset. In contrast, the 'non' in Non-English Speaking Background (NESB), another common term, is reductive because it does not signify that these people can speak other languages or dialects. It should also be noted that NESB is not synonymous with learners of English. Many multilingual speakers are proficient in English.

Preface

In many countries, such as Canada, USA, Ireland and England, the term ELL (English Language Learners) is increasingly replacing ESL or EAL or EAL/D to encompass this diverse range. Similarly, many international journals now use the term ELL. It is for these reasons then that the term EL learner or ELL is used throughout this book.

Acknowledging a person's bilingual or multilingual skills as an asset for emotional, social and academic reasons will be explored in subsequent chapters. Nevertheless, this book begins by validating the knowledge, experiences and resources young bilingual or multilingual students already have.

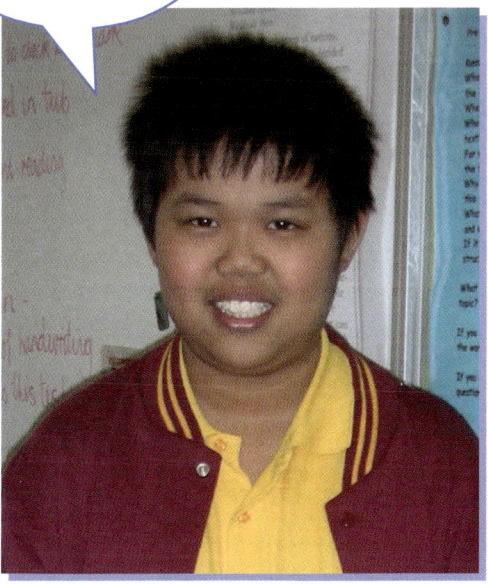

Just some of the languages and dialects children might speak in an Australian classroom

Structure of this book

Chapters 1, 2 and 3

The first three chapters examine the more general ELL theory and thus provide a foundation for the following four chapters that examine specific theoretical principles as they relate to oracy, reading and writing.

Chapters 4, 5, 6 and 7

These four chapters look specifically at teaching and learning strategies to assist students' development of academic English across a variety of subject areas. The suggestions are by no means a definitive list of possibilities but they exemplify major English language learning pedagogical principles as discussed in chapters 1, 2 and 3. In the main, the teaching and learning strategies are appropriate for students in the Developing and Consolidating phases of English language learning (refer to pages 13 and 14 for these definitions). The aim is to assist mainstream teachers who may have minimal or no specialist English language teaching support. The phrase 'focus on' in the title for each of these chapters is used to indicate that the discussion is specific to that mode. That is, each chapter focuses on many of the major theoretical principles related to either oracy or reading or writing and then illustrates how these are translated in practice. However, in reality there should not be an artificial separation and when reading about specific strategies in each chapter, you will see that many strategies incorporate oracy and/or reading and/or writing. This is more explicitly demonstrated in chapter 7: 'Role to communicate: Learning English through drama'. Not only does this chapter highlight how drama is an effective way to use both non-verbal and spoken language to enhance reading and writing, it also makes clear that in practice oracy, reading and writing are linked in teaching and learning sequences.

    The examples are often illustrated with authentic and recent student work samples. Where ICTs (information and communication technologies) are used, they are embedded within the learning activity as a tool and not a strategy in themselves. Similarly, the strategies highlight that assessing learning is an ongoing process as both teachers and students evaluate progress. The student work samples that illustrate strategies result from each teacher's knowledge of each student's entry point and were planned and implemented accordingly. Teachers will need to modify the suggestions according to the specific needs of the students they teach as well as the curriculum requirements for their context.

CHAPTER ONE
LANGUAGE LEARNING AND LANGUAGE USE

Recently I was on a ferry and overheard the following conversation between a grandmother and her eighteen-month-old granddaughter:

Child: *Train!*

Grandmother: *Yes a train on the Harbour Bridge. The trains go on the bridge. We're going under the bridge. Under the bridge goes the ferry. On the bridge goes the train.*

Child: *Under bridge, under bridge.* (As the ferry progressed under the bridge.)

Very young children learn their first language in the context of an authentic 'here and now' situation. I'm fairly sure this grandmother had not started the journey intending to give her granddaughter a lesson on prepositions! Rather, as she interacted with her granddaughter she engaged in a conversation and in so doing was using the language function of position and the prepositions of *under* and *on*.

Learning an additional language at school cannot of course replicate the one-to-one ratio and 'here and now' context between a carer and very young child, but in a classroom we should aim to provide teaching and learning experiences which provide children with many opportunities to practise the target language in situations which are authentic and purposeful. Language learning must therefore occur in all subject areas. Language learning is not just the domain of subject English and/or isolated and segregated skills-based instruction. For example, learning the language of science while engaged in a science activity makes more sense, and so by implication the science teacher is also an English language teacher.

Subsequent chapters will provide strategies that enable students to use language for an authentic purpose within all subject areas. For example, in Chapter 5 there is an idea for teaching prepositions and this occurs within a

PE lesson. Language learners also need frequent reinforcement and good and regular models of the target language (both verbal and written) to assist their progression and again this will be addressed in subsequent chapters. For example Chapter 5, on reading, explains why well crafted factual and fiction texts are important for progress in reading. In addition to this book, teachers are also referred to the Australian Curriculum's *English as an Additional Language or Dialect: Teacher Resource (EAL/D) V1.1* (at www.acara.edu.au/curriculum/eald_teacher_resource/eald_teacher_resource.html). These support materials have been designed to assist mainstream teachers identify the areas where EL learners may require additional assistance.

First however, a brief introduction to the theory of language learning that underpins the method and practice of teaching. The strategies outlined in subsequent chapters are based on the view that language is a social act and that we use language according to the context of the culture. Well known sociolinguistic theorists Halliday & Hasan (1985) argue that within the sociocultural context we then make choices about how we use language dependent on the genre to be used (purpose) and the circumstances. Figure 1.1 illustrates this.

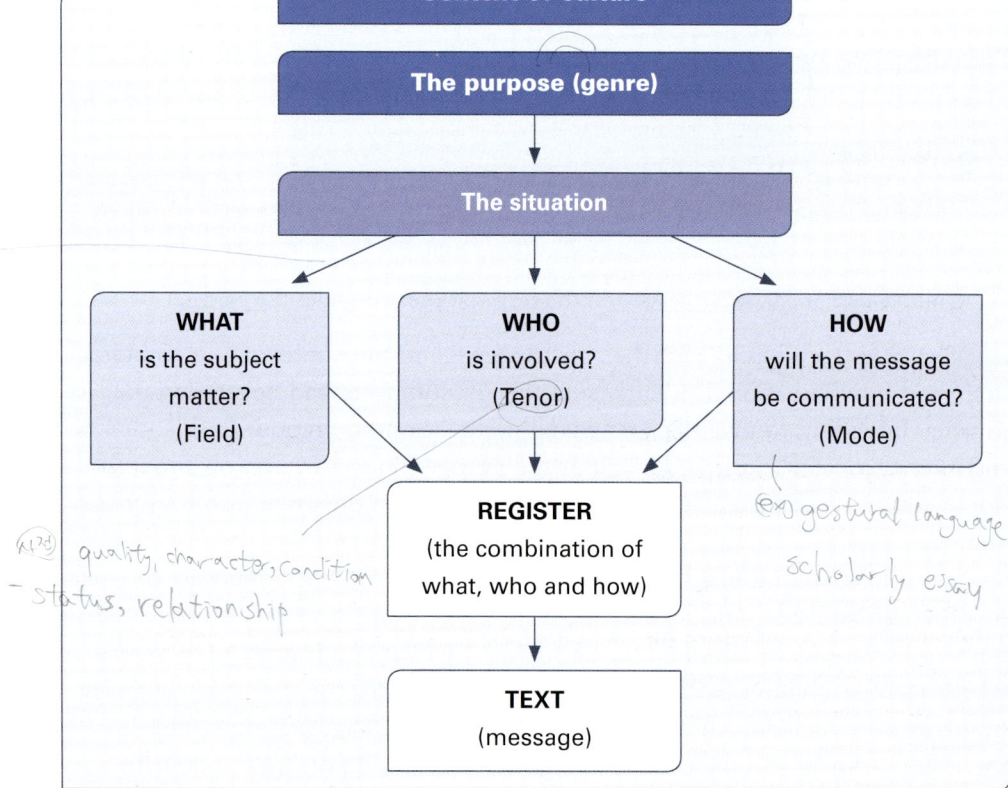

Figure 1.1
Language choices are dependent on these variables

- **Sociocultural context:** This means that choices about the language used will vary and will depend on for example, gender, socioeconomic status, age, education, ethnicity and whether the person lives in a rural or urban setting. For instance, when and how colloquial language is used or the degree of formality between younger and older people will vary according to perhaps one's cultural background.

- **Situational context:** Within this sociocultural context (and then the purpose and hence the genre), the circumstances or situation in which the language is being used will also influence the language choice and will depend on field, tenor and mode.
  - **Field:** Field refers to the topic matter. The topic matter will determine the technical language needed. On a continuum, therefore, the language might range from very common everyday language to very specific and technical language particular to a certain subject.
  - **Tenor:** Tenor refers to the status or relationship between the participants. For example, writing a text message to a good friend informing them of a party might be different from a text message to a grandparent inviting them to dinner. Similarly the choice of language used when speaking to a good friend might be very different to that used when speaking with a supervisor. Knowing the appropriate tenor to use can be difficult for many EL learners and can cause embarrassment.
  - **Mode:** Mode refers to the way a message is transmitted. Communicating the message ranges from face-to-face talk which often includes gestural language, to a scholarly essay.
- **Register:** Collectively, the topic matter (field), the relationship of the people communicating (tenor) and the way the message is communicated (mode) is referred to as the register and the register selected is dependent on the *purpose*. Knowing what the purpose is and then having the appropriate language for this purpose presents difficulties for many EL learners. For example, the two texts below relate to a car accident and the subsequent reporting of events to a police officer. Both are spoken texts.

> **Text 1 (spoken):** *Well the light went green. Whoosh – right through* (gestures with arms) – *didn't see him and bang!* (Claps hands together to make a banging sound.)
>
> **Text 2:** *I was stopped at the traffic lights right here on Parramatta Road and when they went green I proceeded to go, but that car* (pointing to the car) *came from that road and went through the red light and we collided.*

Both texts are from a face-to-face interaction but the language choices are different. Text 1 relies more on paralinguistic language (non-verbal elements such as body language, gesture and facial expressions) to explain the situation. However, to convey the event more precisely (in this case, for the police officer to write a report), it would be better to provide both more detail and use more complex language for accuracy. That is, the language needs to be more **lexically dense**. Since the situation is face to face, the police officer would be able to ask questions to elicit the required information, but Text 2 would be more expedient and useful. That is, the register for the purpose (genre) is more appropriate. While Text 2 still relies on face-to-face interaction with its absence of clear directions, it is further advanced in providing information and is progressing towards 'talk written down' which on an insurance claim form might be written thus:

> **Lexically dense** in this case means that there needs to be more subject-specific vocabulary (collision, traffic, intersection, proceeded and so forth). Written language is usually more lexically dense but formal spoken language usually needs to be as well.

Text 3: The collision occurred at the intersection of Parramatta Rd and Norton St. I was stopped at the traffic lights on Parramatta Rd. When these lights changed to green I accelerated, but the car from Norton St went through the red light and we collided.

Figure 1.2 illustrates the different spoken and written modes along a continuum from most informal and contextualised to most formal and decontextualised. If we plot these three texts on the continuum, Text 1 is the most informal and relies on the immediate 'here and now' context to convey much of the information, whereas Text 3 must rely on written language (with perhaps a diagram) to explain precisely because the communication is occurring devoid of a 'here and now' context – it is a decontextualised situation.

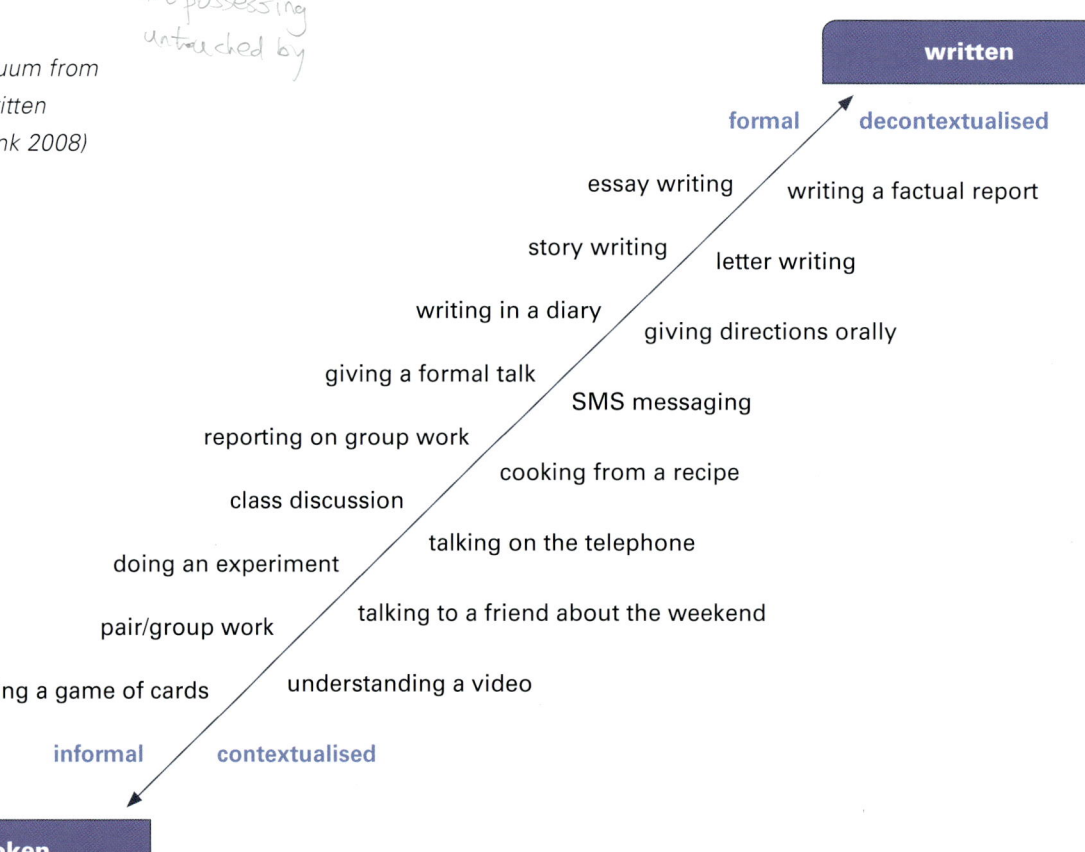

Figure 1.2
Mode continuum from spoken to written
(© Cruickshank 2008)

Many English language learners in our classes would be able to relay the event in a similar way to Text 1, but Text 2 might present difficulties and certainly the written text with its use of, for example, **nominalisation** (collision) could be problematic.

Cummins (1979, 1981, 2008) explains the learning of a language as progressing from BICS (basic interpersonal communication skills) to CALP (cognitive academic language proficiency). Since about 2007, Cummins has been using the term 'conversational English' to replace BICS and 'academic language proficiency' to replace CALP. These later terms will be used throughout this book.

> **Nominalisation** is when a verb or adverb is made into a noun (eg collide becomes collision). It makes the sentence or paragraph more compact and sophisticated, but can be more difficult for ELLs to both read and write.

Cummins argues that it takes about one to two years to attain conversational English (which is sometimes called playground English) and about five to eight years to develop 'academic language proficiency'. It therefore takes anywhere from about six to ten years to acquire academic language proficiency, which Thomas and Collier (2002) suggest is often dependent on the amount of formal schooling in the home language, an important point that will be returned to. Research by Hakuta, Butler & Witt (2000) found that for students with disrupted schooling (such as those from a refugee background), it could take from seven to ten years to acquire academic proficiency *with* specialist support.

Academic language proficiency

Being competent in basic social interactions is not enough for academic achievement. Academic language proficiency refers to the language choices (both grammar and vocabulary) needed within a particular field (subject area) and it is this academic language proficiency that must be addressed in our teaching. In Text 3 on page 8, not only is the detail clear, but using the word *intersection* to define position, nominalising the verb *collide* and using the term *accelerate* makes the message more condensed. At the same time it can be understood away from the immediate context.

Using this everyday example, we can apply the same concept to all subject-specific areas across the curriculum. Requiring students to report back to the class or group on an activity is common and useful. EL learners may be proficient in doing this informally and especially with the aid of gestural language and/or a picture or model to aid them. The difficulty comes when required to rely only on the academic language (meaning the technical language and supporting structures of the content or subject area) as the example below illustrates.

> **Text 4 (nine-year-old girl giving her sport report at assembly):** *Yesterday the girls in the Under 10's Netball won against Bluevale Primary School. Nada won the 'player of the match' because she was the best one at getting a ball into the goal when the other team missed at getting the ball into the goal. But all the girls played really well and Ms Fisher said they are getting much better at keeping one foot still as they turn around to get the ball.*
>
> **Text 5 (nine-year-old girl giving her sport report at assembly):** *Yesterday the Under 10's Netball Team beat the opposing team, Bluevale Primary School. Nada won the 'player of the match' award because she got the most rebounds. However, Ms Fisher said that all the girls should be congratulated because their pivoting had improved.*

Without the specific teaching of both the subject-specific vocabulary and syntactical structures, many students are at risk of 'fossilisation'.

Fossilisation

Fossilisation is another term common in ELL literature. The strict definition is:

> … a process which sometimes occurs in which incorrect linguistic features become a permanent part of the way a person speaks or writes a language. (Richards et al, 1992: 142)

The metaphor of a fossil is often also extended to describe those students who remain stuck at the level of informal or casual language and/or who do not use the technical language pertaining to subject-specific content. That is, with the absence of teaching and learning experiences that explicitly focus on the academic or technical content language, EL learners are at risk of remaining entrenched at the level of conversational English. Teaching the technical vocabulary begins early, as evidenced in my visit to a kindergarten class (five- to six-year-olds) in their third week of formal schooling. Many of the children were EL learners. They had been reading the book *Grandpa and Thomas* (Allen, 2003). When asked why they liked the book so much, one child replied that he *liked the onomatopoeia* in the repetitive refrain 'Swish, swash, swoosh sings the sea'. The teacher had taught this term to provide students with the technical (academic) vocabulary associated with literary techniques. In a student essay in later years, a statement that 'the author's use of onomatopoeia provides a clear image of the sound of waves' is going to be superior to 'the author uses groups of words to make the sound of the waves'.

But it is not only the teaching of subject topic vocabulary that is important. Understanding how to use complex grammatical structures is also important, as well as opportunities to use high order thinking skills such as comparing, synthesising, evaluating and inferring. Subsequent chapters will provide specific strategies, but in order to know what to teach and how to teach we need to know our students and the next chapter addresses this.

CHAPTER TWO
WHO ARE OUR ENGLISH LANGUAGE LEARNERS?

An English language *learner* (ELL) is someone still attaining native or near-native proficiency in English. Near-native proficiency means that the student can very competently use the *academic registers* specific to the field (subject matter) to communicate and so some bilingual or multilingual students in the middle schooling years may meet this proficiency. This is explained in Figure 2.1. These students might only need minimal EL learning support but in many cases will need cultural support, especially in terms of content that is very culturally specific. This will be discussed further in Chapter 3.

Nevertheless, and as explained in Chapter 1, being able to use the academic registers within specific curriculum fields is the critical aspect for success at school. Because it can take seven to ten years to attain near-native proficiency, most students will need targeted and systematic ELL support and the amount and type of support is dependent on many factors, discussed further in this chapter.

At the time of writing, the first version of the Australian Curriculum and Reporting Authority (ACARA) *English as an Additional Language or Dialect: Teacher Resource (EAL/D)* was published on its website (at www.acara.edu.au/curriculum/eald_teacher_resource/eald_teacher_resource.html). This resource (which is being updated frequently) will be referred to throughout this book as it aims to assist teachers who are not ELL specialist teachers in many and varied ways. With reference to English language learning progression, the document identifies four phases. These descriptions of phases are reproduced on pages 12–14 and I have also indicated the approximate length of time for each phase. It is recommended, however, that readers view this resource online because the table is just a summary. The resource provides very specific detail to inform teachers about the language learning characteristics typical of EL learners at different stages of schooling (Foundation to Year 10) and within each of the modes (listening, speaking, reading/viewing and writing). Note also that ACARA uses the term EAL/D, which the reader can substitute for ELL.

> ACARA: *English as an Additional Language or Dialect: Teacher Resource V 1.1*: www.acara.edu.au/verve/_resources/EALD_teacher_resource.pdf.

Broad descriptions of the characteristics of learner groups at each of four phases of English language learning

> Depending on age, learning ability and social adjustment an ELL will typically move beyond this phase after a period of about eight months to one year, *with* specialist ELL support.

Beginning English: Some print literacy in first language

The beginning English phase of learning includes a sub category of limited literacy background, to describe the development of reading/viewing and writing behaviours typical of students with little or no experience of literacy in language.

Characteristics of this learner group

Each phase describes a period of significant English language learning development. There will be differences between a student at the beginning of the phase and a student at the end of the phase.

These students are starting to learn English. They can speak one or more languages/dialects other than English and have an age-appropriate level of print literacy in their first language. They have had varying experiences of formal schooling and may be literate in their first language. In a familiar learning environment, they will begin to engage with simple language tasks of the curriculum, particularly with support from a speaker of their first language, and targeted contextual support (eg visuals and gestures). Learning a language requires intense concentration, and students are likely to tire when listening to and speaking English constantly. High levels of explicit teaching of specific EAL/D skills are required from both the specialist teacher and the classroom teacher. These students are capable of understanding the concepts of the curriculum for their year level. However, as they are new to learning in and about English, they will find it difficult to show achievement as described in the achievement standards for their year level, as these rely heavily on English language proficiency to convey content knowledge and understandings.

Age-related considerations

While many of these characteristics are applicable to all students beginning to learn English, older students will have more life experiences as well as more developed cognitive abilities and will understand print in their first language. They draw upon their first language literacy knowledge as they learn English.

Beginning English: Limited literacy background

These students are learning English for the first time, with little or no foundation in continuous, formal education. They can speak one or more languages/dialects other than English, but have little or no experience with print literacy in their first language. Some students may be unfamiliar with books, needing explicit teaching to understand that the print marks on the page symbolise meaning. In a familiar learning environment, they will begin to engage with simple curriculum demands, particularly with support from a speaker of their first language, and targeted

> Depending on age, learning ability and social adjustment an ELL will typically move beyond this phase after a period of about one to two years *with* specialist ELL support. The reason they take longer than those above is because they may have had interrupted schooling and do not have the conceptual understanding of print in their first language.

contextual scaffolds (eg visuals and gestures). Learning a language requires constant focus and attention, and students will tire easily and may experience a high level of frustration. High levels of explicit teaching are required throughout the day both from the specialist teacher and the classroom teacher. These students may be capable of understanding the content of the curriculum for their year level; however, as they are new to learning in and about English, they will find it difficult to show achievement as described in the achievement standards for their year level, as these rely heavily on English language proficiency to convey content knowledge and understandings.

Age-related considerations

While many of these characteristics are applicable to all students beginning to learn English, older students will have more life experiences as well as more developed cognitive abilities. They draw upon their first language knowledge as they learn English.

Emerging English

Characteristics of this learner group

Each phase describes a period of significant English language learning development. There will be differences between a student at the beginning of the phase and a student at the end of the phase.

These students can speak one or more languages/dialects, including basic English, and have a growing knowledge of print literacy in English. They understand and participate in classroom behaviours and school routines. They engage with curriculum demands with some success, but continue to benefit greatly from the use of first language with peers and teachers' assistants to clarify and consolidate understanding. Explicit and focused language teaching will enable them to produce simple written and spoken English, using predictable and learned formulas. They are still in a phase of language learning that requires intense concentration, so they are likely to tire during the day or disengage when the spoken or written texts under discussion are not accompanied by adequate contextual scaffolds. These learners still require extensive EAL/D explicit teaching throughout the school day from both the specialist teacher and the classroom teacher. These students are able to engage with and learn the content of the Australian Curriculum when provided with suitable language teaching and additional time to complete classroom activities. However, they will find it difficult to show their understandings if achievement must be demonstrated through language-reliant activities.

> Again this is dependent on age, learning ability and social adjustment. An ELL will typically move beyond this phase after a total period of about three to five years *with* specialist ELL support.

Developing English

Characteristics of this learner group

Each phase describes a period of significant English language learning development. There will be differences between a student at the beginning of the phase and a student at the end of the phase.

> This is dependent on age, learning ability and social adjustment. An ELL will move beyond this phase after a total period of about five to seven years *with* specialist ELL support.

These students can speak one or more languages/dialects, including functional Standard Australian English (SAE), and have a developing knowledge of print literacy in SAE. They are active participants in classroom and school routines, and are able to concentrate for longer periods. They purposefully engage with curriculum demands with increasing success. Their first language continues to be a valuable support, and these learners understand the value of code-switching; that is, the ability to change from one language/dialect to suit the context. They produce increasingly extended pieces of spoken and written SAE (although they may be more proficient in one mode than the other), which includes their own innovations with the language. However, they are still developing control over English grammar and building their vocabulary; hence, they continue to need explicit language to be taught, and teaching strategies supportive of EAL/D learners, particularly with the academic language of subject disciplines. They are increasingly able to use SAE sufficiently to demonstrate their understanding of content and thus meet some of the achievement standards for their year level, as described in the Australian Curriculum.

Consolidating English

Characteristics of this learner group

Each phase describes a period of significant English language learning development. There will be differences between a student at the beginning of the phase and a student at the end of the phase.

These students can speak one or more languages dialects and have a sound knowledge of Standard Australian English and have a developing knowledge of print literacy in Standard Australian English. They are active participants in classroom and school routines and are able to concentrate for longer periods. They purposefully engage with curriculum demands with increasing success. Their first language continues to be a valuable support, and these learners understand the value of code-switching (ie the ability to change from one language/dialect to suit the context). They produce increasingly extended pieces of spoken and written Standard Australian English (although they may be more proficient in one mode than the other), which include their own innovations with the language. However, they are still developing control over English grammar, and building their vocabulary; hence they continue to need explicit language to be taught, and teaching strategies supportive of EAL/D learners, particularly with academic language of subject disciplines. They are increasingly able to use Standard Australian English sufficiently to demonstrate their understanding of content and thus meet some of the achievement standards for their year level as described in the Australian Curriculum.

This is dependent on age, learning ability and social adjustment. An ELL will move beyond this phase after a total period of about five to seven years *with* specialist ELL support.

The explanation of phases on these pages comes from the Australian Curriculum and Reporting Authority's English as an Additional Language or Dialect: Teacher Resource V 1.1 (www.acara.edu.au/verve/_resources/EALD_teacher_resource.pdf, accessed 3 September 2011).

As stated previously ACARA's *English as an Additional Language or Dialect: Teacher Resource V 1.1* is a general guide and more specific learner characteristics from Foundation to Year 10 (approximately five- to sixteen-year-olds) can be found on the website. Additionally, it is important to consider the individual child. For example, some students may be in the Consolidating English phase in terms of oracy and reading, but their written work may be more within the Developing English phase.

To explain these phases with Cummins's (2008) distinction between 'conversational fluency' and 'academic language proficiency' as explained in Chapter 1, students in the Beginning and Emerging English phases will still be within the 'conversational fluency' phase range. That is, they rely on face-to-face interaction within familiar contexts and/or purposes and often need gestures and visuals to help contextualise the meaning. Nevertheless this does not imply 'low-level' tasks. Rather cognitively challenging and age-appropriate teaching and learning sequences need to be *adapted*. While students in the later part of the Developing English phase and within the Consolidating English phase will be further advanced in achieving 'academic language proficiency', they will still need targeted English teaching in learning how to analyse, synthesise and evaluate cognitively challenging concepts that may well be less contextualised and more linguistically demanding.

Additionally and importantly, the number of years of instruction given for each phase assumes *specialist English language teacher support* for EL learners. Many mainstream teachers will be in situations where their students are without specialist English language teacher support and so the number of years it takes their students to achieve 'academic language proficiency' is reliant on the mainstream teacher's experience and differentiated mainstream program.

Diversity among EL learners

Having ascertained who the ELLs in your class are and identified their English ability, it is then essential to find out about each student in order to best meet specific needs (both cognitively and emotionally). Students may have been born in Australia *or* arrived from overseas as migrants *or* arrived from overseas as refugees, *and* increasingly Australia is attracting more international fee-paying school-aged students. Figure 2.1 demonstrates this diversity.

The diverse experiences of EL learners have implications for programming. To find out about each student, you might use a survey similar to the one on pages 16–18 to supplement the mandatory forms that most Australian educational systems require and in so doing highlight to parents a respect for their linguistic and cultural heritage and affirm its importance and value in learning English.

This survey could be adapted to meet the specific requirements of individuals. For example, the word child is used on this generic form. It might be preferable to substitute child with the student's first name only because that may alleviate potential anxiety if for instance the carers are not the child's birth parents. Similarly, if you think some of these questions might cause unnecessary anxiety they can be omitted for reasons provided later in the chapter. It should also be noted that this type of survey is not exclusive to new arrivals. It is important to know the cultural and linguistic backgrounds of all your students.

From 2009 to 2010 visas were granted with the following status:
- 168 623 migrant visas (the largest percentage being people from the United Kingdom)
- 6003 refugee visas (the country of origin with the largest percentage was Iraq)
- 7767 humanitarian visas (the country of origin with the largest percentage was Iraq).

As well, 36 519 New Zealand citizens came as permanent or long-term arrivals.
(http://www.immi.gov.au/)

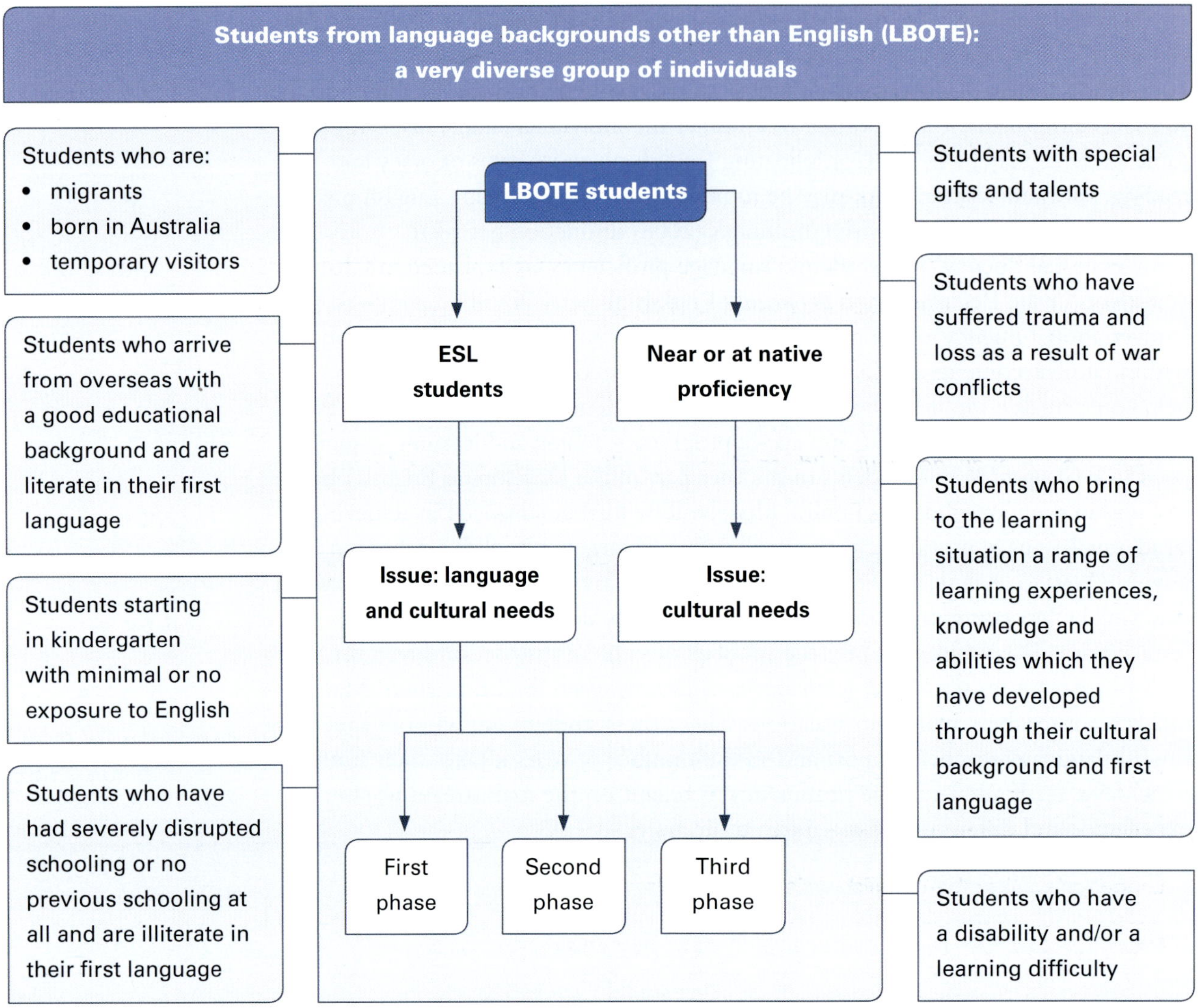

Students from language backgrounds other than English (LBOTE): a very diverse group of individuals

Students who are:
- migrants
- born in Australia
- temporary visitors

Students who arrive from overseas with a good educational background and are literate in their first language

Students starting in kindergarten with minimal or no exposure to English

Students who have had severely disrupted schooling or no previous schooling at all and are illiterate in their first language

LBOTE students
→ ESL students → Issue: language and cultural needs → First phase / Second phase / Third phase
→ Near or at native proficiency → Issue: cultural needs

Students with special gifts and talents

Students who have suffered trauma and loss as a result of war conflicts

Students who bring to the learning situation a range of learning experiences, knowledge and abilities which they have developed through their cultural background and first language

Students who have a disability and/or a learning difficulty

Figure 2.1
ESL learner diversity (© DET NSW)

Language and cultural profile sample survey

Name of student _____

Date of birth _____

Date of arrival in Australia (if born overseas) _____

Date of enrolment in first Australian school _____

All these answers can help your child's teacher prepare an educational program that best suits their needs. You need only answer the questions that are applicable to you.

General

What name does your child like to be called? _____

Who are our English language learners?

Child's country of birth? _____

If your child was born overseas:

How long did your child live in this country? _____

Has your child lived in any other countries before arriving in Australia, and for how long?

_____

Has your child been to another school in Australia? _____

Language background

The ability to speak another language is an advantage for learning English. It will help your teacher if she or he knows the languages your child can already speak and maybe read and write in.

Languages used regularly in the student's home in the following family situations:

Adult/adult	Adult/child	Child/adult	Child/child

Language(s) child spoke before age five _____

Language(s) used by other caregivers _____

Language(s) other than English which child is able to:

Read	Write

Child's dominant language (the one your child is most comfortable in)

_____

Languages other than English read and/or written by parents or carers:

	Read	Read Write
Mother/carer		
Father/carer		

Language(s) other than English your child is studying _____

Language(s) other than English your child would like to study _____

If your child can read and write in the home language, do you think they are achieving at expected grade level?
_____

If your child can speak English, when did your child first learn English? _____

Cultural background

What is your child's ethnic background (eg Lebanese, Greek) _____

Are there any specific cultural practices that the school should be aware of?

For example:

- are there any dietary requirements? _____
- Will your child sometimes need to be absent from school for religious occasions? _____

Are there any other cultural aspects that you would like the school to be aware of?
_____

Educational experiences (if applicable)

Did your child attend school in your home country? _____

If so, for how many years? _____

Are you aware of any difficulties your child has had at school? _____
_____

Has your child's schooling been disrupted due to unforeseen circumstances? _____
_____

Personal experiences and preferences

What activities does your child enjoy (eg sport, music, art, reading, cooking) _____
_____

Does your child have a favourite television program? _____

What would your child most likely choose to do in their spare time at home? _____
_____

Is there any other information that you think might help me in understanding the needs of your child?
_____
_____

Surveys such as this do not necessarily have to be sent home or completed by the administration staff at the time of enrolment. Rather, the survey might be used as the introduction at the first meeting with the parents or guardians. At this meeting (with an accredited interpreter), other matters would also be discussed and these matters as well as how to use an accredited interpreter are detailed on pages 26 and 27, but the survey is mentioned now to explain why this information is important for teachers.

The importance of student background information

Knowledge about competency in first language

Competence in the home language(s) helps students to learn subsequent languages. This is why teachers need to find out about the child's competency in the first language (L1) and always support the maintenance of L1 because learning English in an English-speaking schooling context is different from learning a foreign language as the student needs to:
- learn English
- learn *in* and *through* English (the concepts about a subject)
- learn *about* English (the grammar).

Usually when learning a foreign language as another subject at school or as an adult, one learns the language and about the language (the vocabulary, grammar and so forth). Learning *in* that language is usually not an objective. That is, one does not have to learn concepts within subject-specific fields at the same time as learning the language, and this is an important distinction to understand when addressing the needs of ELLs in our classrooms.

Contrary to common mythology (that purports that the younger you are, the easier it is to learn a new language at school), theoretically it should be easier to learn a new language at school once the first language(s) (L1) is reasonably well established which is about ten years of age (Collier, 1989; Thomas & Collier, 2002). This, however, is assuming that the student has not had interrupted schooling and/or other social and emotional factors that might impede language development. Students about ten years or older should be able to learn another language more quickly because often it is just a matter of transferring the many fundamental conceptual understandings already learnt in L1 into language two (L2). That is, the student can concentrate on learning about English rather than simultaneously learning *in* and *through* English (Gibbons, 2002, 2009). So, for example, if I was learning Italian and the lesson involved reading a recipe to cook risotto, I would have a conceptual understanding about recipes and their purpose. In addition, and using my previous knowledge of both cooking techniques and many of the ingredients, I could predict the likely procedure. I would therefore just need to learn both the Italian vocabulary and linguistic structures. Furthermore, because

I can read English (and Italian uses the same alphabetic system), I would not have to learn about the process of decoding again. Similarly, if a ten-year-old student is learning the English language vocabulary and structures associated with measurement in maths, but already understands the concept of volume and mass in L1 they have less work to do than the student who needs to learn the *concept* of volume and mass at the same time as learning the English topic language to use when discussing this mathematical concept (Gibbons, 2002). This is why some schools with a large number of students in a particular language group provide bilingual programs. For example, at Lansvale Public School in NSW, some of the students more proficient in speaking Vietnamese cover the same maths content as the English speakers, but in Vietnamese. However, such programs are not feasible in many schools. It is therefore really important that mainstream teachers encourage the use of L1 in the classroom as L1 remains a crucial resource for L2 learning. First language maintenance and the use of L1 does not interfere with learning L2, rather it will aid it (Collier, 1989; Cummins, 2000; Gibbons, 2009; Krashen, 1982).

Furthermore, when students are literate in L1 (as in the Italian lesson above) they already have highly developed concepts about the literacy *process* (albeit in another language). Literate students in L1 only need to learn how to read and write in English; they already understand the concept of what reading and writing *is*. This is in stark contrast to a student illiterate in L1 and hence without knowledge about the reading and writing process. Such students have double work because they need to learn about the concept of reading and writing as well as how to do so in English.

In summary, then, having well developed oral skills in L1 aids acquisition of a subsequent language. Acquisition of a subsequent language is even more enhanced if one is also literate in L1 (Collier, 1989; Cummins, 2000, Gibbons, 2009; Krashen, 1982). Nevertheless, it is common to hear people say that students in the early years of formal schooling (approximately four to eight years) *do* learn English faster than older students and they may well have evidence of this. Krashen, (1982) suggests that one significant reason for this is that the pedagogical approaches used in many early childhood environments provide better *conditions* for language learning. It is not because very young students learn more quickly than older students or adults. Subsequent chapters will explore the methodology and strategies best suited for learning a language – common practices in many **early childhood contexts**.

> **Early childhood** refers to children from birth to eight years. Language and literacy practices begin at birth. Settings within this parameter include students in preschool, family day care, long day care and the early years of formal schooling which in Australia is kindergarten/reception/foundation and Years 1 and 2.

Knowledge about the child's name and preferred name

Our name is part of our identity. It can be difficult to pronounce some names if one has no knowledge of a particular language, but it is important to learn to do so and to then ensure that the student's preferred name is used at all times. The significance of using the preferred name is illustrated very poignantly by the following student's comment:

Who are our English language learners?

> When I came to school (in Australia) the principal suggested to my parents that I use an 'English' name as it would be too difficult for my teachers and fellow students to pronounce and remember my name. My parents were keen to please the school so they decided my name would be Peter (this was the name of one of our neighbours). My name means heroism and strength and I was named after one of my father's best friends, who was killed in the war and who was strong and brave. I would like to be called by that name. Peter does not mean anything to me.

Knowledge about the child's religion and practices

This is important to know in determining excursion dates and other significant school events. The majority Australian religions are accounted for and school holidays organised accordingly. However, for other religions you may need to refer to a multi-faith calendar which many educational systems have on their website. For example, the Greek Orthodox Easter often does not coincide with the Australian Easter holiday period and nor do many non-Christian holy days. As well, some students will have dietary restrictions. Observant Muslims for instance do not eat any pig product and only Halal prepared beef and lamb. These requirements are important to know when planning school functions.

Teacher knowledge about first language

Knowledge about the first language is important because it will have implications for individual planning and, with respect to the particular linguistic and cultural contexts and needs of Aboriginal and Torres Straight Islander learners, information should be gleaned from consultation with the community. The discussion below provides some specific examples from other language groups with their implications for learning English:

Is the script Roman?

English uses the Roman script, as does Spanish and Vietnamese for instance, but Arabic and Greek for example do not. Therefore, a student familiar with Roman script (albeit different pronunciations for certain letters) is likely to learn the English alphabet more quickly. Refer to page 79–81 in Chapter 5 for further discussion.

Directionality of print

Arabic and Chinese do not read left to right. This can cause confusion for students learning English. A quick strategy is to mark each page of paper work books with an X and arrow in the left-hand corner of each page.

Grammar

A basic understanding of the learner's first language can make the teaching of English more expedient as then the differences can simply be explained. With older children, there may well be another child from the same language background who can do this.

For instance, in many South East Asian languages, indicating the plural is different to English. In Vietnamese for example, the noun remains constant (one apple, six apple).

1   Tôi đã một trái bôm.   I bought one apple.

2   Tôi đã saú trái bôm.   I bought six apple.

Hence, the difference needs to be explained and the concept of adding 's' or 'es' to a noun in English taught. In many languages such as Arabic and French, for example, the adjective follows the noun rather than preceding it and again, if one knows this, it can be quickly explained to students from these relevant language backgrounds.

Immigration experience: migrant or refugee?

Many ELL students were born in Australia, including bilingual or multilingual Aboriginal and Torres Strait students. Others will have a migrant or refugee family background. The difference between a migrant and a refugee is that migrants choose to move to another country (albeit because conditions in their home country might make this choice almost imperative). Nevertheless, they have had time to make the necessary legal arrangements as well as saying goodbye to their friends and family. Furthermore, where funds permit, they can return to their home country for a holiday or permanently. In stark contrast, refugees have had to flee their country and rarely have time to say farewell to family and friends, arrange finances, pack belongings and attend to other domestic obligations. Neither are they able to return to their country in the short term and possibly long term.

The remainder of this chapter addresses both general considerations for all ELLs as well as the specific needs of children who are refugees or who were born in Australia, but whose family members were refugees. With the amount of media attention at the time of writing this book, it is important to remember that Australia has a long history of accepting refugees and especially immediately post–World War Two. Although there are more migrant children in our schools than refugees, many children (born in Australia) may have parents who came to Australia as refugees and their experiences can (but not always) have an impact on their children.

> The *United Nations 1951 Convention Relating to the Status of Refugees*, to which Australia is a signatory, defines a refugee as a person who 'owing to a well-founded fear of being persecuted for reasons of race, religion, nationality, membership of a particular social group, or political opinion, is outside the country of his nationality, and is unable to or, owing to such fear, is unwilling to avail himself of the protection of that country' (see www.unhcr.org/pages/49da0e466.html).

There are organisations in every state that can assist in understanding more about refugees. The umbrella organisation is FASSTT (the Forum of Australian Services for Survivors of Torture and Trauma) and the website then directs to the specific organisation for each state or territory: www.fasstt.org.au/members/index.php. STARTTS, for example, is the NSW organisation and, like the other organisations around Australia, prepares informative presentations for teachers on the specific needs of refugee students. As well, the school counsellor should be informed when new refugee students arrive and meet with them when appropriate. Below are some of the specific points to be aware of in relation to refugee children.

Sensitivity to likely circumstances

First and foremost it is important to be aware of, and sensitive to, the likely circumstances of refugee children. Some children may have been born in Australia or were babies on arrival. Although they may not remember the circumstances surrounding the fleeing of their home, their older siblings and parents might well be suffering from their experiences and their anxiety may affect the child. Students who have had direct experience may have encountered or witnessed loved ones and family being killed or hurt or they may know friends or families that have 'disappeared'. Their homes and/or entire communities may have been destroyed. Such students will exhibit varying degrees of trauma and some will be more affected than others. Be aware that their trauma could affect their ability to trust others and develop positive relationships. They may also exhibit, for instance, low self-esteem, survivor guilt, aggressive outbursts or emotional numbness, sadness, withdrawal, sleeping problems. Some of my students' experiences are given below, as examples.

Experience 1: I did a lot of cooking with my Year 5 class (ten and eleven years old) to teach language and in this case the language function of instruction with an emphasis on verb types and present tense. At the same time I aimed to validate the various cultures in the class by cooking a variety of cuisines. All students were ELLs and the majority were late Beginning English phase to late Developing English phase. One day we cooked fried rice. Dan (a timid child and now a specialist doctor) yelled out that he hated fried rice and would not do this activity and burst into uncontrollable tears. Although I did try to calm him down and find out the reason for this unusual reaction (without success), I still went ahead with the cooking. Some of the rice stuck to the bottom of the frying pan and burnt. *That's why I hate fried rice! The burnt bits were the bits they gave us to eat in jail!* (Dan was imprisoned with his father after their first (failed) attempt to escape from Vietnam.) I am not suggesting that I should have had this very specific prior knowledge and neither is it appropriate to pry. In retrospect however, if I had been more attuned to the fact that many refugees exhibit varying degrees of trauma, I may have understood that this unusual outburst was signalling that I should have been more responsive to his needs.

Experience 2: At the end of one school year, I arranged a class picnic which involved a ferry trip. One parent (thankfully) met with me beforehand to explain that her son would not be coming because of his fear of boats after his boat ordeal from Vietnam to Malaysia. I was a better listener by then and had read more carefully about the needs and experiences of refugees. We caught a bus.

> **Experience 3:** Fire drills are regulatory policy and rightly so, but it is important to explain this very carefully to students and forewarn them when one is to take place. Although I had explained the practice of fire drills to my students, on one occasion I forgot to tell them that a fire drill was happening after lunch. The siren sounded. A large number of students instantly fled as far away from the school as possible. The siren's ring was reminiscent of bomb warnings back home. I did not forget in future!

As well as experiencing personal trauma, most refugees have lost family members and friends. Some students may be living with people who are close or distant relatives or non-biological family. They may or may not have known these carers before living with them. Alongside being cautious about the emphasis placed on celebrations such as Mother's and Father's Day, quite common activities such as constructing a family tree may be inappropriate, not only because of the trauma it will cause in being reminded that some or many relatives are dead, but because it is quite likely that the names of family members beyond the most recent generation are simply not known. A student I know was not a refugee, but his parents were survivors of the Pol Pot holocaust. It was a very anxious time for them when constructing a family tree was required for homework, because his parents were distressed. Not only could they not fill in the names, they did not wish to show their misery in front of their child.

Similarly, playing games that include being blindfolded should be avoided, as being blindfolded could have connotations linked to memories of being held captive. We also need to be mindful that some refuges have been incarcerated and may be fearful of being in a room with a closed door and/or a room with blinds covering the windows.

The precautions and examples noted above are certainly not exhaustive and space precludes giving more specific examples, but the examples above should help to provide an understanding of the importance of having a general knowledge of the possible experiences of these students and their families. Again, the FASSTT website is a most useful resource. As well as these more general considerations, it is important to be aware of a student's school experience.

Education

The child may have spent time in a refugee camp before arriving in Australia and so had periods of interrupted schooling. A considerable number may not have ever attended school in their home country and/or had interrupted schooling there. It is possible for instance, that a ten-year-old child will not know how to use a pair of scissors, or will be unfamiliar with other schooling equipment and all the many other classroom etiquette expectations we would expect of a child this age. Nevertheless, expect a lot from these students because they *do* want to learn and above all, fit in with their peers and have *friends*. If a school does not have ELL specialist teachers, it is advised that mainstream teachers meet with students privately to 'up skill' them. For those who show extreme resistance or anxiety, it is really important to refer them to appropriate counselling as quickly as possible.

Some students may have age-appropriate literacy skills in L1 and thus, for the reasons given earlier, will be in an advantageous position for learning English. Others will have experience with written English, but lack oral skills. For instance, it is quite common to find that some students have learnt to read in English, but do not speak the language well and so do not understand what they are decoding. That is, it is important to know whether they are reading (comprehending) or just decoding. This important aspect is explained in detail in Chapter 5.

Meetings and the home/school connection

Developing a positive and constructive home/school connection is important, which is why meeting with all parents is relevant. Earlier in this chapter an example of a survey for families from multilingual backgrounds was provided and it was explained why this information is important for teachers, especially in terms of their language and literacy practices. It was also suggested that this survey could be the introduction for a meeting that would cover other aspects of the child's life. Considerations about setting up the meeting, the use of an interpreter and likely topics to be covered are detailed below. Some of these things apply for all students and others are specific to people from refugee backgrounds.

Parents or carers?

As stated earlier, not all students will reside with their biological parent(s), so the word *carer* is now used throughout this chapter to denote the parent, other relative, friend or adult sibling.

Why more than a survey is important

Aside from the teacher finding out about the child, a face-to-face meeting is important to reassure both the student and carers that the teacher and school have their child's best interests at heart, both emotionally and intellectually. Meetings often make it possible to further ascertain the specific needs of a child which the carer may not have wanted to write on enrolment forms. Being mindful that at times it will be necessary to notify the school counsellor, it is important that teachers make contact quickly because informing carer(s) about general Australian schooling contexts, the school and the class programs in particular, will be very beneficial for both the student and the carer(s). Showing the carer where their child sits, some work samples, explaining regular routines and so forth helps establish a warm, trusting and caring relationship (again relevant to all students), but for carers unfamiliar with Australian schooling contexts it has the added advantage of making them familiar with a situation often markedly different to that in their country of origin. If they are refugees it could be probable that they have had traumatic experiences with persons in authority. For this reason, they might be wary of people in authority (and this includes teachers), which is another reason for establishing rapport.

Considerations when arranging the meeting:

- Do the carers work during school hours? It might be necessary to meet in the evening or early morning. This is why many schools hold open days on weekends to include one-on-one carer/teacher meetings as part of a larger open school event, and with greater success in terms of attendance because although some carers work on weekends they have found that on the whole this is more convenient. A whole day event also means that interpreters from a variety of language backgrounds can be employed for the day, making it more economical than 'one off' arrangements.
- Some carers may not be literate in the first language, because they too have missed out on the opportunity of an education. If unsure, then it is best to arrange for an interpreter to speak to the carer rather than send a translated letter. Large educational departments have access to or provide interpreting and translation services, as do organisations such as FASSTT. Increasingly, Google 'Translate' is also being used (http://translate.google.com/) but be aware that the translations are sometimes imperfect and meaning might be impaired.

Using a trained interpreter

It is desirable to use a trained interpreter because professional interpreters ensure accuracy in interpreting and, importantly, have been trained to be neutral in the process. It can be embarrassing and compromising for the carer to have a friend or child interpret, as confidentiality could be at risk. Using the child also alters the hierarchical position and can cause humiliation for both carer and child.

How to conduct the interview

- Try to arrange for the interview to be in the student's classroom so that carers can both observe and sense the safe, secure and happy environment and, as mentioned previously, it helps to familiarise them with some of the Australian educational practices as you show them around the classroom and then ideally the rest of the school.
- Be aware that for some carers who have been subjected to torture and interrogation, closed doors and drawn blinds might be reminiscent of 'interview rooms'. To this end, it is suggested that the door be left open and blinds are up.
- The triangular seating orientation shown in Figure 2.2 ensures that everyone is seated at an equal level and distance.
- Always maintain eye contact with the carer(s) and not with the interpreter. A professional interpreter understands the need for this and will not be offended.
- Allow enough time to brief the interpreter beforehand about the purpose for the meeting and the agenda. This avoids unnecessary conversation between the teacher and the interpreter during the meeting, which can in itself be very disempowering for the carer(s).

Figure 2.2
The ideal triangular seating arrangement for conducting interviews with an interpreter. note that the blinds and the door are open

- Be conscious that the power relationship between teacher and carer in some countries is different to that in Australia and carers may be hesitant to ask questions of someone in perceived higher authority. When explaining the purpose or agenda for the meeting, make clear that questions are encouraged throughout and that time is also allotted at the end for further comments and questions or clarification.

What might be discussed

As well as reassuring the carers that you have the child's best interests at heart and reporting on the student's progress to date, explain the Australian schooling system and your school's specific context and requirements. As well as showing them the child's classroom, resources and work samples it is also important to explain some of the more common wide-ranging procedures of Australian schooling as these could be very different to those in their home country. These could include:

- *Assessment and repetition of grades* Accurate communication about both assessment procedures and academic results is critical. In contrast with Australia, in some countries students repeat a year or a term if they do not pass examinations and they do not progress until they do pass. Sometimes parents assume that their child is meeting Australian grade/year/stage expectations because they have been progressed to the next year level and standardised testing results such as NAPLAN will not be relevant if the child has been in Australia less than twelve months and/or was not in Years 3, 5 or 7. It is important to explain your school's assessment and reporting practices because the child may in fact be achieving below the grade expectations and this can cause confusion and/or misinformation.

- *Excursions* Explain why excursions are an important learning experience, as in many countries excursions are not a common feature of the curriculum. Nevertheless, some carers will still be hesitant even once the learning opportunities are explained. Notwithstanding the expense, there are other reasons for being anxious about excursions. Often it is because carers are not familiar with the venue and are fearful. It is useful to try to put ourselves in their shoes. You might, for example, arrange an excursion to a nearby local reserve with a lake and bushland, knowing that the chances of being bitten by a snake or funnel web spider are extremely remote and (unless in the far north of Australia) there are certainly no saltwater crocodiles, but if carers are not familiar with this reserve, they might be fearful of snakes, spiders or crocodiles. Similarly, the thought of their child going on overnight excursions (avoid using the word camp with its connotations of refugee camps for those from a refugee background) can be very stressful for many carers because they may not have had this experience. Showing a video of the excursion venue, mode of transport, variety of food alternatives to cater for religious beliefs or health conditions and accommodation is constructive and commonplace in many schools. Inviting parents to attend the excursion is also a useful option, and many schools do this, but be aware that you need to arrange this well ahead of time, to ensure that parents complete Child Protection documentation and so forth.

To conclude, this chapter has focused on the importance of understanding that EL learners are a very diverse group. Hence it is essential to glean as much information as possible about each individual to ensure that the individual's social, emotional and academic needs are met.

The common thread for all EL learners is that a well established home language supports rather than hinders the learning of a second language, which is why maintenance of L1 is so important and the teacher can play a significant role in both sanctioning and encouraging the use of L1 at home and at school. As well, an introductory knowledge of the home language is valuable for teachers because this knowledge will help when supporting the student's English learning. A great deal of information can be gained from communicating with parents or carers. Working *together* with families and communities will not only enhance the student's social, emotional and academic success, but provide parents and carers with a better understanding of current Australian schooling contexts.

This chapter began by exploring why the pedagogical conditions prevalent in many early childhood contexts is suited to language learning and suggested that these practices need to be emulated with older students. These pedagogical conditions will be explored in the following chapter.

CHAPTER THREE
PEDAGOGICAL CONDITIONS FOR LEARNING A LANGUAGE

It's not fair. We have to do a project on how Easter is celebrated in Greece. It's easy for the other kids 'cause they already know what Easter is about, but I don't so I have to do double work. I know about Easter eggs, but I don't know the religion bit.

(Alan: Ten-year-old child from a practising Buddhist background, talking to a teacher in the playground.)

This chapter explores a variety of pedagogical conditions best suited for learning an additional language at school. As stated in Chapter 2, if students have established good oral and literacy skills in L1, then theoretically they are in a better position for learning a subsequent language. However, it could well be that in practice, students in early childhood classes *do* learn English more quickly than their older counterparts. This is not because they are more efficient at learning the language (excepting acquiring a better accent), but because the pedagogical conditions in many early childhood contexts are superior language learning environments to some environments in the later years of primary and high school (Krashen, 1982). Many of these conditions will be further explored, but Alan's comment above demonstrates the importance of ascertaining what prior knowledge students have and then building on this knowledge to achieve new knowledge (Cummins, 1996) can alleviate the amount of double work. This is just one of the strategies that many early childhood educators consistently use.

This is not to suggest that students should not learn about the majority culture of a country and/or other cultural practices or anything else that is out of their 'comfort zone'; to the contrary. But Alan was lamenting that he had double work to do because he did not have the same background knowledge of the topic as most other students in his class, making the task more difficult for him to achieve. The purpose of this social studies unit was to gain an appreciation and respect for global diversity and one task was to research the way Christians around the world celebrate Easter differently. Alan's group was researching how many people in Greece celebrate Easter. Perhaps in a predominantly Christian society such as Australia, a working knowledge of traditions such as Easter might be assumed, but Australia is both a linguistically and culturally diverse society and such assumptions can place students from minority linguistic and/or cultural backgrounds at an unfair disadvantage in terms of academic achievement.

Another example comes from a multiple choice comprehension task based on a poster advertising the events at the student's school fete. Devonshire tea at the tuckshop was listed (without a picture) as one of the events. This is a good example of an authentic task, but is also an example of a task that (quite unintentionally) privileges certain background knowledge.

Question: What would you be able to get at the Devonshire tea?

Answer: a) chips; b) scones and jam; c) devon; d) cakes

An eleven-year-old Sudanese student in the Developing English phase chose answer c: devon, which although incorrect is a logical inference. Being aware of each student's background knowledge and hence their ability to achieve is the crucial element and is one reason why culturally inclusive practices are important.

Culturally inclusive practices

The population of Australia is both culturally and linguistically diverse and we all have a cultural and linguistic background. In many schools across Australia the dominant cultural and linguistic background is Anglo-Celtic and English speaking, but even within this group there is diversity. There are also other areas where the dominant culture will be Australians from, for example, an Indigenous, Greek, Vietnamese or Lebanese background and again it is important to note that there will be diversity within these broad categories. Culturally inclusive practices mean acknowledging the diverse heritage of *all* Australians and are important because culturally inclusive practices incorporate and build on knowledge, skills, experiences and values that students bring with them. Culturally inclusive practices alleviate double work and/or confusion and mean children can arrive at academic success more quickly. As mentioned previously, many early childhood contexts do this well and the commercial market is also aware (maybe inadvertently via the cash register) of this principle. For instance, walk into any book store in Australia and many of the books for very young children contain content familiar to many Australian children (Australian animals, and events and activities around going to the beach for example). Conversely in Canada, many books deal with adventures in the snow and North American animals. But of course there are also affective reasons for incorporating culturally inclusive practices. Although the affective cannot be artificially partitioned from the cognitive reasons, the major affective reason for providing resources that validate the variety of cultural and linguistic groups in the class is because it promotes a person's sense of identity. It affirms a respect for each student's

Pedagogical conditions for learning a language

linguistic and cultural heritage and is supported by research confirming that a positive self identity is important for learning (for example, Delpit, 2006).

The photos below show just some examples of resources and/or materials that are culturally inclusive with the aim of enhancing both affective and cognitive development. Readers are also directed to the Australian Curriculum's *English as an Additional Language or Dialect: Teacher Resource* (EAL/D) V 1.1 (at www.acara.edu.au/curriculum/eald_teacher_resource/eald_teacher_resource.html).

Figure 3.1
This chart shows the Aboriginal seasons of the Dharawal people and was a resource used in a Year 7 class when different climatic conditions were being studied in geography. Some of the students in this class were Dharawal people.

Figure 3.2
The students in this Year 4 class were reading the book *Are We There Yet* by Alison Lester, which maps a family's journey around Australia. The students made a map showing the countries they came from.

Figure 3.3
The equipment in this kindergarten class's dramatic play corner includes items from different cuisines. These children are preparing sushi for lunch.

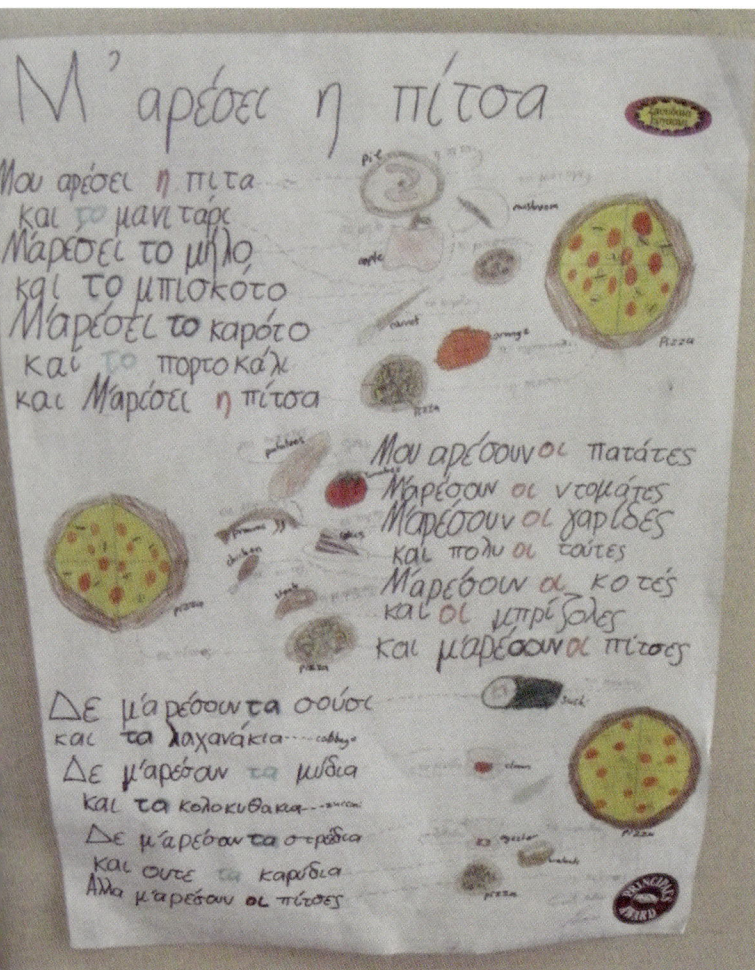

Figure 3.4
Students in this Year 6 class were encouraged to write recipes in their home language. Many of the students at this school attend Saturday school to learn Greek.

Figure 3.5
Equipment for dramatic play: Shopkeepers

Figure 3.6
'Hello' in different languages to represent the immediate community languages and those spoken globally

Figure 3.7
Examples of multilingual texts

Pedagogical conditions for learning a language

<designer, please insert the photo showing beliefs and values>

Figure 3.8
Beliefs and values

The reader might think that there is an error in the box above because that the photo has not been included before going to print, but it is intentional. The other photos above do highlight an important aspect of a class program but only explain what we can 'see' about a person's cultural and linguistic background. However, a person's cultural and linguistic background is not only described by looks and artefacts alone. The beliefs and values that 'make' a person often cannot be visually represented. We could perhaps put a photo of a poster saying 'Free speech is a right not a privilege', but why the person believes this would take more than a slogan to explain. This is why culturally inclusive practices (which are not just about artefacts and what can be 'seen') are markedly different and far more important than one-off multicultural or harmony celebratory days. While such celebrations might go some way to fulfil the aim of acknowledging the cultural and linguistic diversity of the school's population and the wider community, such celebrations do not enhance a student's language learning. However, an ongoing program that has as its overarching principal an awareness that a student's **schema** will assist or hinder their acquisition of new information and skills will enhance language learning.

Schema theory

Schema theory (Anderson & Pearson, 1984) is important for teachers to understand, because its thesis is that our understanding of events is based on our social, cultural and linguistic backgrounds – all the prior experiences we have had. It has particular relevance to reading and is why the *Australian English Curriculum* (www.acara.edu.au/curriculum.html) uses a sociocultural framework (as discussed in Chapter 1) to inform its curriculum. The student's concern about double work (in the quote at the beginning of this chapter) confirms this, but the ramifications can be more profound when one's schema really interferes with comprehension or distorts understanding (as in the Devonshire tea example discussed earlier); but this is not just the case with Beginning English learners. Steffenson et al (1979) conducted a study with university students from

A person's **schema** (the plural is schemata) refers to one's pre-existing knowledge. So, for example, in order to answer questions about a Devonshire tea correctly (refer to page 30) one's knowledge of what a Devonshire tea is, is necessary. Similarly, our understanding of certain values will be underpinned by our cultural context; for example, child-rearing practices.

American-Anglo and American-East Indian backgrounds. All students read two different articles about wedding ceremonies. One article was about an East Indian wedding ceremony and the other about an American-Anglo wedding ceremony. The American-Anglos took longer to read the article about the East Indian wedding and vice versa. Importantly, the two groups' comprehension of the text was affected. For example, the American-East Indian students incorrectly inferred that because the Anglo bride was wearing her grandmother's wedding dress she must be very poor. On the other hand, the American–Anglo students misunderstood the dowry tradition interpreting it as mutual gift giving.

Similar misunderstandings occurred with primary aged students when Lipson (1982) gave students from Jewish and Catholic day schools articles to read on Bar Mitzvahs and Communion. The Jewish students took less time than the Catholic students to read the article about Bar Mitzvahs and more accurately answered the questions, and the Catholic children read and comprehended the text on Communions more quickly and precisely. Other anecdotal evidence confirms this analysis. For example, a NSW final High School English comprehension paper (1998) required students to read and respond to an article about chokos (a vegetable). There was much media attention (*Sydney Morning Herald*, 1998) due to public outcry about the subject matter (chokos) in this public examination, because many students, teachers and parents felt that students who did not know what a choko was were disadvantaged and especially in answering the inferential questions. That is, their prior knowledge about the literal or concrete information was missing or limited and interfered with their analytical skills.

Building up knowledge of the topic

Related therefore to schema theory is the important pedagogical strategy of activating or stimulating a student's prior understandings and then building on from that point for, as Cummins et al (2006) state:

> Prior knowledge, skills, beliefs, and concepts significantly influence what learners notice about their environment and how they organize and interpret their observations. Prior knowledge refers *not just to information or skills previously acquired in a transmission-oriented instructional sequence but to the totality of the experiences that have shaped the learner's identity and cognitive functioning* (author's emphasis). This principle implies that in classrooms with students from linguistically diverse backgrounds, instruction must explicitly activate students' prior knowledge and build relevant background knowledge as necessary.

There are many teaching strategies to help students recall what they already do know and suggestions are made in Chapters 4, 5, 6 and 7. These strategies not only affirm to students that they are not an empty vessel, but act as a valuable assessment tool for the teacher in terms of knowing the *starting point* for planning intellectually challenging tasks. Additionally, alerting students that in fact they do know something about the subject and/or quickly re-familiarising them with the fundamental vocabulary and language structures enables them to engage more quickly with intellectually challenging experiences or as Cummins (1996: 77) states, 'it frees up brain power'. Of course there may be instances where there is very little prior knowledge and this makes building up knowledge of the topic even more crucial. Many of the strategies that can be used to do this will be explained in later chapters, but an essential requirement is the importance of *talking for learning*. Early childhood educators spend a lot of time building up knowledge of a topic. For example, before reading a book for shared reading, teachers commonly begin with what is often termed *prediction activities* or before conducting a science experiment, time will be spent with an explicit focus on the purpose of the experiment, the type of equipment to be used and the associated vocabulary and language structures. This is but one of many pedagogical approaches that are needed for all EL learners in all year levels. Furthermore, the emphasis in early childhood contexts is on collaborative group work and in Australia for example *The Early Years of Learning Framework* (DEEWR, 2009), stresses the importance of this through play-based learning. Play-based learning is 'a context for learning through which children organise and make sense of their social worlds, as they engage actively with people, objects and representations' (DEEWR, 2009: 6). It is beyond the scope of this book to explore play-based learning in detail, although dramatic play (just one form of play) is discussed in Chapter 7, but of significance here are the carefully planned structures that teachers set up to encourage active and collaborative communication.

Collaborative group work interaction

It is well-nigh impossible to get very young children to speak if they don't want to. Many new learners of a language are silent and Krashen (1982) refers to this as the 'right to remain silent', but in this silent period, children are still processing the language. They are very capable receptive learners. This is not to say that children should not be encouraged to speak (produce language) and the strategies in Chapter 4 in particular detail how to do this, but in early childhood environments quiet (silent) children spend much of their day working and interacting with peers in oracy (talking and listening) rich learning environments. Just as beginner speakers of English might be hesitant to speak, the same often applies to students in the Developing and Consolidating English phases when in situations that are linguistically challenging for them, or as one child in the Consolidating English phase explained to me, *I let Nathan (native speaker) do all the talking because he can say it better than me.*

Another of Krashen's conditions – a 'supportive and stress free environment' – is often referred to in the ELL literature, and teachers of older students do aim for this, but stress free also means that the emphasis is away from isolated skills based language learning lessons which for many students can be daunting or embarrassing when they are asked to produce language. Conversely, when language learning occurs for an authentic purpose with other goals incorporated, many students may feel more confident to interact. For instance, the kindergarten class who read Pamela Allen's book *Grandpa and Thomas* (which is about a grandfather and grandson building sandcastles at the beach) made sandcastles from play dough and innovated on the existing refrain in the book (refer to the text innovation strategy on page 105 in Chapter 5).

Figure 3.9

Child from a kindergarten class who read Pamela Allen's book Grandpa and Thomas *and made sandcastles from play dough and innovated on the refrain in the book*

Figure 3.10

Another play dough sandcastle and innovation on the refrain. Note all the other writing as well.

A child who rarely spoke was actively participating in the activity, and listening and smiling while other students at his table chatted as they completed the task. They were recalling their experiences at the beach. One child was explaining that his family ate fish and chips at the beach. *Yum … Yummy* chorused the others, including the quiet student. Now of course we want students to be able to say more than 'yummy' and furthermore as explained in Chapter 1 we want them to move beyond playground or conversational language and learn the academic discourses of subject specific fields, but providing opportunities for children such as this boy to *take a risk and speak is vital*. Social situations with peers such as the example above allow for this (Pica, 1994) and when the groups can be constructed so that ELLs are with native speakers, they will be hearing good models. Nevertheless, as just stated, incidental chat is not sufficient and no matter how well intentioned, neither is a supportive and stress free environment alone, for as one principal said, 'if care was all there was, schools would not be educative in the ways they ought to be' Hayes et al (2006: 61).

Scaffolding language learning

Scaffolding (Wood, Bruner & Ross, 1976) and Zone of Proximal Development (Vygotsky, 1986) are pedagogical concepts familiar to mainstream teachers, and their significance for EL learners is of similar importance, especially when we link these concepts to Cummins's model (1984: 139) as adapted in Figure 3.11.

When one reads both the vertical and horizontal lines as continuums, it is possible to analyse a task's language demands. The horizontal line runs on a continuum from language that is context-embedded to context-reduced. For instance, a face-to-face explanation of directions to your house with the aid of a map would be context embedded, whereas providing directions over the phone would be context reduced because there is no visual or contextual support. Increasingly, however, the internet helps to make these everyday conversations

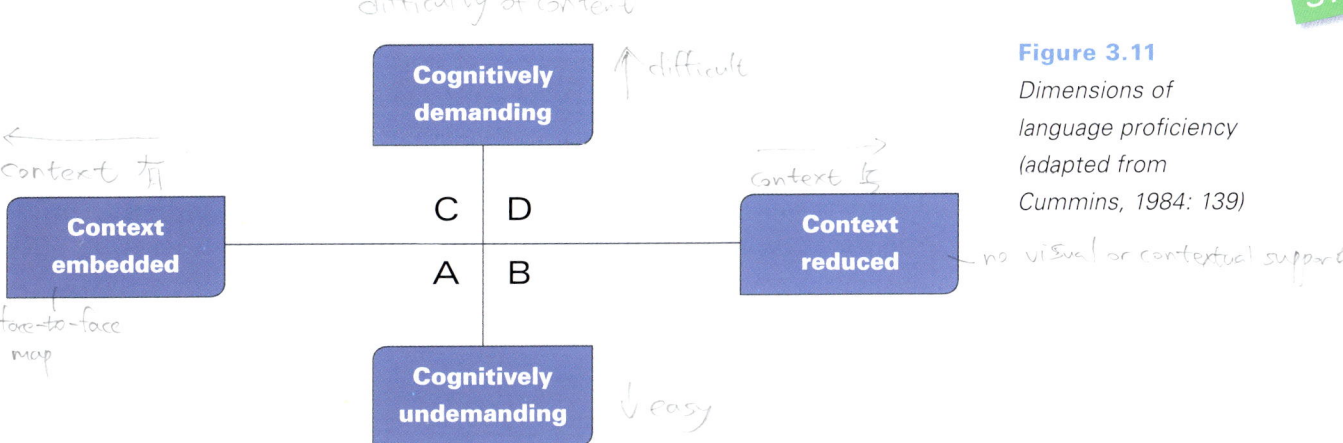

Figure 3.11
Dimensions of language proficiency (adapted from Cummins, 1984: 139)

more context-embedded. When a marketer is selling you a mobile plan over the phone, you are likely to be clicking and viewing the various options on the website as she or he talks to you. Understanding this mobile plan without this visual help would be more context-reduced.

Similarly, the vertical line runs on a continuum from demanding to undemanding in terms of the difficulty of content. Depending on the age group and their English language proficiency, the examples will differ of course. With a ten-year-old student in the Consolidating English phase in mind, writing an argument against deforestation is more cognitively demanding than writing a recount of a recent birthday party they attended.

The A, B, C and D quadrants are very useful therefore when analysing the language challenges the activity might demand; for instance, when thinking of an eight-year-old Developing or Consolidating English phase student (usually in Year 3), the activities about littering shown in Figure 3.12 would be relevant.

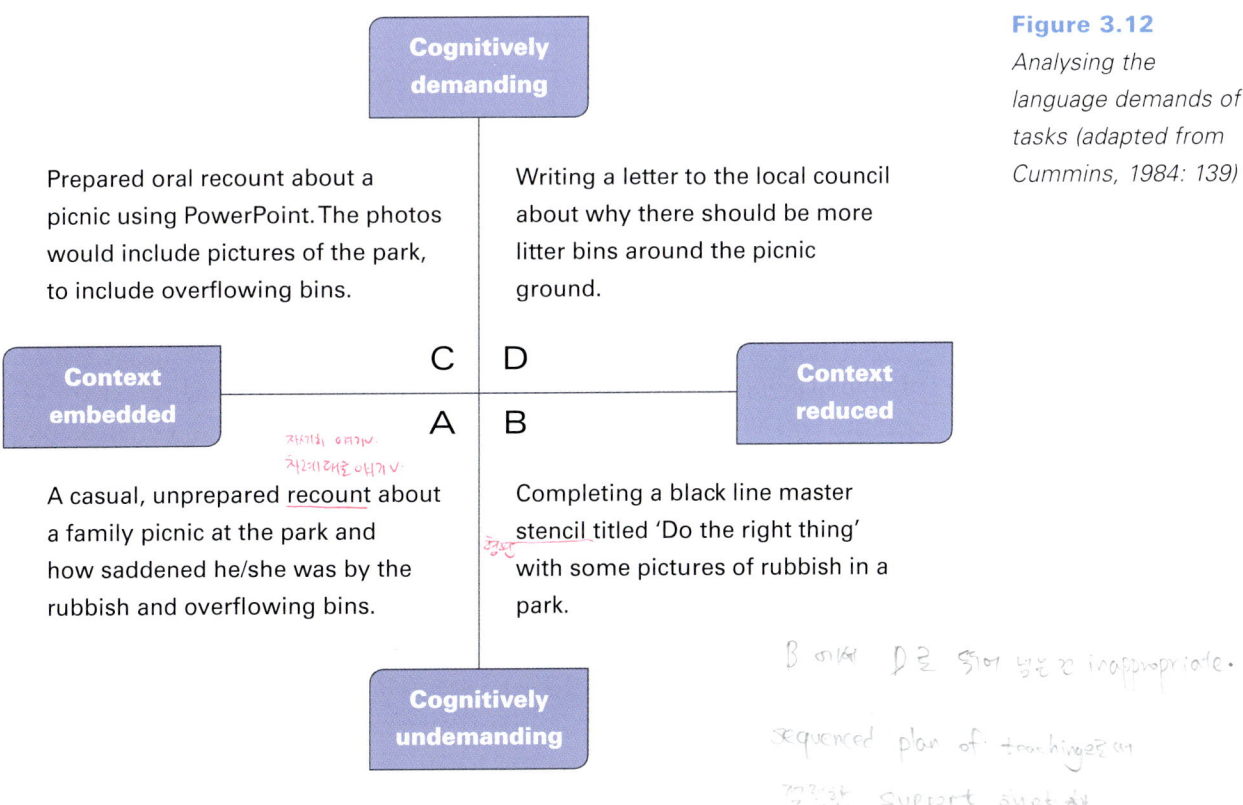

Figure 3.12
Analysing the language demands of tasks (adapted from Cummins, 1984: 139)

Plainly the activity in quadrant B is not academically demanding as neither thinking nor producing is done by the child and clearly jumping straight into quadrant D without any support is pedagogically inappropriate – thus the need to provide the appropriate *support* usually by way of a sequenced plan of teaching and learning experiences. Based on a teacher's assessment of what the student can do, these teaching/learning sequences build on existing knowledge to a place of unknown possibilities, but achievable ones.

The scaffolding cycle

The term scaffolding has become a bit of a buzz word and is sometimes incorrectly used as a synonym for help. It is important to understand that scaffolding is not just any sort of help. It is carefully constructed *support* provided by teachers to facilitate students in tasks that will extend and challenge them for as Maybin et al state:

> [scaffolding] is not just any assistance which helps a learner accomplish a task. It is help which will enable a learner to accomplish a task which they would not have been quite able to manage on their own, and it is help which is intended to bring the learner closer to a state of competence which will enable them eventually to complete such a task on their own. (Maybin, Mercer & Steiner, 1992: 188)

To this end, many ELL teachers use a scaffolding support framework which highlights specifically the planning of activities for the language demands. The sequence, which can ebb and flow, is from 'controlled support' to 'guided support' and then 'independent support'. Importantly, the independent support section does not mean that a student necessarily works alone. The maxim that 'two heads are better than one' should be the regular feature of classroom organisation. That is, most of the time students will be working in pairs, triads or quads on any given task. In many cases I have found that pairs or triads are optimal because these groupings often allow for more involvement by each of the participants.

Controlled support (full scaffolding)

The term 'noticing' (Swain, 1995) is the feature in this phase. This means that teacher preparation is aiming for students to notice the target language (both vocabulary and likely language structures) through explanation and modelling. The focus therefore is on *language input*.

Because building up a knowledge of the topic is a prime objective, activities might include for instance, brainstorming, floor storming, modelled reading and deconstruction activities (refer to Chapter 5 for examples). Explaining clearly the purpose for the activity and the expectations or goals is also important; and this purpose may well be negotiated between the teacher and students. For example, some thirteen-year-old students were learning about the ancient Egyptian number system and the students suggested they make games (with written

Pedagogical conditions for learning a language

instructions) based on this number system for ten-year-old students at a near by primary school. The assessment criterion was also negotiated between teacher and students (Fair Go Team, in progress).

Guided support (partial scaffolding)

The activities at this stage are designed to enable students to share their knowledge with a deliberate focus on students using (producing) the target language by *recycling* or *appropriating* the language gathered from the controlled support phase to enable long-term *language intake*. Many of the communicative strategies mentioned in Chapter 4 apply to this phase.

Independent support (minimal scaffolding)

The activities in this phase are designed to enable students to use the now familiar target language and *recast* it or *reformulate* it to enable long-term *language uptake*. Often activities are designed so that students need to transfer this language uptake within a similar but different context or content area. Importantly, 'independent' does not mean that students always work alone. Students will often be working in pairs or groups. It is the support from the teacher that is reduced.

Theory to practice

The Australian Curriculum's *English as an Additional Language or Dialect: Teacher Resource (EAL/D) V 1.1* provides annotations to the content area learning descriptions for key learning areas to suggest modifications for planning, developing and implementing appropriate activities for EL learners.

In the example of a scaffolding cycle (page 40), it is envisaged that the students are in the late Developing to mid Consolidating English phase and about ten years or older. They are analysing an oral description (with an accompanying transcript) in order to produce their own. This example not only highlights the gradual removal of support towards independent completion of tasks but also indicates how the cycle can ebb and flow between controlled, guided and independent as new concepts are introduced within a specific subject.

The example highlights how the task has been scaffolded so that students become producers rather than reproducers of knowledge (Hayes et al, 2006). In contrast to regurgitating what someone else has already solved, students are provided with models and resources to enable them to problem solve and produce original and intellectually demanding work. Hammond and Gibbons use the term 'supporting up' students to counteract a 'dumbed down curriculum' (Hammond & Gibbons, 2005: 6). Gibbons (2009) stresses such an approach, advocating that teachers must provide challenging tasks for academic language learning. By implication, deep thinking and problem solving are involved and she terms this 'learning in the challenge zone' (ibid.: 17). She lists seven intellectual practices which are not intended to be read sequentially or in order of priority (page 41).

Example of scaffolding cycle

Aim: Students to research and prepare an oral description report.

Controlled support: Teacher provides target language by:

- constructing a chart which shows students the steps in preparing a descriptive information report
- asking students to listen to an information report from a podcast or vodcast which also has a written transcript (the Behind the News website is a useful resource www.abc.net.au/btn/)
- explaining and demonstrating some active listening strategies that can be employed when listening to a talk, eg note-taking, mind mapping, questioning
- explaining the importance of varying voice, intonation and volume, pausing (and gestures and eye contact if applicable) and then students listen and rate the speaker's use of these skills using a rating scale.

Guided support: Students practise target language by:

- re-reading the transcript of the podcast or vodcast
- in groups producing a semantic map of main ideas and then analysing and categorising it according to the chart presented in the controlled support phase
- in pairs, completing a written cloze based on the podcast or vodcast, focusing on nouns and noun groups. While completing this, students discuss possible inclusions based on how the information in the text aided them in coming to this consensus.

Independent support: Students use target language by:

- working in pairs to research a topic, they take notes and use these to practise their talk before presenting it to an audience; concentrating on how to engage the listener by varying voice, using intonation and volume, pausing, using gestures and eye contact
- working in quads, each pair listens to other pair's reports, summarising their main points.

Controlled support

Building on from the above sequence, the students might then move back to a controlled support situation where the focus is on presenting a written description. The teacher provides models that demonstrate how and why a written description is different to an oral description. For instance, attention to how the absence of verbal and non-verbal language calls for more use of nominalisation, modality and so forth should be a focus. (And so the scaffolding sequence is repeated.) (Adapted from NSW, Department of Education and Training, Multicultural Programs Unit (2005), *ESL Steps: ESL Curriculum Framework K–6 Stage 3*, NSW Department of Education and Training, Multicultural Programs Unit, Darlinghurst, NSW, p. 10.)

Refer to chapters 4, 5, 6 or 7 for explanations of the strategies mentioned here as well as Derewianka, 2011.

- Students engage with the key ideas and concepts of the discipline in ways that reflect how 'experts' in the field think and reason.
- Students transform what they have learned into a different form for use in a new context or for a different audience.
- Students make links between concrete knowledge and abstract theoretical knowledge.
- Students engage in substantive conversation.
- Students make connections between the spoken and written language of the subject and other discipline-related ways of making meaning.
- Students take a critical stance toward knowledge and information.
- Students use metalanguage in the context of learning about other things.
(Gibbons, 2009: 21–30)

Mariani's (1997) research is also important to consider because he similarly argues for a pedagogical approach that offers challenging and engaging activities with appropriate support. Mariani explains scaffolding as one of the tenets for support (a concept previously explained in this chapter). Of equal significance, he emphasises that support also includes the *interactions* we have with students and thus the messages we convey. Using examples from his own learning experience Mariani concludes that while one of the activities was high challenge there was a 'ridiculously low level of support, both in terms of task, and perhaps more importantly, in terms of interaction, that is affective support. The result, at least as far as I was concerned, was anxiety, insecurity, discomfort, and even aggressiveness – not to mention the long-term effect on my self-confidence'.

For low challenge with low support Mariani uses the words 'boredom, apathy, indifference and demotivation'. Conversely, for a high challenge and high support activity he concludes that he had 'a feeling of satisfaction at the end of the day – my self esteem had been boosted and I had learned that I could achieve something even in a subject I wasn't particularly interested in'.

Figure 3.13 shows Mariani's original diagram, which demonstrates what he terms the 'four basic types of challenge/support patterns'.

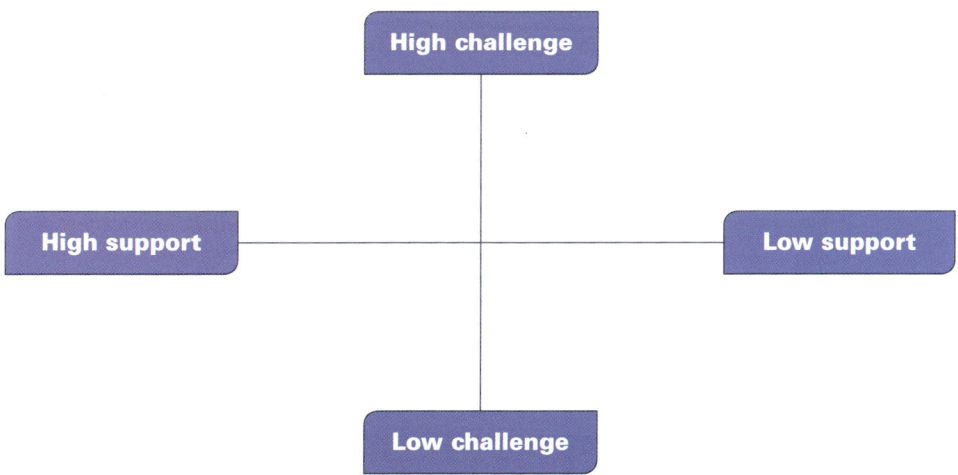

Figure 3.13
Mariani's (1997) diagram demonstrating the 'four basic types of challenge/support patterns'

In Figure 3.14 on page 42, I have adapted Figure 3.13 by including explanations within each quadrant to align it with another research project which is explained immediately preceding this figure.

Figure 3.14
Framework of challenge/support patterns (adapted from Mariani, 1997)

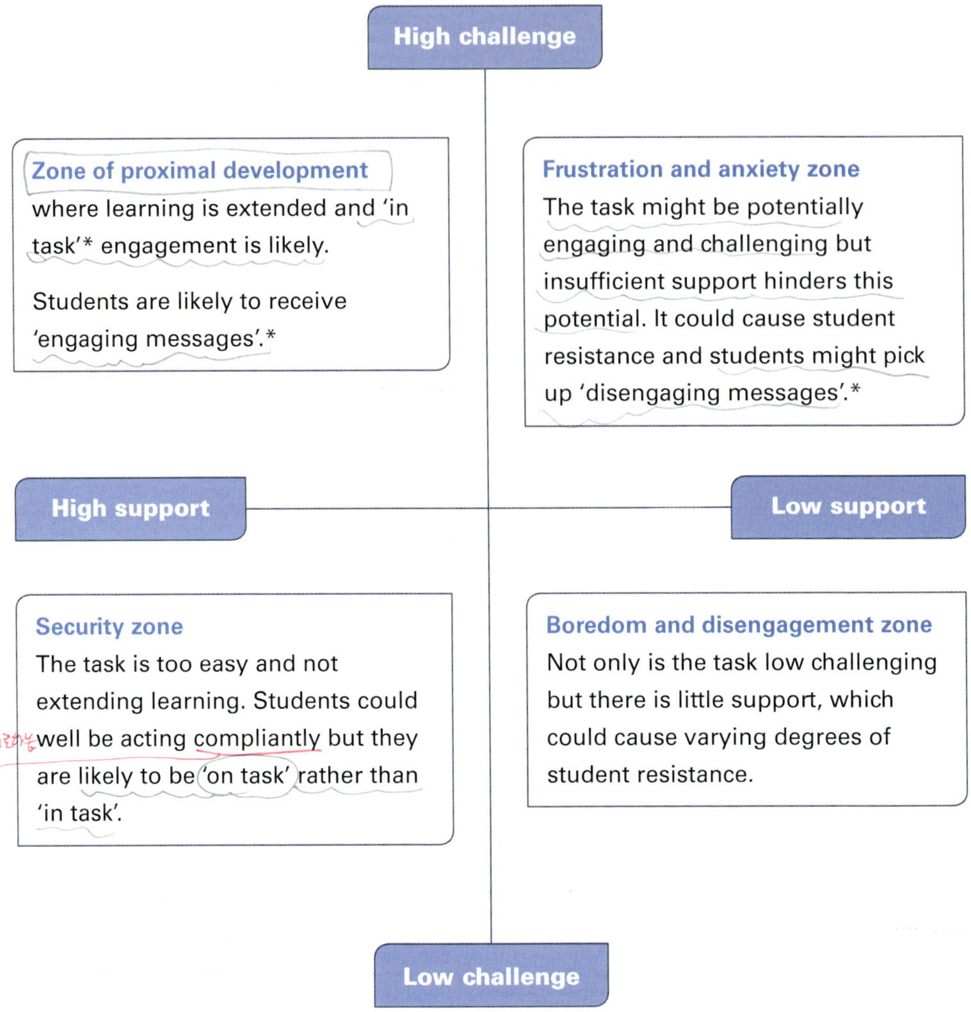

* 'On task' and 'in task' and 'disengaging messages' and 'engaging messages' are explained in the next section.

High challenge

Zone of proximal development
where learning is extended and 'in task'* engagement is likely.

Students are likely to receive 'engaging messages'.*

Frustration and anxiety zone
The task might be potentially engaging and challenging but insufficient support hinders this potential. It could cause student resistance and students might pick up 'disengaging messages'.*

High support — **Low support**

Security zone
The task is too easy and not extending learning. Students could well be acting compliantly but they are likely to be 'on task' rather than 'in task'.

Boredom and disengagement zone
Not only is the task low challenging but there is little support, which could cause varying degrees of student resistance.

Low challenge

A research project that I have been involved in for over ten years, called the Fair Go Project (FGP), has been examining how the choice of pedagogy has an impact on student engagement and there are correlations with Mariani's research, as documented in Figure 3.14 and now detailed.

The Fair Go Project's pedagogical framework for student engagement

Influenced and informed by the research of both 'authentic' pedagogy (Newmann & Associates, 1996) and Productive Pedagogies (QSRLS, 2001) as well as Bernstein's (1996) important research about how the type of curriculum planning can convey messages to students that influence their attitude to learning, the Fair Go Project investigates in more depth what 'engagement' is.

The notion of engagement became the central focus of the FGP because the project was based on the premise that student engagement is a critical condition for improved academic outcomes. It set out specifically to examine what engagement looks like in classrooms and especially for students from socio-economically and educationally disadvantaged backgrounds (in future referred to as low **SES**). In most of the research schools (all in NSW) there was a high percentage of EL learners (in some schools as high as 98 per cent) and these learners were from a diversity of backgrounds and experiences, including Indigenous students and students from refugee family backgrounds (FGT, 2006).

There is always the risk of stereotyping, but it is the case that a fair proportion of students from low SES backgrounds are academically disengaged, confirmed by data from teacher interviews in which the consistent message was that for many students, engaging with school, and by implication learning, was problematic (FGT, 2006; FGT, in progress). Many teachers *did* have high academic expectations for their students, but many students resisted the challenge because they did not have a sense that academic achievement was their prerogative – it was seen as the domain for advantaged groups, but not part of their reality. It could be said that at times a vicious circle ensued. Students resisted challenging work (were not 'in task'), but were willing to participate (be 'on task') in low challenging activities. And so a sense of compliance set in. With few exceptions, classrooms were peaceful places, but learning was below expectations.

SES: socio-economic status

The FGP's definition of engagement

The FGP centralises student engagement as the driving force to enhance both learning and social outcomes, so that students will 'buy into' the educational experience and hence have a long-term belief that educational achievement *is* a realistic aspiration. It defines engagement in learning as something more than 'compliance' or 'on task' behaviour. The FGP uses the term 'in task' as opposed to 'on task', because the word 'in' suggests more of a commitment – that one is inside the metaphorical space. Conversely, the word 'on' suggests being on the surface of a metaphorical space.

Further, the FGP identifies two forms of engagement; small 'e' engagement and big 'E' engagement. Small 'e' engagement is when students are involved in a *substantive* learning task (in task) rather than procedural tasks with little challenge (on task). Engagement is viewed as a feeling or an emotion – something that is internalised, and so the FGP asserts that when students are engaged over *extended* and *sustained* periods of time (usually longer than a year), big 'E' engagement might be achieved because students have developed a personal commitment and trust in themselves. That is, the students might have a long-term belief that 'school is for me' and so the FGP team uses the term 'future in the present' based on the concept of future (school is for me) within the present (in task).

In terms of pedagogy, the FGP contends that to achieve small 'e' engagement (in task as opposed to on task or compliance), the pedagogical process needs to be 'high cognitive' (a task that requires deep thinking and by implication problem solving), 'high affective' (a task that promotes positive feelings while doing) and 'high operative' (actively doing or active involvement). In classes where this process is occurring there appears to be an inextricable link between all three (Munns, 2007; FGT, in progress) as illustrated in Figure 3.15.

Figure 3.15

The Fair Go pedagogy

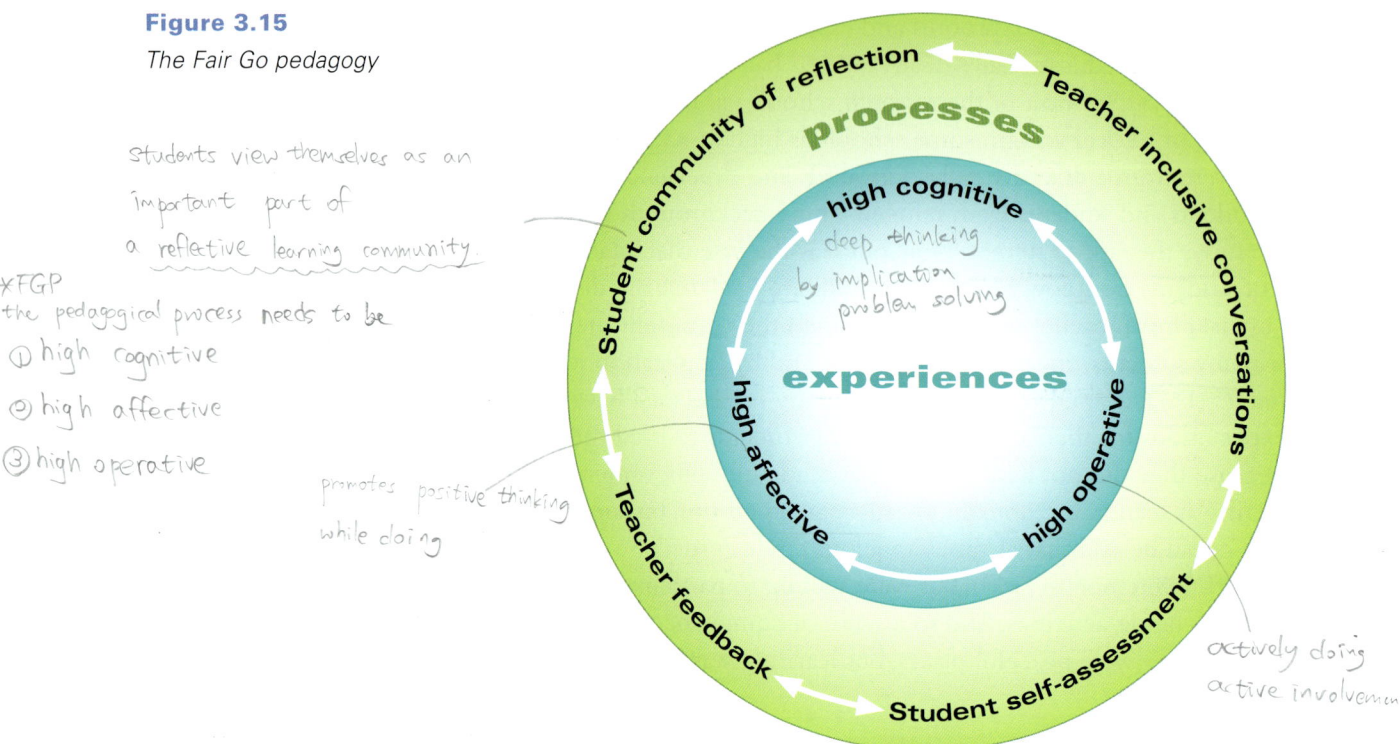

The outer circle of Figure 3.15 describes what the FGP refers to as 'insider' classroom processes. These processes are inextricably linked to and support the learning experiences, because students view themselves as an important part of a reflective learning community driven by teacher inclusive conversations, student self-assessment, and teacher feedback.

Achieving this high level of engagement is realised because of this reflective learning community, one where teachers send messages that both validate and respect the student's role in the pedagogical process. Figure 3.16 illustrates five messages that the FGP identified as 'engaging messages' for low SES students, contending that when students receive messages about their knowledge, their ability, their role in classroom control, their place and their voice they have a feeling of empowerment and hence the term 'discourses of power'. Conversely, the 'disengaging messages' are as presented in Figure 3.17.

As stated previously, the FGP research has been conducted in low SES schools with high proportions of EL learners in the case study schools, but this pedagogical framework has relevance for all ELLs irrespective of SES circumstance. One reason for this may well be the links between it and the theory underpinning ELL mentioned in this chapter and Chapters 1 and 2. How the FGP pedagogical framework conforms to many ELL principles in terms of the 'discourse of power – engaging messages' (Figure 3.17) are summarised below and on page 46.

- That *place* is important. It is alright to be a kid from a particular community and cultural and linguistic background, links with the concept of culturally inclusive practices as well as the importance of the home/school connection.
- That *knowledge* should be contextualised so that connections can be made, support both scaffolding and schema theories and principles.

Pedagogical conditions for learning a language

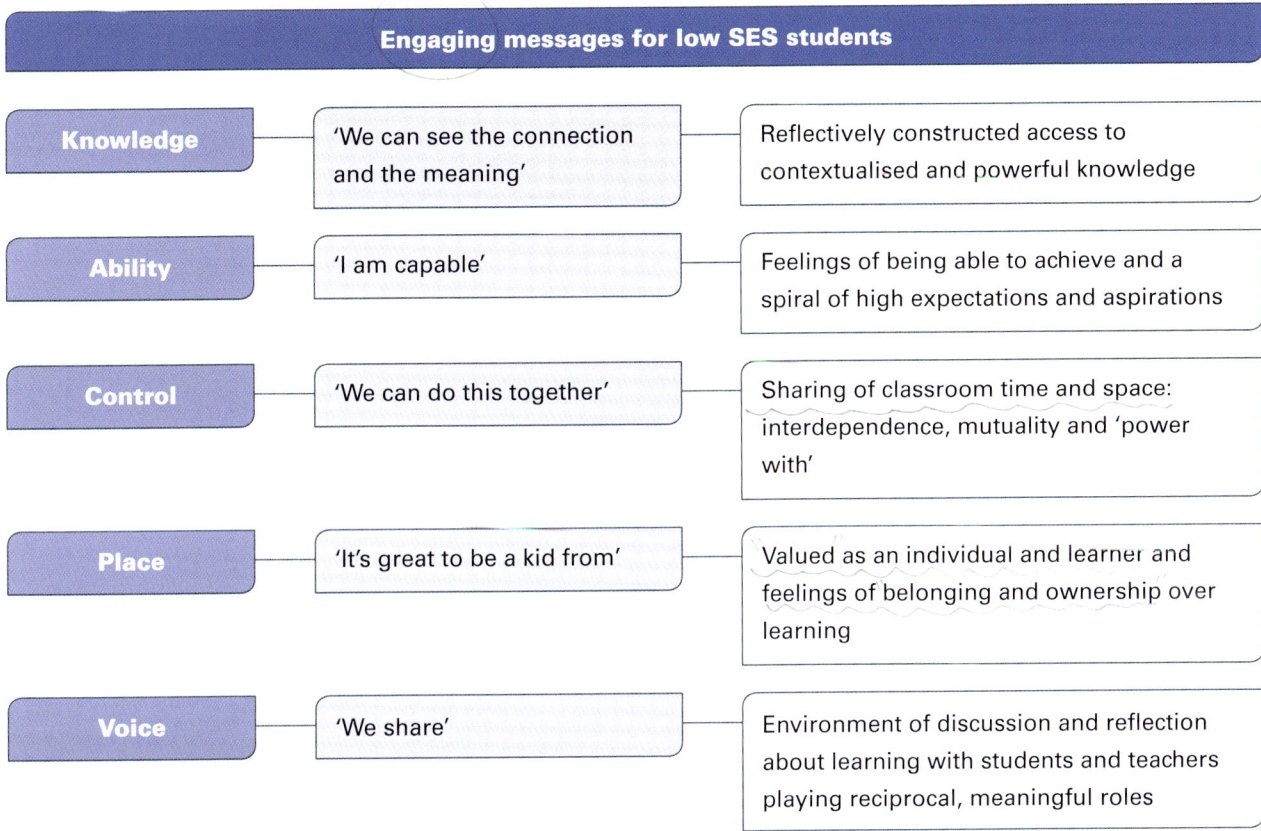

Figure 3.16
Discourses of power and engaging messages for low SES students

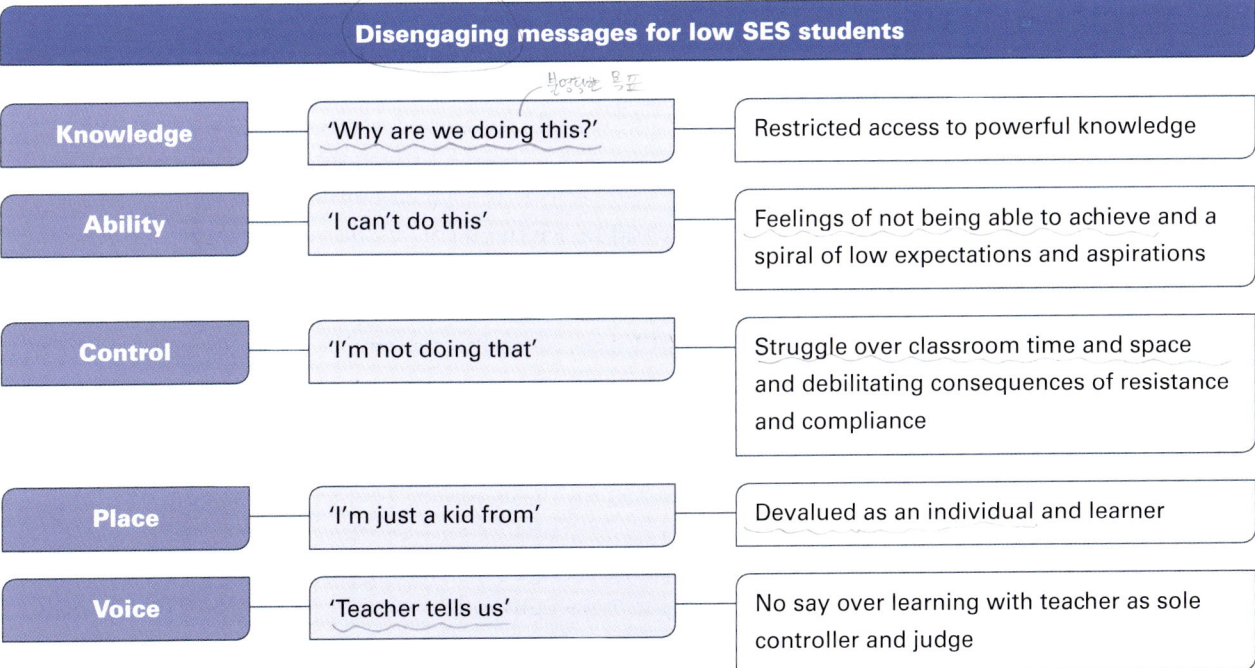

Figure 3.17
Discourses of power and disengaging messages for low SES students

- That it be *powerful knowledge* is one of the tenets of sociolinguistic theory and supports for example Cummins's, Gibbons's and Mariani's positions as discussed earlier on the importance of a cognitively demanding program.
- That feelings of *ability* and a belief that *I am capable* and can achieve at an aspirational level when combined with *control* and *voice*, echoes the importance of both negotiated and collaborative learning where there are many opportunities for students to practise the target language with peers and teachers.
- Similarly, *small 'e' engagement* (in task) requires high cognitive, high affective and high operative learning experiences and this supports ELL pedagogy which advocates highly challenging tasks with an emphasis on students actively participating and producing in order to achieve academic language proficiency.

Additionally, the FGP model explicitly attends to the importance of the connection and interplay between these three processes (see Figure 3.15). In its most recent project (FGT, in progress) the FGP researched thirty exemplary teachers in low SES communities across NSW. Although teaching in geographically, culturally and linguistically diverse contexts and across age groups (three years to eighteen years) all of the teachers viewed this connection and interplay as critical. In particular, the *affective* domain was viewed as crucial because it provided students with positive feelings which in turn promoted risk taking – which is such an important aspect in the language learning process. Finalising the analyses of all data is still being undertaken at the time of writing this book; however, five teachers have been analysed closely (FGT, 2011). All five teachers have a high percentage of EL learners. The following themes are common to them all.

Their pedagogy is *high cognitive* because:
- it is appreciating (valuing and understanding) that classroom experiences are intellectually challenging
- learning is a priority and is explicitly considered business
- teaching and learning are seen as sustained and ongoing classroom conversations.

Their pedagogy is *high affective* because:
- it is authentic learning that connects and builds community
- teaching is seen as a creative process, producing new imaginations about learning
- there is emotional and social safety for students.

Their pedagogy is *high operative* because:
- there are links built between cognitive, affective and operative processes
- there is a developed status for thinkers and learners that targets and minimises student resistance
- there is a thoughtful and dynamic repertoire of practices.

(Adapted from Munns et al, 2011: 170.).

Furthermore, what is implicit in the FGP model and the wording of the themes from an ELL perspective, but explicit in the data, is both the importance and variety of scaffolding and other support (FGT, 2006; FGT, in progress).

Pedagogical conditions for learning a language

In subsequent chapters, snap-shots of practice from teachers within this project, as well as other teachers, are used to explain how the pedagogical conditions for supporting English language learning explained in this chapter translate into practice.

To conclude this and previous chapters that have examined the more general ELL theory, and thus position the following chapters that examine specific theoretical principles as they relate to oracy, reading and writing, I share a reflection emailed to me by a beginning teacher after a tutorial about teaching EL learners.

> My own experience as a refugee starting school in Year 5 was very traumatic which made me feel like a complete outsider. I had a stressful time getting here (Australia) but I don't want to dwell on that just now. During that period (Year 5), I felt slow and stupid as the lessons were taught at a very fast pace and it was structured in a way which seemed to cater only for those students who were fluent in English. I constantly felt I was left behind because I could not speak or understand English. As this happened a long time ago I am not certain if all the bad experiences caused me to delay my development in the new language but I am definite it was not a welcoming and comfortable environment to be in, especially for a new arrival. And this was worsened by the racist remarks made by other students in the class and school. Therefore it is vital that teachers who have refugees in their class develop a positive and secure environment for them. This is done by the teacher discussing what difficulties a newcomer would be experiencing when he or she enters the class and how the children in the class might help him or her adjust better to the new environment. Helping children develop positive attitudes towards the new arrival will help her or him to feel accepted and part of the class. This secure environment will motivate the new arrival to be involved in classroom activities and to interact with other children, which will encourage him or her to learn and speak the new language faster.

We then met and discussed her reflection, and I transcribed what she said at that time:

> I wish my teacher had met with my parents so she could know what happened and why I felt so sad and I might not have felt so helpless. I dropped out of school as soon as I could in Year 9 (at fifteen years old), not because I thought I was stupid, but because the language barrier by then was just too great …Then I went back to TAFE and did my HSC. I'm pleased to have the opportunity to go to Uni now and I'm really looking forward to teaching because if we can make a difference, we can save the anguish. I have not heard the term culturally inclusive before, but it makes a lot of sense because it helps validate all the kids in the classroom. And I can really relate to the importance of building up the field (knowledge of the topic) because for example the teacher just assumed that I understood what a birthday party was, but I'd never been to one so I didn't know anything about them. It's just all these little things that build up and up and so I just decided to give up!

The following chapters now look specifically at teaching and learning strategies to assist students' development of academic English language across a variety of subject areas.

CHAPTER FOUR
FOCUS ON ORACY

This chapter demonstrates the importance of programming to include a major focus on talking and listening in the classroom and especially prior to reading and writing and then in tandem while reading and writing. Throughout the chapter, ideas and strategies are presented to enhance oracy in English, with the assumption that using L1 is a very useful and legitimate tool. Many students (and especially if there is a group from the same language background) might, for example, use L1 in order to enhance their understanding of the concept being explored. Teachers and/or other adults should also use the student's first language where possible.

The term oracy has been used as the title for the chapter because oracy denotes both the productive (talking) and the receptive (listening) aspect of language. In this book the type of listening referred to is termed 'active listening'. Just as psychologists use strategies to engage people in active listening for the purposes of learning to communicate with others better in their personal life or in business situations, we need to provide situations in classrooms for active listening, in terms of learning English. This means providing situations where the listener has to process what they hear by either talking or writing in order to indicate their understanding.

As explained in Chapter 1, very young children learn their first language by interacting with other people in a 'happening here and now' context. It is realistic and authentic. Children both listen to the language (receptive) and produce the language (productive), primarily with parents, carers and older siblings. These people (from now on referred to as carers to encompass the range of people) support the learner by talking *with* the child, and the language used is relevant to the context and situation. This talking covers a range of modes. Much of the time it will be language accompanying action. This type of talk is usually informal. So, for example, while on the swings at the park, the language associated with swings will be used:

Focus on oracy

Child: *Push me ... make higher.*

Carer: *Okay! I'll make you go higher but hold on tight.*

But although this is informal spoken language, the carer is providing the appropriate form of language. They are providing a correct model. This is called reformulating the student's language or recasting it. Carers seem to do this almost intuitively and so do many teachers. Concentrate on listening for this next time you hear a young child talking with their parent or when you are interacting with a student.

> Notice how the carer is both 'recasting' and 'reformulating' the language.

Similarly, many carers read books to young children and again are modelling the language. The register is usually more formal because it is spoken words in written form as the following example demonstrates:

Sonia and her mother went to the park to play on the swings. Sonia asked her mother to push her so that she could go higher.

Hold on tight warned her mother, *or you will fall off*.

The language needs to be more formal because although there may well be pictures to accompany the words, it is still more *context reduced* than the spoken transcript where the word 'swing' is not used, because they are 'here and now' on the swings. With reference to Cummins's model of the dimensions of language proficiency (page 37 of Chapter 3), playing on the swings is context-embedded and the reading of the story becomes more context-reduced.

Furthermore, very young children are not expected to learn to talk and read and write simultaneously. When carers read with very young children, they model the reading process and provide incidental 'lessons' such as *that word there says beach ... can you see the beach in the picture?* and similarly when writing. 'Let's put Vegemite on the shopping list: look v-e-g-e-m-i-t-e and it starts with 'v'! But the expectation remains that the very young child learns to speak the language rather than learning to read and write it.

A classroom context cannot replicate this home language learning situation and the expectation is that the student learns to talk and read and write simultaneously. Nevertheless, the implication that one masters a language by listening to it and speaking it is paramount. Teachers therefore must allow significant time for purposeful oracy learning across the *entire range* of spoken modes (see Figure 4.1) because oracy is fundamental to reading and writing progress.

In Australia, and with the emphasis on national testing that at the time of writing this book only tests reading and writing, it is crucial that teachers understand that oracy is fundamental to improving reading and writing progress because, as for example, both Halliday (1985) and Vygotsky (1986) suggest, talking in particular allows students to *think* in different ways. Vygotsky used the terms 'inner speech' and 'outer speech', to explain how important verbal interaction is for learning. Inner speech can be described as the abstract thoughts – the use of mental talk one does self to self. Outer speech is the external interactions one has with other people. This external interaction allows one to continue to explore and problem solve in order to clarify ideas or concepts with self (inner talk). For example, as a teacher you might talk with a colleague about how to best program

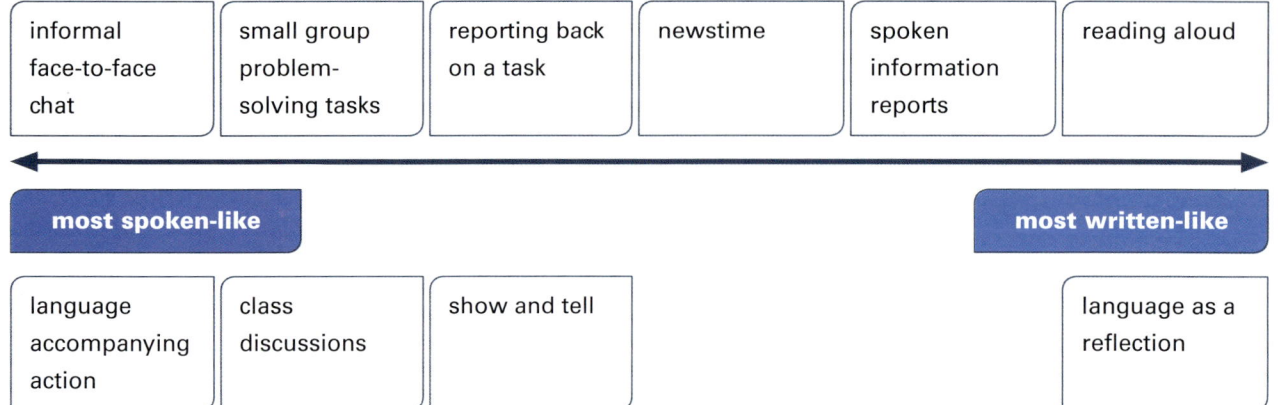

Figure 4.1

The mode continuum
(Jones, 1996: 13)

a unit of work on climate change. As you talk (which involves listening to the other person), you will possibly clarify the pedagogical approach you will use as well as some of the content to be covered. Then later on you will think about this more and problem solve with yourself. Vygotsky argues that 'outer speech' assists a person's abstract thinking process as they engage in this 'inner speech' to attain a more in-depth understanding. Therefore, providing a learning environment which positions oracy as a fundamental part of any teaching and learning sequence is necessary for any student irrespective of their English learning needs. For EL learners in particular though, we need to provide teaching and learning experiences that enable students to interact for a variety of purposes in the target language (English). This range of purposes might not be immediately or directly aligned to the curriculum as many of the purposes for communicating relate to exploring and negotiating our relationships with others. This is why drama is such a useful strategy, and this is discussed more in Chapter 7.

In the ELL literature, the purpose for communicating is often referred to as the language function and many of the most common ones are listed in Table 4.1. Many common language functions involve more complex thinking (sometimes referred to as higher order thinking) and these include, for example, expressing an opinion, predicting and hypothesising, generalising and evaluating.

Table 4.1 Common language functions

We communicate in a variety of ways dependent on the purpose or the function we want to perform

To agree or disagree	To apologise	To ask permission	To ask for assistance
To ask for directions	To classify	To describe	To clarify
To define	To express position	To express cause and effect	To report
To evaluate	To give instructions	To sequence	To express an opinion
To generalise	To enquire	To justify	To explain
To warn	To speculate	To compare and contrast	To predict or hypothesise

The need to use these functions (to communicate one's ideas) is common in subjects such as history, geography, maths and science and is why *integrating language learning across all curriculum areas* is so important. Furthermore, a range of language structures for each function needs to be presented to students. For example, and to draw an analogy, most teachers will be familiar with learning experiences that highlight to children that there are more interesting ways to say the word 'said' (whispered, exclaimed, yelled and so forth) . Similarly, when examining the language function of for instance generalisation, students need exposure to a variety of structures such as: usually …, as a rule …, by and large …, they are all …, many are … In the same way, and in order to predict or hypothesise, students would be exposed to structures such as: It is likely that …, I suspect that …, because of …, the result might be … On page 64 a strategy is explained to highlight how children attended to a range of language structures for the function of comparing and contrasting after reading the book *Mirrors* (Baker, 2010).

Classroom talk

The initiation, response, feedback (IRF) pattern familiar in many classrooms is useful but not sufficient in English learning classrooms, because it may limit the amount of talking the student will produce, especially in a whole class situation (Mercer, 2000). However, the IRF model is useful to quickly clarify knowledge. For example, when studying the water cycle, the following IRF might occur:

> Teacher: *Yesterday we read an article about why evaporation is an important part or process in the water cycle. Why is this so?*
>
> Student: *Because without evaporation there would be less rain.*
>
> Teacher: *Good answer and what might the likely consequence be?* **What might the result be? That is, what might happen? What will be the consequence?**

Rather than asking the whole class with one child responding, this IRF model can be manipulated to allow *all* children to *think* and *speak* using the think-pair-share strategy.

In *think-pair-share* (sometimes called 'talking buddies'), students work in pairs. The teacher (or another student) might ask a question, then individuals think for several seconds before anyone talks (wait time) and pairs then discuss. Pairs may report back to the whole class or group. You might also consider asking one person to report back on what their partner was saying and so encourage 'active listening'. The wait time (also termed 'think time') is important because studies such as Rowe (1986) found that an extra two or three seconds can allow for more in-depth thinking and hence more complex responses. Furthermore, it often takes EL learners longer than proficient English speakers to *produce* what they know. Without this time, some EL learners 'give up', for as one student explained, *I don't try to answer because I can never think of [how to say] the answer as quickly as the good speakers.*

> Notice how the teacher is reformulating 'tricky' vocabulary, which is discussed further in this chapter.

The importance of teacher/student talk

Both teacher guidance and scaffolding are important, as explained in Chapter 3, but in the main these are preferable in small groups or one-on-one to allow for greater interaction. The teacher's role when interacting is to talk *with* the students by probing and questioning. This probing and questioning requires the student to explain in more detail and allows the teacher to recast or reformulate what the student says and thus model new language as the example below demonstrates. These students were preparing a sculpture for drama (refer to page 146 in Chapter 7) and the teacher began to interact with them.

> Teacher: *What is your sculpture **portraying**? What is it **showing**?*
>
> Alan: *I'm making Sam look like Mari when she's being teased.*
>
> Teacher: *So you're **portraying** Mari when Patrick teases her.*
>
> Sam: *Yeah, I'm Mari so my face has to be sad.*
>
> Teacher: *Your face has to be sad? Have a look at the instructions.* (A chart on the wall that explains how to do sculpting.) *What is the phrase that explains this?*
>
> Sam and Alan: *Facial expressions!*
>
> Teacher: *Great! And what sort of facial expressions have you decided on?*
>
> Alan: *Looking sad.*
>
> Teacher: *So he'll be **frowning** will he? Do you know what **frown** means?*
>
> Alan: *Yes, he'll need to, you know, make his face look sad.* (Alan makes a frown.)
>
> Teacher: *So can you say what you'll do again but this time use the word frown?*
>
> Alan: *Yeah! I'm going to make Sam frown.* (Sam overacts and they both laugh.)

> Note for example how the teacher introduced the word *portray*, but reformulated it using the more common term *show*.

Later on when required to explain their sculpture to the group, they used the words *portray*, *facial expression* and *frown*. That is, they were appropriating and recasting the language from this previous conversation. As well, the teacher had asked all pairs to introduce their sculpture by starting with the clause 'Our sculpture portrays Mari …' (focus on language functions of explaining and describing).

Partner work

Partner or group work is essential for EL learners, not only because it promotes more learning opportunities through talk, but also for affective reasons. Pica's research (1992) suggests that students often feel more comfortable interacting with their peers than with teachers. She terms this 'equality of speaker status'. Working in cooperative friendship groups encourages students to take more risks and thus make more attempts to practise the target language. The implication therefore is for a lot of cooperative work with peers in small groups, with activities that make

Focus on oracy

it possible to speak purposefully and negotiate the meaning. As stated earlier, oracy tasks should precede and then continue to be an integral part of a reading and/or writing teaching and learning sequence. Many of these strategies are termed communicative activities.

Communicative activities

Communicative activities are based on the premise that students acquire language when they understand *what's* said; that is, they understand the content.

Krashen (1982) uses the term 'comprehensible input'. This is not to be associated with simplified language. To the contrary, and if we link it with the principles of 'scaffolding' and the 'zone of proximal development', it means raising the bar just a little higher than where the student might be at, but doing so with the aid of many of the conditions mentioned before (use of translation from L1, visual aids and concrete materials, gestures, building on prior knowledge and so forth).

This premise also means that the focus is on using language in authentic contexts. That is, that oracy tasks will occur within the context of content learning (across all curriculum areas) and not in isolated drill practice.

Communicative activities are also based on the premise that language is learned through use. Not only is comprehensible input important, but so too is 'comprehensible output' (Swain, 2000), and the emphasis should initially be on approximation rather than accuracy to encourage the student to feel more confident and take risks, and practise communicating (output). Swain uses the terms 'stretched' or 'pushed' language to explain that we need to provide situations and learning experiences that require students to both problem solve and negotiate meaning through extended and sustained conversations. *How* it is said (whether the grammar is correct) is secondary. This does not mean that the grammar is not important, but *initially* the emphasis should be on what the student produces to indicate an understanding of the concept. Then attention can be given to further developing both tasks and teaching strategies that model and teach the correct language form, and Chapters 5 and 6 highlight this.

The following checklist is helpful when deciding how useful an activity may be:

- Is talking necessary?
- Is there an information gap?
- Is interaction necessary? Are all children in a group involved, either in speaking or in listening?
- Will the experience involve the students in natural, meaningful conversation?
- Are reliable models of language readily available for students who need support?
- Are relevant 'chunks' or stretches of language being reinforced?
- Is there sufficient visual and contextual support to enable beginners in English to interpret meaning?
- Is thinking involved?
- Are relevant areas of the curriculum being reinforced?
- Does the experience allow for the involvement of all participants?
- How does this learning experience link to the mainstream program?
- Is the pace right, with enough variety within a given time span?

© Adapted by Kerrie Reid and Helen West, Catholic Education Office, Sydney

What it looks like in practice

The following activities are examples of just some strategies which should occur within the context of an *extended learning sequence* rather than as isolated 'one-off' lessons. Some strategies are referred to again in later chapters and other oracy activities will be introduced, especially in Chapter 7. Communicative activities are frequently planned for Beginning and Emerging English learners, but as the following examples demonstrate, they are also suitable for those in the Developing and Consolidating English phases. Furthermore, commercial examples may at times fit perfectly with the planned area of study, but by and large the learning potential is heightened when a generic idea is modified to directly relate to the learning objectives as demonstrated in this chapter.

Communicative activities can be classified generally as either collaborative or information gap.

Collaborative tasks:
- Group members usually receive the same information (eg article to be read, commercial game to be played such as Monopoly).
- Students are organised to work collaboratively on the task.
- The degree of interaction among students is variable.

Information gap activities:
- Students do not all possess the same information (commercial games such as Battleships and Guess Who? are examples of these).
- All students need to exchange their differing information to complete the task. That is, they need to negotiate to ensure they receive accurate information.
- Every student must talk.

Examples of information gap activities

Barrier games

As the title suggests, there is both a physical barrier (a school bag, for example) so that students cannot see their partner's information, because there is also an *information* barrier (refer to Figures 6.9 and 6.10, page 125). Each person has separate information that requires their partner to ask questions in order to obtain information so that they can complete the task.

> Refer to Figures 4.2 and 4.3.

Example 1: Landmarks of Australia

This barrier game was constructed as just one of many activities within a unit of work for seven-year-old students in the Emerging English phase when reading the book *Are we there yet?* (Lester, 2004). It's an adaptation from an activity developed by ELL teacher Caterina Batieri. The students were required to attend to the literary aspects of the book and at the same time it was integrated with

Focus on oracy

Figure 4.2
Player A
(NB student has a copy of the book to refer to)

Ideas for asking and seeking information:

A: *It's a really fun place to go to.*
B: *Is it in Queensland?*
A: *No, it's west of there.*
B: *Is it in the Northern Territory?*
A: *No, it's west of there.*
B: *Western Australia?*
A: *Yes.*
B: *Do they look like fingers?*
A: *Yes!*
B: *The Pinnacles!*
A: *Yes!*
= 3 points

Figure 4.3
Player B (NB student has a copy of the book to refer to)

Ideas for asking and seeking information:

A: *It's a famous building.*
B: *Is it in New south Wales?*
A: *Yes.*
B: *Do people go there to see plays?*
A: *Yes and they also go to listen to orchestras.*
B: *It's the Opera House!*
A: *Yes!*
= 3 points

a study about Australia and significant landmarks. This activity came towards the end of the unit sequence to consolidate their learning about significant landmarks.

The objective is for Player A to describe the location of a site and for Player B to identify the significant site. This is modelled for the student on their worksheet. A way to ensure that there is a lot of describing and clarifying is to have a point score – one point if the answer is given after only one question and three points if they have to ask at least two questions before answering.

The predominant language functions being used are describing and defining but the conversation doesn't necessarily stop there. For example, when some students were playing this game, they also began to talk about their experiences demonstrating the opportunity for more varied language use than in most isolated specific skills-based lessons.

Student 1: *Have you been on the Harbour Bridge? I have. My dad took us for a walk on it.*

Student 2: *Yeah, I've been on it heaps because sometimes I go with my Dad in his truck but I've never walked on it.*

Example 2: Communicative crosswords

These crosswords are designed so that one person has the crossword with all the down answers and the other person has the same crossword but they only have the across answers. Each person is required to both talk and listen to seek information.

This activity is suited for all curriculum areas and aids and consolidates topic vocabulary and spelling for a specific content area. The language focus is on describing, explaining, clarifying and negotiating for information, but when observing students you will often note that the discussion does not just revolve around solving the clue. Students usually talk about other concepts and topic content as they work together. This crossword was made by Kerrie Reid and Helen West at the Catholic Education Office, Sydney using www.puzzlemaker.com. If you are using this program, select the 'criss cross' option.

Completing this crossword came towards the end of a unit of work on the circulatory system and so the clues were not provided by the teacher as the aim was for students to independently practise the target language. As such, it also formed a useful assessment tool. The sequence is as follows:

1. Building knowledge of the topic: Students receive a concept map outline and in pairs record known information.
2. Teacher reads a text (several times) that explains the circulatory system.
3. In pairs, students complete the concept map and form quads to share information.
4. Students complete crossword using their concept map to aid them.

Note that the students are also using the function of comparison with language structures such as 'not as big as' and 'they're bigger'.

This is a good example of a sequence from controlled to guided to independent support (see page 38 of Chapter 3). For example, to explain the word 'veins', the student might refer to their concept map from the guided support stage and say: *They're thin tubes which carry blood around the body but they're bigger than capillaries, but not as big as arteries.*

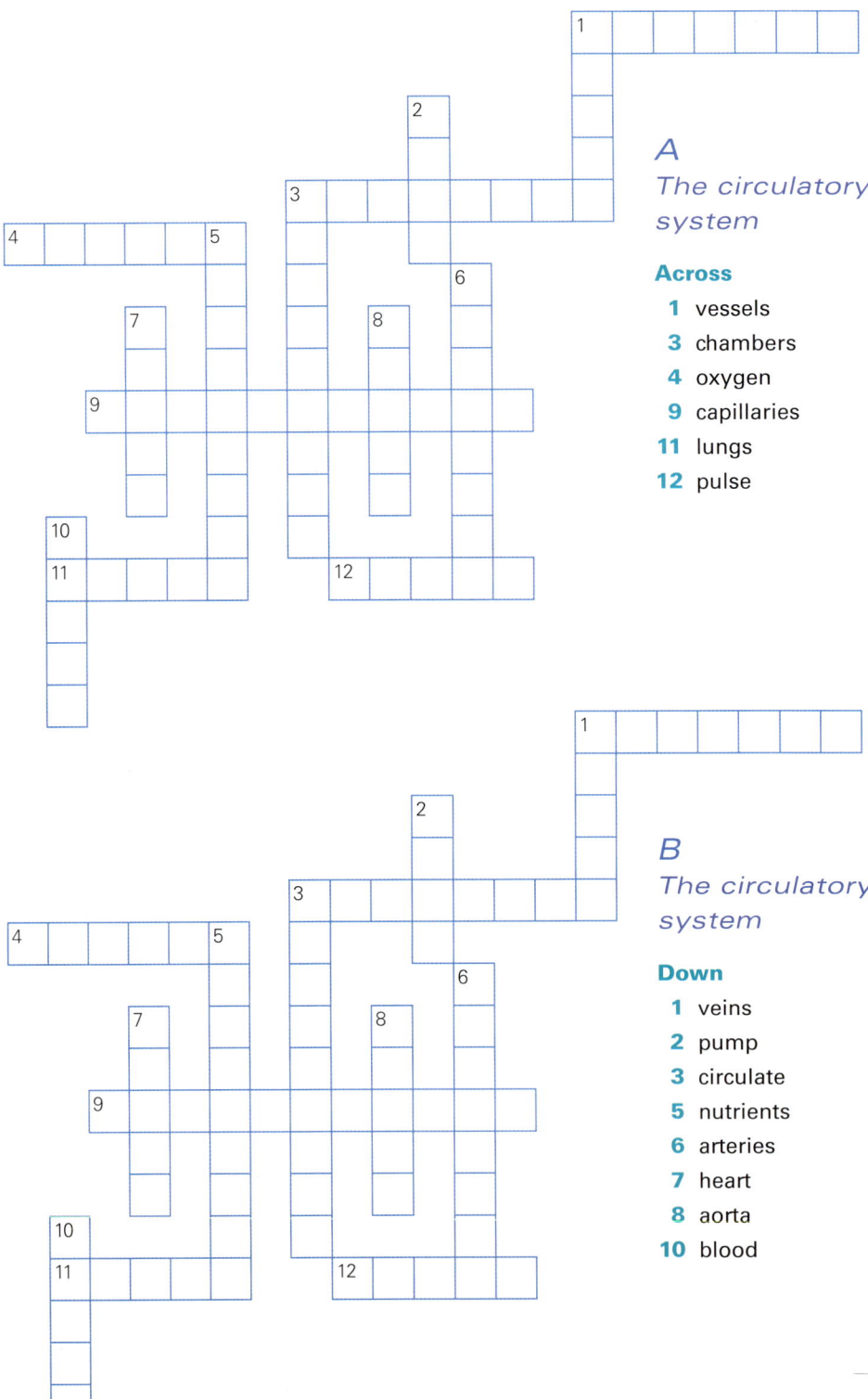

Figure 4.4
Crossword A, 'The circulatory system' ©Kerrie Reid and Helen West; Catholic Education Office, Sydney

A
The circulatory system

Across
1 vessels
3 chambers
4 oxygen
9 capillaries
11 lungs
12 pulse

Figure 4.5
Crossword B, 'The circulatory system' ©Kerrie Reid and Helen West; Catholic Education Office, Sydney

B
The circulatory system

Down
1 veins
2 pump
3 circulate
5 nutrients
6 arteries
7 heart
8 aorta
10 blood

Focus on oracy

A similar sequence was planned for twelve-year-old students studying Federation.

A
Should Australia have been federated in 1901?

Across
- 3 exconvicts
- 7 federation
- 8 nation
- 9 issue
- 10 tax

Figure 4.6
Crossword A, 'Should Australia have been federated in 1901?' ©Kerrie Reid and Helen West; Catholic Education Office, Sydney

B
Should Australia have been federated in 1901?

Down
- 1 opinion
- 2 population
- 4 patriotic
- 5 resident
- 6 colony

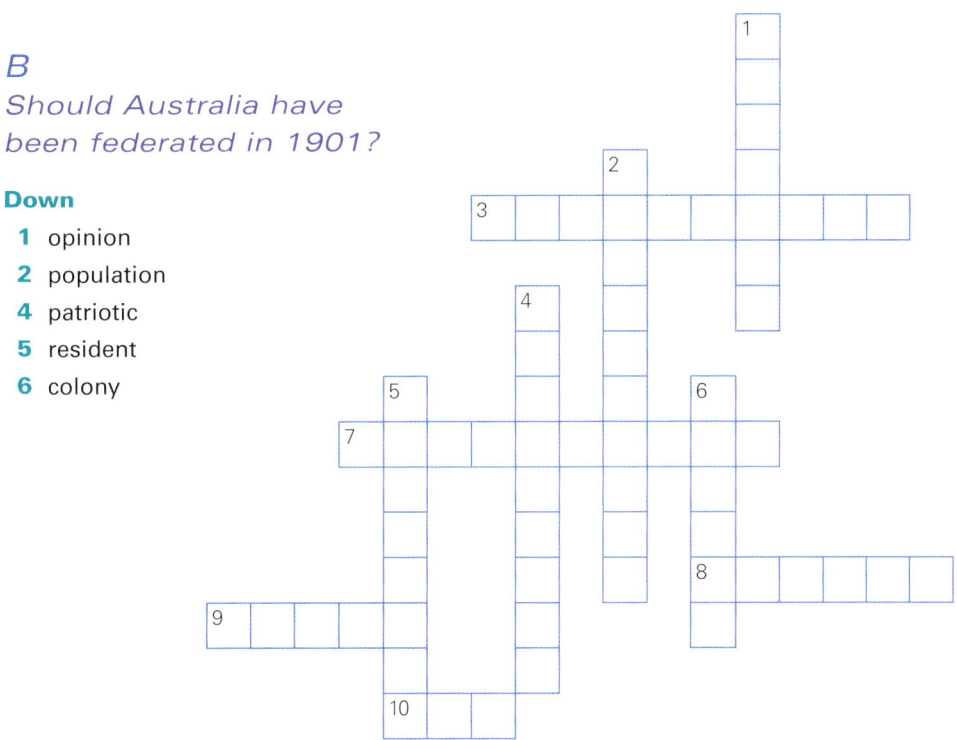

Figure 4.7
Crossword B, 'Should Australia have been federated in 1901?' ©Kerrie Reid and Helen West; Catholic Education Office, Sydney

How to

Make a complete crossword with answers and clues. This becomes the master sheet and can be used as the marking guide for students later:
- Cut and paste this crossword to make two more crosswords.
- Label one of these *Crossword A* and the other *Crossword B*.
- *Crossword A*: delete all down answers (and down clues if applicable). Retain across answers (and across clues if applicable).
- *Crossword B*: delete all across answers (and across clues if applicable). Retain down answers (and down clues if applicable).
- Person A then gives the clue for 1 across.
- Person B then gives the answer, if known. This is verified by Person A and they both write the word on their crossword.
- Person B then gives their clue for 2 down and so on.
  You might like to laminate these for future use.

Variations and extensions

Having provided sufficient teacher modelled examples, encourage students to make their own crosswords. They should do this in pairs so that they talk as they negotiate the construction. Students enjoy this and it is a valuable language learning experience. For instance, some twelve-year-old learners in the late Emerging English phase made a communicative crossword for seven-year-olds who were reading *Mum goes to work* by Libby Gleeson (1992) and in this case they wrote clues as well. The activity ensured that the twelve-year-old children read the book carefully in order to write the clues. This book is not age-appropriate and in other circumstances one could not expect twelve-year-olds to be engaged with its content. However, because the purpose was to provide a crossword for seven-year-olds, the students were engaged in a story which was at their reading ability.

Example 3: Taronga zoo map

Before going on an excursion to the zoo, ten-year-old students downloaded a map of the zoo (see Figure 4.8). The teacher made about twenty clue cards to go with this map. Another aim was to consolidate their understanding of the maths concept of coordinates.

How to play

Student A picks up a card and reads the information to Student B. Student B then finds the coordinates and provides the answer. Examples of clue cards are shown on page 61.

Spot the Difference

Often Spot the Difference is played using pictures and students need to find the differences in the pictures, but it can also be used for reading. For instance, when learning about the features of procedural texts some eleven-year-old children

Focus on oracy

Figure 4.8
Taronga Zoo map

Taronga Zoo clue card

Explain and ask:
The coordinate is 13 G. What is the name of this area and what is the name of the animal shown in the picture?

Answer:
African Waterhole and the name of the animal is Giraffe.

Taronga Zoo clue card

Explain and ask:
Find the Lower Entry/Exit area at the southern end of the map. Now find the disabled sign. What would be the closest coordinate?

Answer:
The coordinate is T 21.

made tabouleh for their end of term BBQ party. They sourced recipes from the internet and used one of these to make their tabouleh. As well, the different recipes were printed and used for the following activity.

Student A used the first recipe and Student B used the second recipe:

> 1 bunch of fresh parsley
> 3–4 medium tomatoes, diced
> Juice of 1 lemon or to taste
> 3 tablespoons fine bulgur
> (and so forth)

> 3 tablespoons fine bulgur
> 3 medium firm ripe tomatoes, diced into small cubes
> 1 cup chopped flat leaf parsley
> Juice of 1 to 2 lemons
> (and so forth)

Student A: *My recipe says juice of 1 lemon or to taste. Does yours?*

Student B: *No my recipe says juice of 1 to 2 lemons.*

On each of their sheets (which were laminated for reuse) they wrote 'same' or 'different' next to each ingredient. A cloze activity was also made from the procedural section to focus on the action verbs within a cooking recipe (refer to page 98 of Chapter 5 for information about the cloze strategy).

Bingo

The following topic words were used to play bingo. The words below were on the call-out sheet. Refer to instructions for playing bingo at for example www.dltk-cards.com/bingo/instructions.htm.

Figure 4.9
Bingo master sheet

knife سكينة	mint نعناع	bowl طاسة سلطانية	salt ملح
tablespoon كبيرة معلقة	parsley بقدونس	tomato بندورة	water ماء
lemon حامض ليمون	cutting board لوح خشب للقطع عليه	olive oil زيت زيتون	utensils اوعية وعاء
garlic ثوم	ingredients المحتويات	tabouleh تبولة	measuring cup كوب قياس
bulgur برغل	shallots بصل اخضر	black pepper فلفل اسود	garlic crusher ثوم سحاقة

Focus on oracy

Back-to-back viewing

Kerrie Reid and Helen West from the Catholic Education Office, Sydney developed this strategy for students studying Antarctica.

Back-to-back Viewing

Students sit in two lines and back-to-back to view a DVD. Students in line 1 face the screen and students in line 2 face away from the screen.

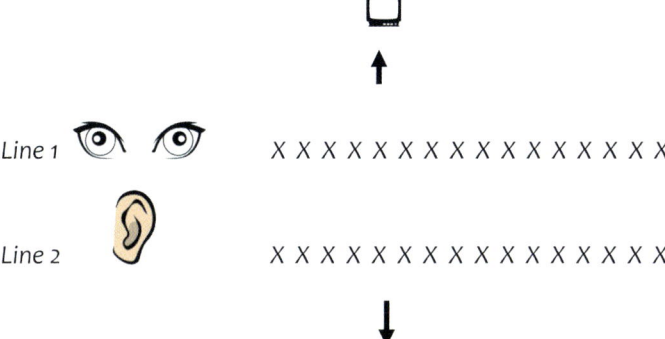

Students listen or view a short section of the DVD and then in pairs share what they a) heard and b) saw. Students can be given a matrix to record. Students swap positions and view the next section of the DVD and repeat the process.

Example of recording matrix:

	What did you see?	What did you hear?
Why is Antarctica a unique environment?		
How can the environmental damage be managed?		
What is being done to ensure Antarctica will be protected in the future?		
New or unfamiliar words…		

Module 6.0

ESL Matters

Figure 4.10
Back-to-back viewing © Kerrie Reid and Helen West; Catholic Education Office, Sydney

Other information gap strategies

The above examples are not exhaustive and other strategies that fit into this category include 'Kim's game', 'describe and draw' and 'enquiry and elimination' tasks. Many examples can be sourced from the internet, but as can be seen above, it is easy to use a generic idea found elsewhere to make activities that integrate with your existing program; that is, match directly to the concepts you are teaching.

Collaborative tasks

- Group members generally receive the same information (eg article to be read; commercial game to be played such as Monopoly).
- Students are organised to work collaboratively on the task (pairs or triads are usually best).
- The degree of interaction among students is variable.

Spot the Difference as a collaborative task

Previously Spot the Difference was demonstrated as an information gap task. Below is an example of Spot the Difference as a collaborative task. A group of ten-year-old students were reading the book *Mirrors* by Jeannie Baker 2010. Using only pictures it tells the story of two contemporary families: one in inner-city Sydney and the other in the Valley of Roses in southern Morocco. Students used this information to focus on the language of comparison and contrast. The following structures were written on cards.

both	in comparison	whereas	the main differences are
is the same as	neither	are similar	is similar
the main difference is	unlike the	compared to	in contrast to

The cards were placed face down and students had to pick up a card and make a statement which they then wrote as illustrated in Figure 4.11.

In the example on the next page (see Figure 4.12), the students worked in a group of three. This is a good example of language learning in maths. These ten-year-old students in Rebecca Hillis's class were in the Developing English phase. Two were from a Vietnamese language background and the other from a Cantonese language background. The conceptual understanding about the features of prisms is correct and well explained. In terms of grammar, however, it is evident that these students had not fully mastered the use of plurals and articles. This work sample therefore provides the basis (assessment) for planning further tasks that will directly attend to these grammatical features.

Focus on oracy

Figure 4.11
Spot the Difference using the language of comparison

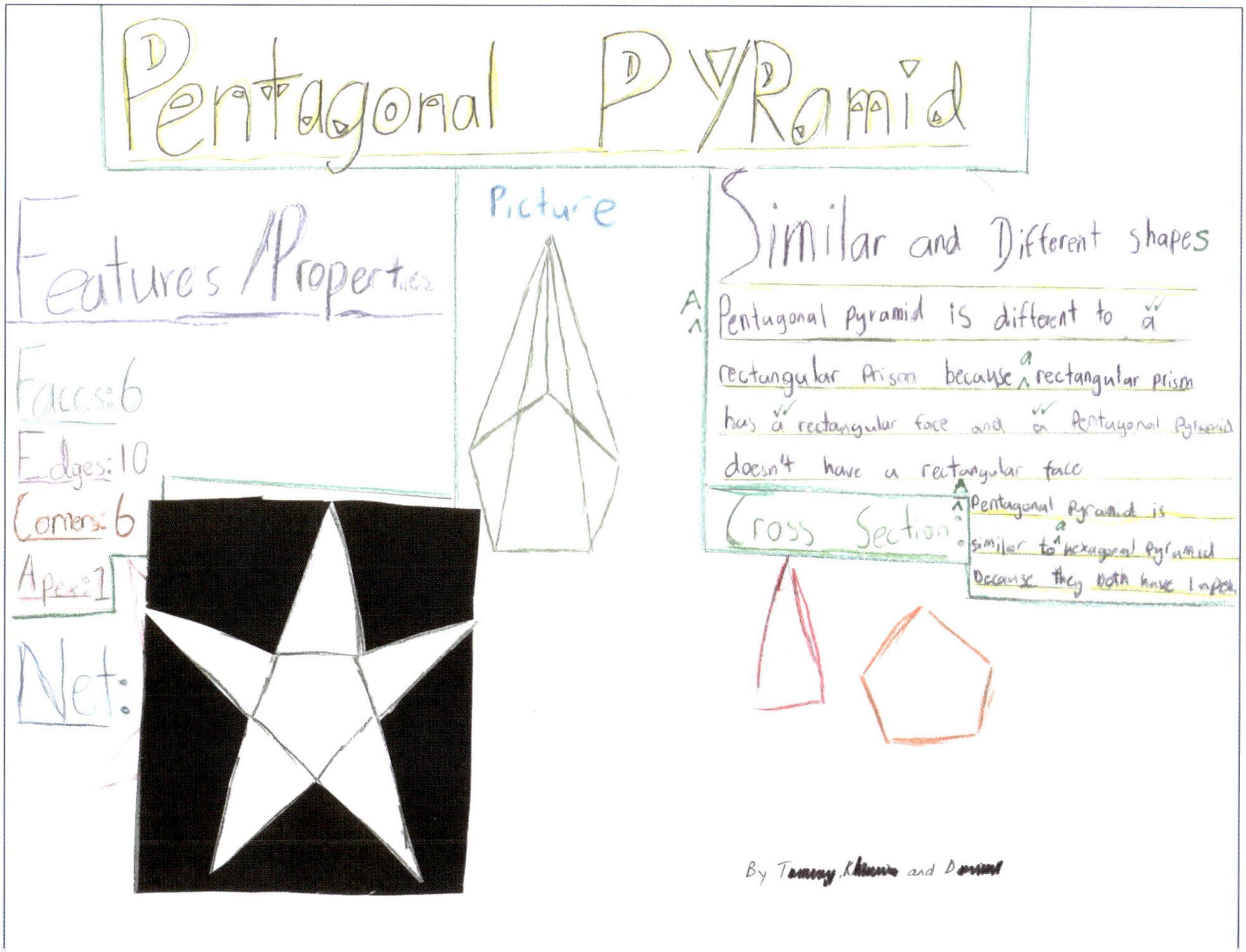

Figure 4.12
English language learning occurs in all curriculum areas

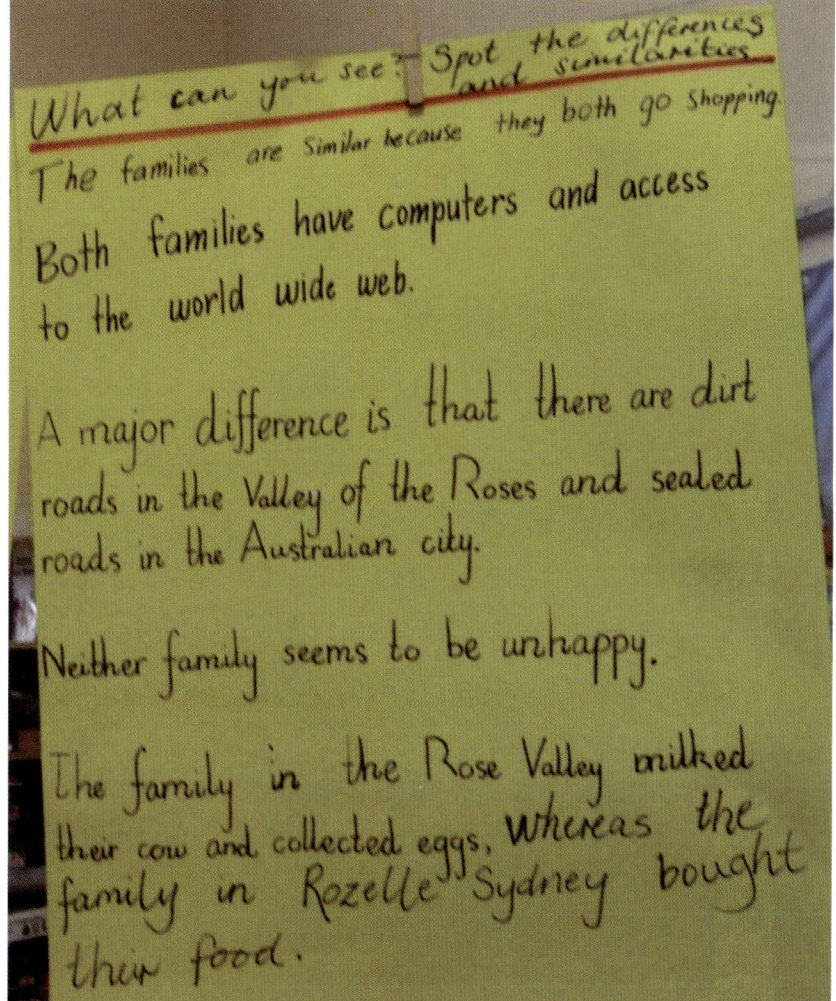

Graphic organisers

These are ways of collating and presenting information diagrammatically, dependent on the purpose. For instance, a concept map (see page 92 in Chapter 5) may be used to begin a new unit of work to ascertain what students already know. Information is then added as the unit progresses, or conversely it might be used at the end of a unit to ascertain what content the student now knows. Venn diagrams (see page 102 in Chapter 5) are useful for comparing and contrasting. There are numerous websites that illustrate the variety of organisers and explain both their purpose and use in far more detail than space allows here. The following graphic organiser sites are very useful.

- http://vels.vcaa.vic.edu.au/support/domainsupport/thinking/organisers.html
- www.writedesignonline.com/organizers/index.html.

Here we will focus is on just one organiser: the matrix, to demonstrate its many possibilities across subject areas.

The matrix organiser

A matrix is a way of organising and collating information. Matrix activities can also be made as information gap activities, as was demonstrated in the 'back-to-back viewing' example (Figure 4.10 on page 63), but can also be constructed as collaborative tasks where students have the same information. Together they need to talk about the content, consolidate their conceptual and/or vocabulary knowledge and glean the relevant facts that might then be used for further written work.

As for all graphic organisers, there are many variations, and the examples below illustrate just some options. The benefits of this strategy are dependent on the purpose, but in general terms listening, talking, reading and writing are all utilised.

Example 1: Matrix to collate weather information to both focus on the language of weather and past, present and future tenses

The language focus is on describing using vocabulary about weather (minimum/maximum temperature, Celsius and so forth). This also formed the basis for a cloze exercise to focus on past, present and future tense as the following example demonstrates. In this case, the students needed to read the online weather map

Today's weather for capital cities of Australia (excerpt from matrix)					
	Minimum (min) to maximum (max) temperature	Rain	Cloudy	Partly cloudy	Sunny
Sydney	19 to 25	no	no	no	yes
Melbourne	13 to 23	yes	yes	no	no
Perth	18 to 28	no	no	yes	no

Focus on oracy

for the day's forecast to complete the matrix. Then, using the information from the matrix, as well as reading the table on the same screen that reported yesterday's temperatures, they completed a cloze.

> *Excerpt of cloze exercise following completion of the matrix*
>
> Use both your matrix for today's expected weather and the table reporting yesterday's forecast to insert the following information:
>
> The maximum temperature in Sydney today will be _____ degrees Celsius.
>
> The maximum temperature in Perth today _____ _____ 28° (degrees) Celsius.
>
> Yesterday the _____ temperature in Adelaide _____ 15° (degrees) Celsius.
>
> Yesterday the minimum _____ in Sydney _____ 19° (degrees) Celsius.
>
> It is expected that the _____ temperature in Melbourne _____ _____ 23° (_____) Celsius.

Note that unless you are using cloze for testing purposes, aim to always have students work with a partner to enable them to talk about the content. You can find more information about cloze passages in Chapter 5, page 98.

Example 2: Collating information for an information report

The language focus is on the topic vocabulary and information specific to some Australian animals. In pairs, students researched information and completed the matrix.

Australian animal information report (excerpt from matrix)							
Animal	General classification	Appearance	Habitat	Diet (carnivore, omnivore, herbivore)	Movement	Reproduction	Other interesting facts
Kangaroo	marsupial				Hops on back legs and uses tail for support		
Black snake							
Koala				Herbivore; mostly eucalyptus leaves and some flowers	Crawls slowly on 4 legs		
Echidna							

The completed matrix was used for many purposes including the writing of an information report on one of the animals, and the language function of generalisation was used, but it was also used to consolidate students' use of the language of comparison. For example:
- *Although* kangaroos and koalas are both marsupials their ability to move is quite different. *Whereas* kangaroos can hop very quickly, koalas move more slowly.
- Snakes are carnivorous but koalas are herbivores.

Example 3: Junk mail – don't curse it use it!

The aim of this matrix was to classify items in a shopping brochure in order to:
- consolidate the mathematical concepts of greater than and less than
- calculate savings on specials
- match maths symbols to the written word.

Classifying greater than (>) and less than (<)				
Greater than (>) $4.99	Less than (<) $12.99	Between $1.50 and $3.99	Saving more than than $1.00, but no more than $1.48	Saving more than $10.00
Box of chocolates				Jumper Great saving! Was $39.99 now only $19.99!

This matrix was just one activity during maths groups. Following the completion of the matrix, the students presented their findings as an oral report.

Dictogloss

This is a technique adapted from Ruth Wajnryb (1990). The teacher or another student reads aloud a passage (usually about 100 words) at normal pace several times and students reconstruct it. While the initial focus is on listening skills, it is particularly valuable because it integrates listening with talking, reading and writing. This is not a traditional dictation. Rather the aim is for students to reconstruct for meaning using key grammatical structures and vocabulary and this is made clear in the following explanation.

The four stages in the procedure are building up content knowledge, listening to the text, reconstruction of the text and comparison of versions of the text. This is now explained using volcanoes as the topic, and specifically what happens in a volcanic eruption.

Stage 1: Building knowledge of the topic

In this phase, the context was provided by:
- Visual stimulus relating to the topic of text (see Figure 4.13).
- Brainstorming about the topic. Using the think, pair, share strategy, students brainstormed their existing knowledge and began filling in the following matrix on the interactive white board (IWB).

Focus on oracy

What we already know	What we want to know	What we found out

At the same time, they were prepared for likely unfamiliar vocabulary such as eruption and substance.

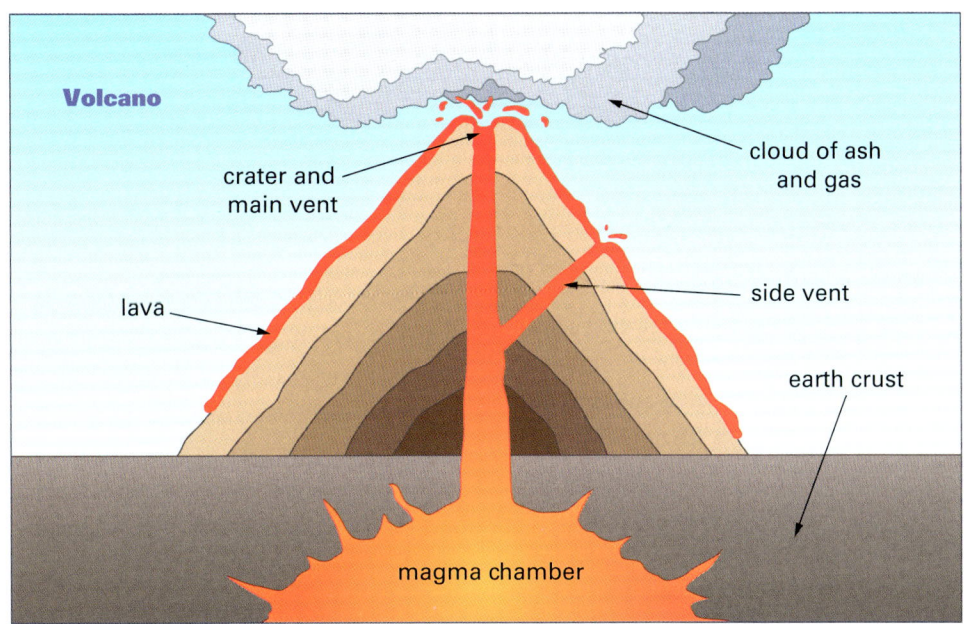

Figure 4.13
Visual stimulus relating to volcanos

Stage 2: Listening to text

First the teacher read a short piece of text twice at normal speed. The first time, the students just listened to the entire text to get the gist of the passage as a whole. The second time, they (individually) jotted down key topic words. As well, students might write some of the syntactical information (function words) surrounding the key words, but the teacher needs to emphasise that the aim is to paraphrase as opposed to verbatim dictation.

Stage 3: Reconstruction of text

In groups of three (selecting one person to be the scribe), students recreated the text they heard using the key words they had individually jotted down and their collective understanding of what the text was about. Again it was explained that their text did not have to be exactly the same as the original. Rather, it should capture the meaning and intent of the original.

Stage 4: Comparison

Having reconstructed the text, each triad joined with another triad to share and compare texts, at which time they made alterations or corrections. The original text was then displayed on the IWB and returning to their group, they compared their reconstructions with the original and discussed their accuracy in terms of topic content.

Some benefits

Apart from familiarising students with different genres, the teacher can identify difficulties for future English lessons. Importantly also, students learn that they can glean main ideas and then write them in their own words rather than copying.

Original text

What happens in a volcanic eruption?

Deep below the Earth's surface it is so hot that some rocks slowly melt and become a thick flowing substance called magma. Because it is lighter than the solid rock around it, magma rises and collects in magma chambers. Eventually some of the magma pushes through vents and breaks at the Earth's surface. Magma that has erupted is called lava.

The force of the explosion depends on how runny or sticky the magma is. If the magma is thin and runny, gases can escape easily from it. When this type of magma erupts the lava flows slowly and so the eruption rarely kills people because they have enough time to escape. If the magma is thick and sticky, gases cannot escape easily and so it is a violent explosion and often kills people.

(Adapted from http://vulcan.wr.usgs.gov/Outreach/AboutVolcanoes/how_do_volcanoes_erupt.html)

Students' example: Pia, Holly and Nadia

What happens in a volcanic eruption?

Deep below Earth it's so hot that some rocks melt and become a thick flowing substance called *magma*. It's lighter than the solid rock around it and the magma rises and collects in magma chambers. Eventually the magma pushes through vents and breaks at the Earth's surface. Magma is called *lava*.

When the magma is thin and runny, gases can escape easily from it and the lava flows slow and doesn't kill many people but if it's thick and sticky, gases cannot escape easily. This violent explosion can kill people.

Annotations:
- The students have done a good job. The tense is consistent and accurate and the main ideas of the text have been reconstructed.
- The title was displayed and the students copied it down. (Example of focus on nominalisation.)
- It would be more accurate to have written the word *surface* as well but this is not a major problem.
- The students use the contracted form for pronouns. At a later stage it will be explained that traditionally this is not acceptable in academic writing but at this stage I want to concentrate on accuracy of information and sentence structure.
- This sentence is ambiguous and this was discussed.
- The students left out the first sentence but meaning is retained.
- A very common mistake with EL learners, indicating more lessons on how to use adverbs are necessary.

Posing questions to advance oracy

Asking questions that promote students to think critically about what they are reading, viewing or listening to, not only provides a focus for students but also provides them with something substantial to talk about. Monica Palmer is a teacher educator at Immaculate Heart of Mary Primary School in Sefton, Sydney where 90 per cent of the nine- to twelve-year-old students are in the Developing and Consolidating English phases. Monica has developed the 'Palmer Plan for Productive Participation and Purposeful Perceptive Talk about Texts' (Palmer Plan) and is conducting an action research project at her school at the time of writing this book.

The sequence, which can be recursive, is:

Focus on oracy

- **Pose** the question(s) to focus the students' thinking before reading and/or viewing and/or listening.
- **Share** the text.
- **Pause** after reading, viewing or listening to the text and ask the question again.
- **Ponder**: think about the question.
- **Pair**: discuss the question with a partner using the 'Language Prompts' cards.
- **Panel**: join with another pair and continue to discuss the question.
- **Present**: share answers with the class.

© Monica Palmer, 2011

The questions for middle years students include those shown in Table 4.2.

Table 4.2 Comprehension through conversation language prompts

Evaluating	Analysing and synthesising	Identifying the main idea
Would you want to read another book by this writer? Why? Why not?	How is the information from the text similar or different to other texts you have read?	What is the message in this text? How do you know?
If you were the writer, what part of the text would you feel most proud of having written? Why?	How do the main ideas in the text fit with your own point of view?	What is the main thing the author wants us to think about?
	How would you use this information in another situation?	What were you wondering about at the end of our reading?

Identifying the author's purpose	Inferring	Visualising
Why did the author write the text?	What do you think is really happening here? What did you have to do to make those inferences?	How can I see, feel, hear, taste, or smell parts of the text in my mind?
Who was this text written for? How do you know?	What are the clues in the text that confirm your ideas?	What image do you see in your head?
What is the author's point of view? How do you know?	How do the illustrations give you extra information?	How has the author created this mental image?

Self questioning	Verifying predictions	Making connections
Suppose? Imagine? Why do you think?	What information in the text proves that your prediction is correct?	How does this text remind you about things you already know?
Tell me a question you tried to ask yourself before you read this part of the text. How did you try to find out the answer?	After reading a little more, I now predict that …	How does this text remind you about others texts you have read?
What were you wondering about as you were reading?		

© Monica Palmer, 2011

In addition, as shown in Table 4.3, students are provided with language prompts to help them construct their ideas when discussing with peers. Note that 'read' can be substituted for 'listened' or 'viewed'.

Table 4.3 Comprehension through conversation language prompts

Evaluating	Analysing and synthesising	Identifying the main idea	Identifying the author's purpose
I would definitely read another text by this author because …	A similarity between this text and … is …	The main idea the author wants us to think about is …	The author created this text because …
I believe that this author is a talented writer because …	This text is comparable to … because …	The message the author wants us to think about is … I know this because …	Due to the use of the language features … we can determine that the author's point of view is …
I strongly believe this text was poorly written because …	There are distinct similarities between this text and …		The author generated his/her point of view by …
	A significant feature of this text I would use in my own life is …		The text was created to …

Inferring	Visualising	Self questioning	Verifying predictions
The illustrations gave me clues about the meaning by …	When I read the text, I created an image in my head that looked like …	Throughout the reading I was wondering why …	The information in the text that proves my prediction is accurate was …
I know about the character because the texts gave me clues. These clues were …	The words the author uses to create the imagery were …	During the reading I was wondering how …	The information in the text that proves my prediction is inaccurate was …
The phrase the author uses to give us extra clues about the meaning is …	The author has created a sensory experience by …	As the text unfolded I was pondering about …	
The author has used the metaphor … to express …			

© Monica Palmer, 2011

What this looks like in practice

As part of their reading program, a class of ten- and eleven-year-old students at this school listened to a podcast on the Ballarat Goldfields Diary at http://sheducationcom.ascetinteractive.biz/?id=untitled_2. The sequence was:

Focus on oracy

1 Before listening, the following visualising question prompts were *posed* on the IWB and remained there for children to see as they listened to the podcast.
   - How can I see, feel, hear, taste or smell parts of the text in my mind?
   - What image do you see in your head?
   - How has the author created this mental image?
2 Students listened to the podcast.
3 After listening the students paused and pondered (thought about the questions), and listened to the podcast at least once more.
4 In pairs, students discussed their mental images using the questions which were turned into statements for this discussion.
   - When I listened to the diary entry, the images that came into my head were …
   - Some words I heard the author use that sparked images in my head were …
   - When I heard the diary entry, I imagined that the gold rush time would feel like …
5 Students then formed a panel group of four, discussed their ideas and created a glog (www.glogster.com) on a computer.
6 Groups presented their glogs on the SMART Board to the class. Note that glogs are multimodal; the pictures below only illustrate the written and visual modes. Students also used audio and video to communicate their message.

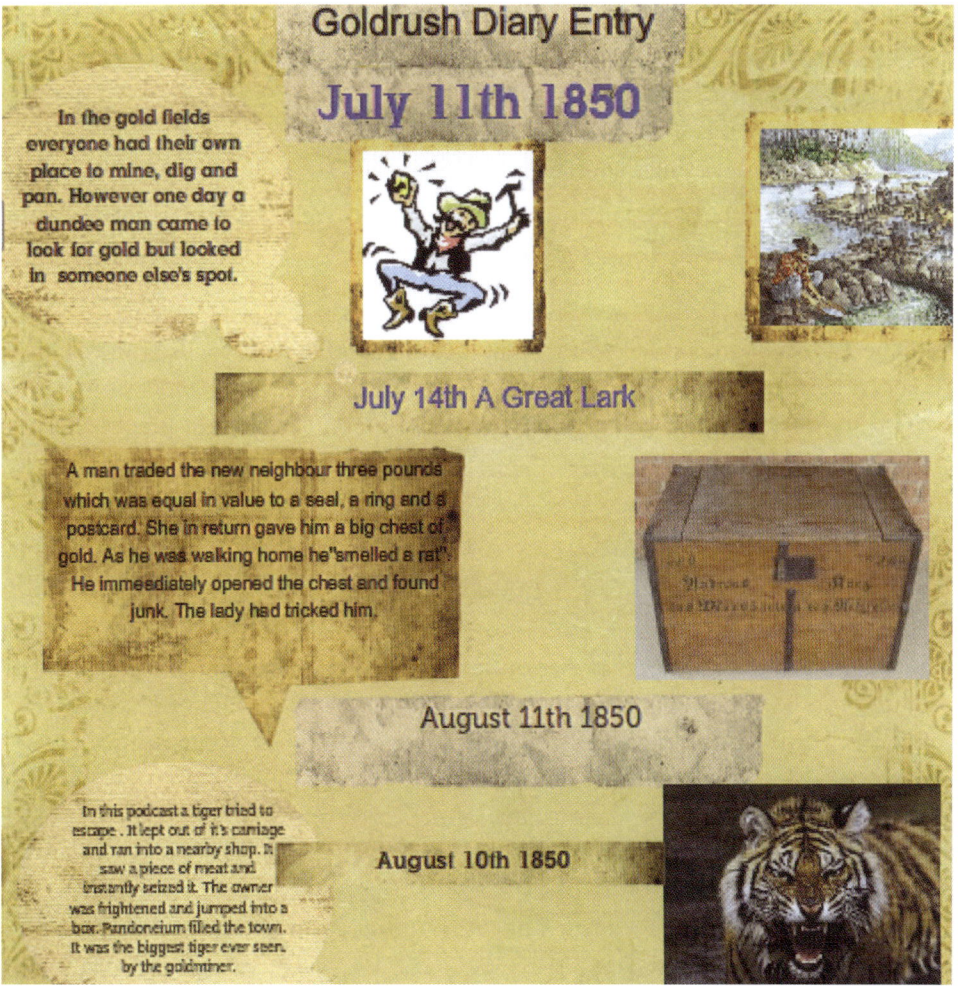

Figure 4.14
Collaborative group (four students) glog about life on the Goldfields

Figure 4.15
Collaborative group (four students) glog about life on the Goldfields

The Palmer Plan is referred to in the next chapter, which focuses on reading. As stated before, but reiterated now, the modes of oracy, reading and writing are artificially isolated in this book so the focus can be on each but in practice they are *not* isolated.

Other oracy activities

The examples in this chapter present just some of the strategies that can be used to ensure that students actively talk and listen using a range of language functions. Some of the strategies suggested below will be explored in further chapters:

- Text reconstructions (refer to page 104 in Chapter 5).
- Vocabulary clusters and clines (refer to pages 120–21 in Chapter 6).
- Cloze (refer to pages 98–101 in Chapter 5 and pages 121–23 in Chapter 6).
- Drama forms such as Readers' Theatre, improvisation and puppetry (refer to Chapter 7).

- Drama strategies such as sculpting, still image and voice collage (refer to Chapter 7 and the PETAA website for more information).
- Readers are also referred to Dufficy (2005) and Gibbons (2009) for further examples such as the enquiry and elimination, and describe and draw strategies.
- In addition, the Australian Curriculum's *English as an Additional Language or Dialect: Teacher Resource (EAL/D)* section will be updated continuously to include resources (www.acara.edu.au/curriculum/eald_teacher_resource/eald_teacher_resource.html).

The critical issue for EL learners is that these activities should be done in pairs, triads or quads and in rare cases larger groups but never as an individual activity because this negates the purpose and that purpose is fundamental for language learning success … talk *before*, *during* and *after* reading and writing. The next chapter, on reading, explores this further.

http://www.petaa.edu.au/

CHAPTER FIVE
FOCUS ON READING

> Digital texts are texts viewed and read on the screen of a computer or a hand-held mobile digital device (Walsh, 2011: 105).

The term reading is used throughout this chapter in a broad sense, and recognises both the reading and the viewing of a variety of texts, from print based hard copy books to **digital texts** and other existing and emerging technologies.

Reading on screen

Although students need the same skills to read the *written word* in digital texts, reading on screen does call for more complex skills and other processes (Coiro et al 2008; Zammit, 2008). Many print based texts such as picture books and factual texts are multimodal, and usually the combination is the printed word and static visuals. The choice of modes on screen, however, is usually greater with, for instance, the combination of the printed word, sound and moving and static images. In order to read (comprehend) digital texts, students need to know how these multiple modes combine to construct meaning. Navigating can also be more complex. Unlike hard copy texts, where for instance, pages are turned and usually sequentially, most web pages have multiple pathways and involve a knowledge of, for example, different URL domains, how to use hyperlinks, mouse hovers, and the role of bolding or highlighting. Therefore, the reader needs to skim and scan, and rely more on pictorial, typographical and organisational features than in print based texts to obtain information (Callow, 2008; Callow & Hertzberg, 2006).

Taking into account this complexity, a useful resource, that enables students to critically read on screen, and in particular the internet, has been developed by Dwyer and Harrison (2008) and Dwyer (2009). Working in threes, students take on the respective interchangeable roles of 'questioner', 'navigator' and 'summariser', emulating Palinscar and Brown's (1984) concept of these reciprocal roles with hard copy texts. Dwyer and Harrison designed these roles to help students achieve the following 'challenges', which are:

1 Developing effective questions for online inquiry.
2 Generating and revising search strings.
3 Investigating search results with a critical eye.
4 Previewing the website and locating online information.
5 Critically evaluating the relevance of online information.
6 Summarising, transforming and synthesising information.
7 Communicating information to others, using Web 2.0 technologies for literacy.

Another valuable resource is Maureen Walsh's recent PETAA publication *Multimodal literacy: Researching classroom practice* (2011). It details a wide variety of teaching and learning sequences for reading and viewing on screen and importantly, as Walsh explains, 'we need to realise … that we cannot just consider the differences between reading print and reading on screen as static comparisons' (Walsh, 2011: 10).

It is therefore beyond the scope of this chapter to discuss all aspects of both reading and viewing – that is a book in itself. Rather, this chapter's focus is on how students read the alphabetic text, because research shows (for example, Wallace, 1988) that EL learners tend to over-rely on graphophonics and this interferes with their ability to comprehend.

Learning to read and reading to learn

For beginners, learning to read and reading to learn are simultaneous acts. That is, while learning how to read, they also use the reading material to learn something, and this applies to both factual and fictional texts. However, as discussed in Chapters 1 and 2, we need to be mindful that texts differ, depending on, in particular, *register* and *purpose*. As well, the student's sociocultural background and schematic knowledge will affect how they read a text. Correspondingly, the author's sociocultural background and schematic knowledge can affect how they write the text.

This chapter begins by isolating the learning-to-read process, but in practice this should never be separated from reading to learn and, by implication, comprehend. Similarly, in practice, oracy will always be a part of the reading teaching and learning experience. We will start by discussing some aspects of early reading development, as this informs reading to learn. Moreover some students in the Developing English phase do still struggle with learning to read. The important (and often tricky) task is to choose texts that are at an appropriate and engaging emotional and social level – see the suggestions on the PETAA website: www.petaa.edu.au.

Reading *with* students

Reading with students on a daily basis is common practice in the early grades and should be given the same prominence in later grades because *hearing* a proficient model read a text and at the same time *seeing* the text allows the student to:
- become familiar with the reading process
- hear and see a good model of written English.

While there might be a place for independent student silent reading – commonly termed DEAR (Drop Everything And Read) or USSR (Uninterrupted Sustained Silent Reading), some students find it difficult to remain engaged during this activity (Bryan, 2007). With a crowded curriculum, I argue that the priority should be for daily modelled reading either in 'real time' or digitally. This is because reading *with* an experienced reader is a fundamental aspect of learning to read (Clay, 1982; Holdaway, 1979). This in part is why some students come to formal schooling already reading in English or another home language, while others are at least familiar with the process of reading and some of the associated skills. That is, these monolingual and multilingual students have this familiarity because they have read hard copy and digital texts with carers at home and/or preschool.

While many parents may not be aware of the technicalities and skills involved in the reading process, they do in fact teach these. With digital texts they demonstrate clicking and scrolling and the use of hyperlinks, for example. With hard copy books, they demonstrate skills such as book orientation and page turning; and with both types of texts they point to words, pictures and other visuals and discuss what is happening. If the child loves the text, then the parent will often read it multiple times, which ensures that repetition of language structures takes place – and this is not confined to fiction. Many children request repeated readings of favourite factual books. So while DEAR might have a place in the daily program, perhaps more important for EL learners is the acronym that I use: DEALTS (Drop Everything And Listen To Stories) – which also assumes they can see the text. As well as hard copy texts, podcasts or vodcasts can also be used, but it is important to make the transcript available for students to see and follow. This strategy uses many of the features of Holdaway's (1979) 'shared book experience', which is common in many early childhood classes. In shared book experiences students are *hearing* a good model (usually the teacher) of English syntax and fluency and at the same time observe and follow both the visual and printed text. Seeing the text is especially important because it enables the students to observe all the modes used, which might include visual and pictorial information, and the combination of all modes contributes to meaning – understanding the content.

Focus on reading

Learning to read: the process

Reading or decoding?

To begin, it is important to delineate the difference between reading and decoding and in so doing demonstrate the position this book takes on not only what reading is, but how to teach reading and in particular graphophonics – information related to letters and sounds.

> ### Example 1
>
> In Danish, the letters 'f' and 'a' and' r' put together say 'far' as in car. Do you know what it means in Danish? If you don't, then you are not reading you are just decoding (saying the word). That is, you do not comprehend the word. (By the way, it means father.)
>
> ### Example 2
>
> Here are some Hebrew letters.
>
> א   The name of this letter is Aleph and its sound within the word below is 'u' as in **up**.
>
> ב   The name of this letter is Vet and its sound within the word below is 'v' as in **love**.
>
> Here is the word אב , so it is pronounced **uv**. Hang on! Is this a typo? It should be **va**!
>
> Well ... no, because in Hebrew as for Arabic, one reads from right to left along the horizontal line. And what does it mean? It means father. Again, unless you know Hebrew you are simply decoding and unless you understand the *directionality of print* in this language then you do not possess that important principle of the reading process either.

From these two examples therefore, we can establish that *reading is synonymous with comprehending* as distinct from the various sub-skills needed in the reading process (two of which have just been mentioned – decoding and directionality).

Understanding that reading (comprehending) is *different* to decoding (saying the word) is a critical aspect that we must explain to students. Of course, to read (comprehend), one needs the various skills that make up the reading process. Students with limited literacy skills in L1 will need to learn the various sub-skills needed in the reading process, *but* if a student can already read in another language then they will have mastered much of the process. This is another reason for maintaining L1 and is also why older literate students with the right language learning conditions can master reading a new language better than younger students. Students literate in L1 may, for example, already understand the concept of print (albeit in another language), the conventions of using a particular text (directionality, page turning, clicking and so forth), the purpose of different texts (genres), and how to use prediction skills to gain meaning. They do not need to be retaught the skills and concepts they already know. Rather, they need to be reminded to use these skills when learning to read English.

Some students may have been learning English before arriving in Australia. In some cases their reading *skills* may be better than their oracy and written work because they have had more tuition in reading, but assessing whether they decode as opposed to read is important. I once taught a high achieving eleven-year-old Filipino girl. She read a passage from *The Twits* (Dahl, 1980) quite fluently. When asked what the passage was about, she had very little idea. She was decoding. Furthermore, many students when reading aloud (regardless of reading ability), concentrate on decoding rather than comprehending and especially on the first reading. This important point is addressed later in the chapter.

However, for all EL learners, irrespective of their ability to decode and so forth, assessment of their linguistic and schematic knowledge is crucial to ensure that they approach a text understanding not only the *purpose* of the text, but also the cultural *nuances* within it. Readers are reminded of the example in Chapter 3 where schematic knowledge affected some American students' reading of texts about wedding traditions. We will return to schematic knowledge later in the chapter, but first some of the important principles of learning to read as they relate to EL learners.

Graphophonics

> Graphophonics is the relationship between the printed letter (grapho) and its sound (phonology).

For students from language systems that use characters rather than letters (eg Chinese and Japanese) or connected scripts such as Arabic, teaching the Roman alphabet is an obvious first step. However, a literate student from a language background that uses the Roman alphabet may have different pronunciations for the *names* of some of the letters. For example, in Australia the name for 'z' is 'zed' as in 'zebra' and in America it is 'zee'. In Finnish the *name* for the letter 'h' is 'ho' and in Portuguese it is 'aga'.

If students don't know the names for the letters in the alphabet, many teachers find it useful to link this learning with learning to handwrite and use the Carnine Order (Carnine et al, 2004):

```
a  m  t  s  i  f  d  r  o  g
l  h  u  c  b  n  k  v  e  w
j  p  y  T  L  M  F  D  I  N  A
R  H  G  B  x  q  z  J  E  Q
```

Nevertheless, a rigid adherence to this order is problematic and there is a need for flexibility to ensure that the learning is authentic and purposeful. Take for example the kindergarten class (referred to in Chapters 1 and 3) who were reading *Grandpa and Thomas* (Allen, 2003) in Week 3 of Term 1. The language structures within this book are very repetitive with a concentration on the letters 't', 's' and 'g' so these were the letters used in handwriting that week for all students. Learning the written name correspondence was then followed up with explicit guided reading instruction with those who needed it – eleven of the twenty students already knew their alphabet (as distinct from knowing how to do foundation handwriting) and three of these eleven students were already independent readers. Nevertheless, in the teacher's program all students were learning the mechanics, be it handwriting and phonics or just handwriting, using a text of literary merit as the resource.

Phonology

Phonology is the study of the sound system, and as a broad term includes concepts such as syllables, rhythm and rhyme; and the next section explores the importance of teaching phonology *in context* and using well written material.

Teaching and learning the sounds of vowels within the context of a whole word

The sounds of vowels will vary according to their placement within a word. We cannot know the sound a vowel represents until we see it in context. Take for example the letter 'a'. Often the letter 'a' does not sound /ae/ as in hat. It often sounds /ar/ or /ay/.

For example, in the book *Grandpa and Thomas* referred to above, there are two different sounds for the letter 'a' in the one sentence: 'Thomas carries his bucket and spade'. In *carries*, the letter 'a' represents the /a/ sound as in *hat*. In *spade*, the letter 'a' represents the /a/ sound as in *day*. And the same vowel sound differences occur in the majority of structured texts for beginning readers found in many reading schemes. Take for example the sentence 'A train has wheels'. ('A' as in *but*, and 'a' as in *ay* and then 'a' as in *hat*).

Teaching and learning sound patterns in the context of a whole text and using the cueing system

Learning familiar sound patterns is important but it must not be done in isolation. It needs to be taught by examining the word within the context of a whole phrase, clause or sentence.

For example the word 'wind' with its rhyme (rime) 'ind' can be pronounced two different ways depending on its meaning:

> 1 *The wind blew fiercely.* (The word 'the' is a definite article used within a noun group. Whether you knew this grammar before reading about it just now is not relevant. Your experience with English syntax helped you, and in combination with your semantic knowledge about the words 'blew' and 'fiercely', you knew how to pronounce the word correctly. You were therefore reading (comprehending) as opposed to just decoding.
>
> 2 *You'll need to wind up the ropes on the parachute carefully so they don't get tangled.* (Again both syntax and semantics support the reader to predict the word. 'You'll need to', indicates that something to be done must follow (ie a main verb). Looking at the picture and reading the words 'the ropes' also assists and is further supported by the word 'parachute'.)

So, to pronounce 'wind' in each sentence correctly, you used a variety of cues to achieve meaning, as demonstrated in Figure 5.1. You used three cues to read 'The wind blew fiercely' (graphophonics, syntactic and semantic) and when reading 'You'll need to wind up the ropes on the parachute carefully so they don't get tangled', you may also have attended to the pictorial cue. In other words, to comprehend, we need more than graphophonics and this must be clearly and carefully explained to our EL students so that they understand that they need to rely on all three or four cues. One teacher for instance uses a modified version of Figure 5.1 to explain this critical concept to her students.

Figure 5.1

Cues for achieving meaning (ie reading)

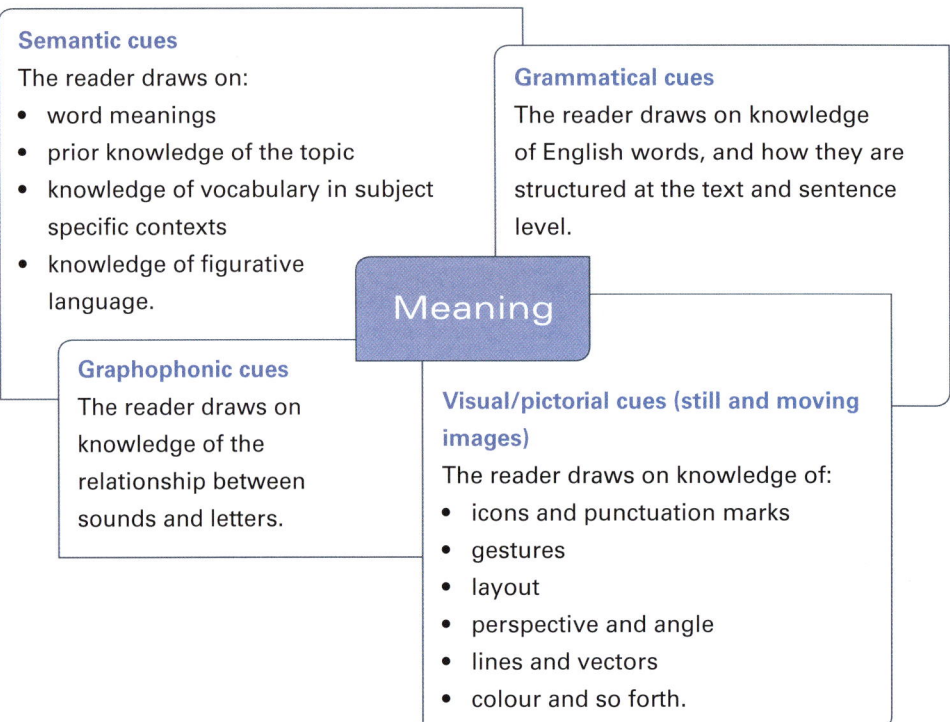

Using authentic words within the context of authentic texts

Importantly, the word 'wind' is a real word and can be explained, but the use of nonsense words is really problematic, which is why using well written authentic texts is so important. Regrettably, at the time of writing, some commercially available programs still use nonsense words and often in isolation as word lists. In one example and to practise c-v-c (consonant, vowel, consonant) words, 'words' include, 'fid', 'nev', 'joz' and for blends 'glant' and 'smat'. Monolingual students might recognise this nonsense, but EL learners often cannot distinguish the real from the nonsense. This added confusion complicates language learning and is detrimental to reading progress.

This is not to argue against the practice of word recognition, but the purpose *must* be authentic and aligned with a text being read for either its literary merit alone or linked to a topic being studied. Practice for c-v-c words, for example,

Focus on reading

might be linked to the words used when reading *The very hungry caterpillar* (Carle, 1981): *sun pop big fat*, or for *Grandpa and Thomas* (Allen, 2003): *bag rug big put dig tip pat*.

While the quantity of words may not be as great as in some commercially available lists, the *quality of the language learning is superior*. Attention should focus on 'onset' and 'rime' which is an important sub-skill of phonological awareness.

(here, 's' is the onset and 'un' the rime)

sun	pop	big	fat
run	top	dig	rat
fun	hop	pig	sat

The same principles apply with older students needing the same assistance but using texts that appeal to their age. In the example below, a group of ten-year-old students were reading 'Little Red Riding Hood', one of Roald Dahl's *Revolting rhymes* (1980). It was age- and interest-appropriate and is a good text for examining onset and rime. The table below was constructed. The words in red are from the text and the words in blue were ones that students provided.

eel as in **feel**	*eal* as in **meal**	*in* as in **grin**	*ough* as in **tough** and **enough**	*air* as in **hair** and **chair**
peel kneel	real veal	fin tin	rough	hair fair

The students also used other authentic texts to look at these concepts. For example, when one of the boys had a birthday, a selection of rhyming messages in commercial birthday cards were analysed and students then wrote their own rhyming messages to the birthday boy.

> Happy Birthday to Blake
> Who isn't a fake
> He's a friend
> Who often loses his pen
> But he's fun to be around
> Especially on the soccer ground

Another group of students, when studying the Australian Gold Rush, read (through singing) a variety of poems, including 'The unsuccessful swell' and 'Look out below' by Charles Thatcher (1852–78), as these poems also have good examples of onset and rime. They sang these ballads many times; and repetition is necessary to enhance reading development.

Using authentic repetitive texts

As for learning to drive a car, tell the time or bake cakes, repeating the activity (in this case, re-reading words) is necessary to achieve competency. This is why so many books for beginning readers are repetitive. Usually, however, quality literature which uses repetition as a literary feature has more repetition in it than simplified texts in many commercial reading schemes. For instance, I compared *Time for bed* (Fox, 1994) to a reading scheme reader which is also about going to bed on time. Just two examples were the number of times the word 'bed' and the word 'time' were repeated. In the reading scheme text, 'bed' is written five times and the word 'time' twice. In Fox's book both 'bed' and 'time' occur thirteen times. Furthermore, many students would prefer multiple readings of Fox's book, because of its imaginative storyline, as opposed to the reading scheme's five bland pages describing a child in bed.

Repeated readings

Not only is repeated reading of individual words important, so too is repeated readings of the whole text to glean meaning. Fox's book is not suitable for older students, but Dahl's (1980) parody of 'Little Red Riding Hood' is. Its appeal to students (as well as its focus on rhythm and rhyme) lends itself to multiple readings and especially Readers' Theatre (refer to Chapter 7 and the PETAA website: www.petaa.edu.au/). Similarly, poems that can be sung should be used, again capitalising on early childhood pedagogy, where reading is often taught through singing. While songs for early childhood students would not be suitable for older students, singing or choral reading of, for instance, a variety of bush ballads when studying the history of the Australian Gold Rush is suitable.

All the examples above demonstrate the importance of using genuine English words to focus on aspects of phonology within the context of authentic texts. Students can then use all cues to predict a word rather than relying on graphophonics alone. But there is another critical reason for using authentic texts with EL learners: They are usually better written because they do not simplify the language and hence do not make the language unnatural.

Using authentic (natural) language

We need to read the material before using it with students to assess the language structures for authenticity. Thinking that it will make reading easier for students, some reading scheme texts simplify the language but in fact such texts can make understanding more difficult, especially for EL learners (see Moustafa, 2001 for a good example). Simplifying the language often makes the message unrealistic or unnatural. Similarly, reducing the amount of language reduces the contextual support often needed to predict meaning. The table on page 85 demonstrates this. The left-hand column is an example of unnatural language and has been based on the language found in some 'readers' for beginners. The right-hand column illustrates how this contrived text might really (authentically) be written to convey the message.

Focus on reading

	Unnatural or contrived language about a child wanting his father to play with him	Authentic language (a real home conversation)	
The exclamation marks indicate that it is a demand. Therefore *said* is semantically inaccurate. Mark would not say 'come here' he would shout or yell or scream 'come here'.	Dad! Dad! 'Come here!' said Mark. 'Here is my toy.' Dad and Mark are playing with the toy.	Dad! Dad! 'Come here!' shouted Mark. Dad came in from the kitchen. 'What do you want?' 'Nick gave me this toy car for my birthday! Can you play with me?' Dad and Mark played with the car.	If we are asking for someone to come here, then they are somewhere else. This contextual information helps rather than hinders the reader. Providing more semantic detail often aids prediction (Moustafa, 2001).
In English we use the contracted form when speaking in casual or informal situations. In reality, Mark would have said 'here's.			

Many proficient English speakers know and use authentic language, despite exposure to contrived texts but if EL learners spend most of their time exposed to unnatural English models such as in the left-hand column above, then they are deprived of the varied, appropriate and authentic language structures used in English and hence this impedes their progress in learning academic English.

Selecting authentic factual texts

As for narratives, factual texts need to be evaluated and Unsworth's categories are a useful tool for ascertaining how useful a text really is in terms of providing factual content:

1. **Subverters** suggest that scientific knowledge is like playing a game, collecting pieces of information such as are used in quizzes or books of record-breakers. They also suggest that it is like a story you can enter into imaginatively.

2. **Simplifiers** seek to minimise technicality and hence represent mainly commonsense knowledge. In some cases oversimplification results in scientific inaccuracy.

3. **Distractors** include a good deal of localised and/or peripheral information. Much of the information is ancillary, that is, it accompanies and relies on illustrations to make meaning being constituted by the language itself ... In distractors there may also be a good deal of personal interaction with the reader.

4. **Approximators** attempt to reconstruct specialist knowledge for young children. These texts require close examination to determine the integrity of the information and its accessibility to young readers.

5. **Initiators** are the most successful recontextualisations of specialist knowledge for young readers [because they use the appropriate technical language and address the factual knowledge directly].
(Unsworth, 1993: 229)

Some texts that are examples of subverters are just very poorly written, but others are fine works of literature. A good example is *The very hungry caterpillar* (Carle, 1981) – a wonderfully imaginative narrative with beautiful imagery. However, if used to teach something about caterpillars it becomes an excellent example of a text with subverter, simplifier and distractor qualities. The only technical word used is *cocoon*; the egg is described as popping rather than hatching and the caterpillar's wonderful feast distracts in terms of factual relevance. An appropriate text for learning about the life cycle of a caterpillar would be a pictorial flow chart combined with written explanations using accurate scientific terms and there are very good examples both in hard copy and online.

Critically comprehending: The four roles of the reader

Many students in the Developing and Consolidating English phases do have difficulty with interpreting or inferring a written text; usually, but not exclusively, because they lack the background knowledge in English or the content is not part of their schematic knowledge. Using the well known folk tale *The three little pigs*, we could ask the following questions:

- *How many pigs are in the story?* This is called a literal question – it is 'on the line'. It is explicitly stated in the story: 'Once upon a time there were three little pigs'. This question is unlikely to present difficulties for most students
- *Why is the brick house the strongest?* This is an interpretive question because it is 'between the lines'. It is implied; that is, we know it did not blow down, but unless we know what a brick is and what it is made from we cannot answer why. Hence this question could well present difficulties for some EL learners.
- *Why do you think the author used a wolf in the story?* This is an inferential question because it goes 'beyond the line'; that is, we need to make inferences based on our knowledge of wolves. Again, this question could well present difficulties for some EL learners.

An understanding of the four roles of the reader (Freebody & Luke, 1990; Freebody, 2004) is useful for English language teaching, because these roles illustrate that readers not only use the four cues referred to earlier to comprehend a text; they use different roles or resources and practices in order to analyse and critique texts. These different practices are defined below and the resources needed to do the practice are noted (which is why in both this and other books you may see the word 'resources' substituted for 'practice' or aligned to it). Using the two words in sync indicates that one cannot do (practise) without the necessary resources and just as for the cueing systems, they should not be viewed in isolation as the definition below illustrates.

The roles are: code breaker, text user, text participant and text analyst. *Code breaker practices* means having the resources to not only decipher the graphophonic, visual and syntactical codes but also to work out what sort of text it is and hence its purpose and so what to do with it. *Text user practices* are therefore closely aligned to code breaker practices, because students use their prior knowledge resources (and importantly their schematic and semantic knowledge) to help them understand a new text not only literally but also inferentially. In so doing, readers also need to use their *text participant practices* and this involves having the resources to contribute and involve oneself with the text in order to not only know what to do with it, but have opinions that can be shared in interaction with other peers and/or teachers.

This is why the discussion in Chapter 3 is important and 'building knowledge of the topic' is especially important *prior* to reading a text. Using the example of kites, the students first need to be alerted to the genre. Is it a narrative about a girl flying her kite on holidays at the beach or is it an information text about kites? Either way, students need to have the genre explained (not to guess at it), as well as being provided with an explanation about the likely vocabulary they will encounter (as opposed to looking the words up in the dictionary by themselves – which often disengages students).

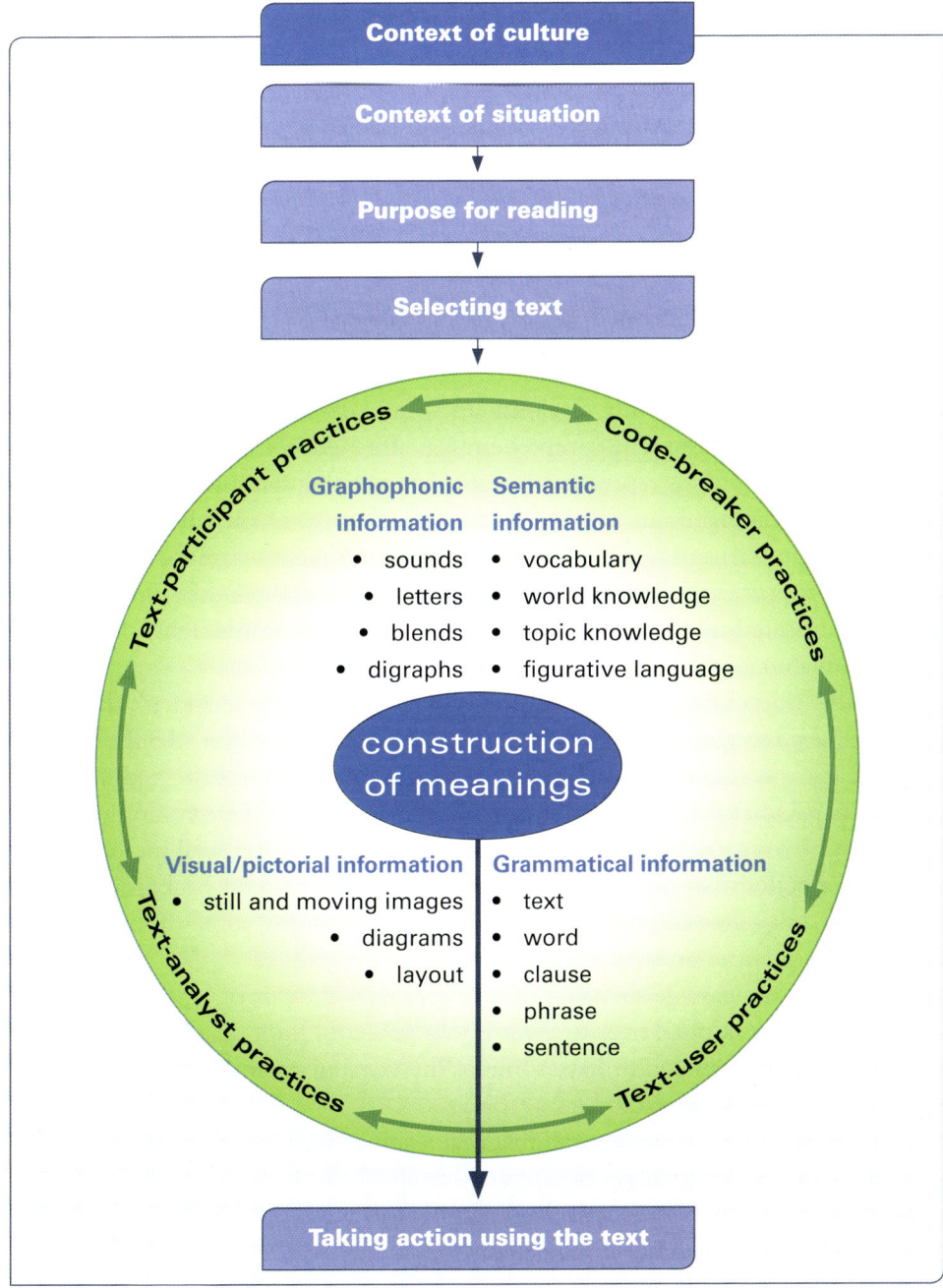

Figure 5.2

A model of reading (from Winch et al, 2010: 44, © Marcelle Halliday, 2006)

The *text analyst practice* becomes the really crucial factor, because being a skilful analyst is necessary to attain academic language proficiency. Having the language as well as the skills to analyse a text and hence understand how the text is positioning oneself (the reader) means that one can both interpret and infer the author's intent and point of view. Furthermore, this depth of analysis enables students to understand that no text is neutral and has been *crafted* by the author to present ideas to the reader. Often the term *critical reading* is used to explain this concept. Examples of how this looks in practice are found in the work samples throughout the book but in particular on pages 96, 97, 105–07 and Chapter 7.

To summarise the discussion on the reading process so far in this chapter diagrammatically, Halliday's model of reading (Figure 5.2, on page 87) is useful, but as Winch et al state:

> It is important to understand that reading is a dynamic process and a static diagram such as [this] cannot fully represent the complexity of the reading process. However, it serves to remind us of the various interconnected elements that make up the reading process. It shows us that descriptions of reading as 'just sounding out the words' are far from accurate or helpful. (Winch et al, 2010: 44)

Reading (comprehending) ... aloud or silently?

> I hate it (reading aloud). My friends think I'm stupid, the teacher thinks I'm stupid and I can't remember what I've read! (nine-year-old ELL boy)

Whether a text is read silently or aloud (and especially on a first reading) can influence how well a student comprehends, as affirmed in the quote above. This student's opinion is representative of many people's sentiments (including adults) about reading aloud, but apart from the affective reason which of course is important in terms of setting up the right conditions for learning, the crucial factor, in terms of comprehension, is that when reading aloud, the student might well be concentrating so much on decoding (getting the words right) that they do not concentrate on the meaning.

Try this. Show the passage at the top of page 89 to a friend and ask them to read it *aloud* to you before they have an opportunity to read it silently, or alternatively you could read it aloud now, imagining that you were reading it to an audience. Don't forget to read it fluently and with a lot of expression!

If you or your friend have some medical training you may well understand the passage better than those without, because it is part of your background knowledge, but other adults would have difficulty decoding some of the words and at the same time understanding what they are reading.

Now read the passage silently. You probably have the gist of what it is about even though you skipped over the words that you could not decode quickly, but of course you would need to have some of the vocabulary and major concepts explained to better understand it.

So it is important to understand that oral reading and silent reading are different and require different skills. In oral reading, one needs to externalise the content to an audience using voice and gesture. It is the most difficult type of reading because one needs to simultaneously read the word as well as scan on

> **Disruption of the CXCR4/CXCL12 chemotactic interaction during hematopoietic stem cell mobilization induced by GCSF or cyclophosphamide**
>
> Hematopoietic progenitor cells (HPCs) normally reside in the bone marrow (BM) but can be mobilized into the peripheral blood (PB) after treatment with GCSF or chemotherapy. In previous studies, we showed that granulocyte precursors accumulate in the BM during mobilization induced by either GCSF or cyclophosphamide (CY), leading to the accumulation of active neutrophil proteases in this tissue. We now report that mobilization of HPCs by GCSF coincides in vivo with the cleavage of the N-terminus of the chemokine receptor CXCR4 on HPCs resident in the BM and mobilized into the PB. This cleavage of CXCR4 on mobilized HPCs results in the loss of chemotaxis in response to the CXCR4 ligand, the chemokine stromal cell–derived factor-1 (SDF-1/CXCL12). Furthermore, the concentration of SDF-1 decreased in vivo in the BM of mobilized mice, and this decrease coincided with the accumulation of serine proteases able to directly cleave and inactivate SDF-1. Since both SDF-1 and its receptor, CXCR4, are essential for the homing and retention of HPCs in the BM, the proteolytic degradation of SDF-1, together with that of CXCR4, could represent a critical step leading to the mobilization of HPCs into the PB in response to GCSF or CY. (Levesque, J.P. et al (2003), 'Disruption of the CXCR4/CXCL12 chemotactic interaction during hematopoietic stem cell mobilization induced by GCSF or cyclophosphamide', PubMed, January, 111(2): 187–96)

silently for what is coming next and depending on fluency and text difficulty there is a two- to four-second delay. Nevertheless, there is a place for oral reading. Aside from being a means for teachers to monitor their students' progress, it is necessary for future vocational reasons such as presenting a report at a meeting. In addition, reading aloud allows the reader to 'hear' the literary devices such as rhythm, rhyme, alliteration and emotive adjectives, verbs and adverbs for, as Booth (1991) suggests, many literary texts really come to life this way.

*However, **always** allow students to read the whole text silently before being required to read aloud.* This applies for *all* reading instruction. For instance, if a small group of students is reading a text together, they should listen and follow a model (eg teacher, podcast) or have the necessary time to read it silently to themselves before reading it aloud to the group.

The same goes for any sort of testing (running records and so forth) because this gives a more accurate indication of the child's ability to read (comprehend) and decode. This is why, with running record assessments for instance, it is now common practice to allow students to read a previously unseen passage silently to themselves before the teacher conducts the running record test (see for instance www.earlyyearsliteracy.sa.edu.au/pages/cg0001086/runningrecords/?reFlag=1).

The chapter so far has concentrated on the 'learning to read' aspect. The remainder of the chapter looks at some strategies for 'reading to learn' using both narrative and factual texts and in the main for those students in the Developing and Consolidating English phases. Readers are reminded, however, that learning to read and reading to learn are not isolated in practice (either during explicit or implicit teaching and learning experiences) – that is, we learn from what we read. And this not only applies to factual texts for, as Barbara Hardy states when highlighting the importance of narrative for learning:

We dream in narrative, daydream in narrative, remember, anticipate, hope, despair, believe, doubt, plan, revise, criticise, construct, gossip, learn, hate and love by narrative. In order really to live, we make up stories about ourselves and others, about the personal as well as the social past and future. (Hardy, 1975: 13)

Reading to learn

The model developed by Nicoll, Unsworth & Parker (1987) is used here. They suggest that activities designed to enhance the reading of a text be categorised as below, but since then I have modified the framework by breaking down the stages in the 'Getting into the text' category.

- Getting ready for the text (before reading the text).
- Getting into the text: Stage 1 (the first reading).
- Getting into the text: Stage 2 (subsequent readings).
- Coming back to the text (subsequent readings).
- Going beyond the text (using the text as the basis for new reading and/or to explain the themes and issues in new ways).

While there may be some overlap, and at times the category 'Going beyond the text' may not be necessary (that is, there is no purpose for it), the benefit of this framework is that it accounts for the varied practices, resources and roles that successful readers use. It should also be noted that writing and reading are often closely linked and this is particularly the case when looking at structural patterns. This aspect will be examined when we focus on writing in the next chapter. Importantly though, oracy and reading are always closely linked and the following strategies focus on this link. In addition, many of the strategies that follow can be classified under the six strategies below, which numerous schools are using at the time of writing. They are sometimes referred to as the 'Super Six' strategies:

- *Making connections* with the text based on their own life experiences or knowledge of events in the world or with other texts they have read.
- *Predicting* or anticipating on the basis of prior knowledge, some key words, diagrams or pictures in the text as they skim and scan.
- *Visualising* by creating a mental image of what they are reading, which may well be translated through music, visual arts, drama or dance.
- *Summarising* the key ideas, themes or concepts, often through graphic outlines.
- *Monitoring* what they are reading as they progress through the passage and, if they feel meaning has been disrupted, stopping to think about how to solve this problem (re-reading or reading on to see if that provides further clues and so forth).
- *Questioning* themselves or others in order to clarify meaning at both a literal analytical and inferential level.

Readers are reminded that strategies such as the Palmer Plan (pages 70–1 in Chapter 4) relate to the above 'Super Six' strategies and to this chapter in general.

Focus on reading

The reading sequence

The activities within each category are just some examples of many suitable strategies. They are not in hierarchical order and the choice of activity will be dependent on both the purpose and the text.

Getting ready for the text

This section is not just confined to predicting what a text might be about by reading the title and/or visuals on the cover of the book, home page or newspaper article. Many of the suggestions that follow can be used at other stages of the reading sequence as well. At this stage, however, they are constructed to position the reader so that their prior knowledge about the topic is activated, and if they have no prior knowledge to develop some knowledge about the topic. At the same time related language structures and vocabulary are introduced before they begin reading the text.

Examples in practice

Tell students what the text is about

An obvious but important strategy.

> Today we are going to be reading an article/story about x. It is a narrative/factual text. It is specifically about … that is, it concentrates on or highlights … There is some tricky vocabulary which I've written on the IWB.

Then ask students if they know the meaning of the key word(s) and, if not, provide a definition. It is important not to treat all the vocabulary in isolation, but rather select vocabulary that will have an immediate impact on understanding. For example before reading the book *Something from nothing* (Gilman, 1992), just one word was explained – 'material', as it is used throughout the book. The teacher explained its meaning within the context of sewing by showing a piece of material. The teacher also modelled the process of sewing with a needle and thread and students then mimed this action.

Various ways to activate prior knowledge (what students already know about a subject) and build up knowledge of the topic

Drama strategy of sculpting

(Refer to pages 146–51 in Chapter 7 about how to do this strategy and for other examples, noting that sculpting can be used with both fiction and factual texts.) To position the students to 'feel' a dominant theme in a text, students might do a quick sculpting activity. For example, before seeing the narrative *Marianthe's story* (Aliki, 1998) or even being told what it was about, students were asked to sculpt their partner to show how a person might feel on their first day at a new school. Furthermore, this first day was in a new country and they could not speak the language. This is a dominant issue in the text. After the sculpting, students brainstormed words to describe this feeling (anxious, nervous etc) and placed relevant words on a cline (refer to page 121).

Progressive brainstorm

Figure 5.3 illustrates this. Each group of three to four students (with a different coloured pen for each group) brainstorms what they know about a particular topic. They are given a couple of minutes to do this at their table and then, leaving their sheet on that table, move to the next group's piece of paper, read that group's ideas and then add to it using their coloured pen. Once they have

Figure 5.3
This progressive brainstorm was constructed by university students midway into their semester course

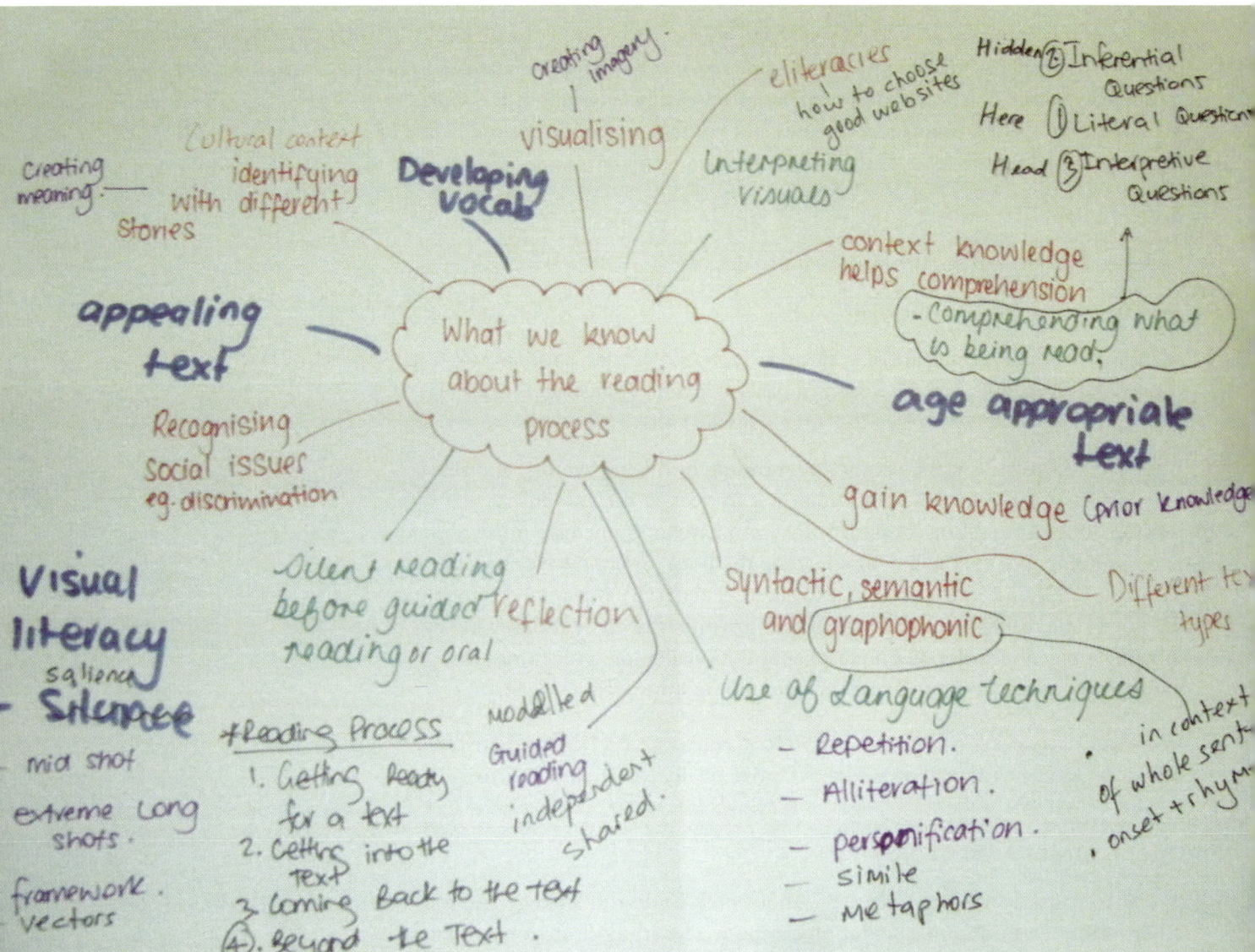

contributed to each group's sheet, they return to their original one and re-read it. At this stage, they might want to make changes to anything they do not agree with and/or add to it. All papers can then be displayed, allowing each group to speak to their concept map, highlighting what they deem to be

Focus on reading

important concepts and reflecting on what they learnt from the contribution of other groups. This is a very useful strategy because it 'helps build shared knowledge in the class and assists the teacher in assessing students' current knowledge and thinking around a topic' (Gibbons, 2009: 65).

Floor storming

Depending on the topic, you might collect a variety of pictures or just one picture related to the topic. For example, when learning about Australian mammals, one class used the pictures they took at the zoo and recorded what they already knew from the excursion before reading an article. In another example, students in Rebecca Hillis's class were given a picture of an Egyptian pyramid and in pairs they discussed and then wrote what they already knew prior to reading an article about pyramids.

Figure 5.4
Floor storming notes written about pyramids

Charting my knowledge

In pairs students complete this table, which they add to during subsequent readings; useful for both formative and summative assessment.

What we know before reading the text)	What we would like to know (before reading the text)	What I learnt (having read the text)	What I still need to find out and where might I go

What I predict

The work sample in Figure 5.5 on page 94 illustrates one pair's work before reading an online article about Tutankhamun (http://homepage.poweru.com.au/~ancient/tut1.htm).

Figure 5.5
Prediction work sample

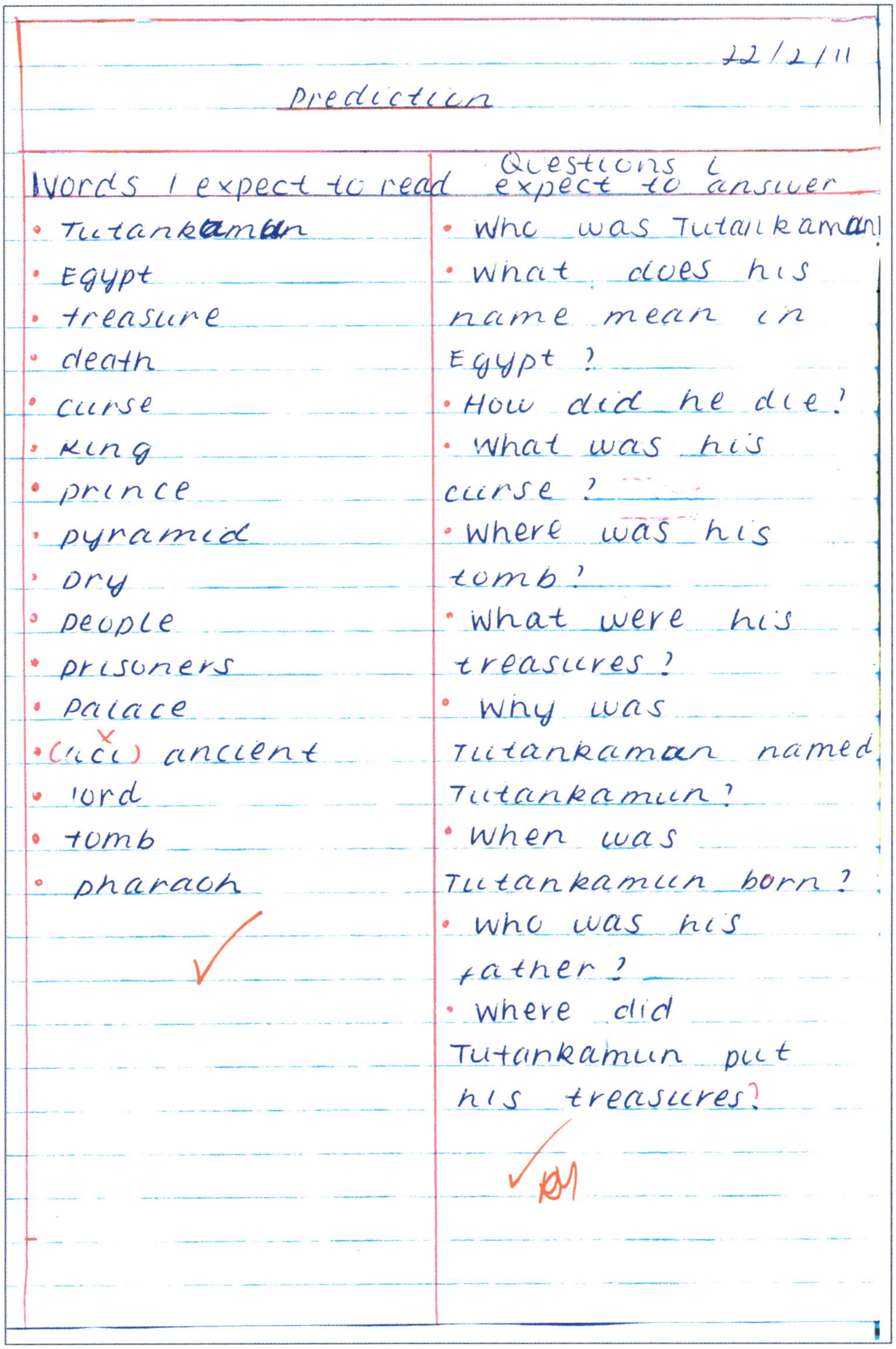

	22/2/11
	Prediction
Words I expect to read	Questions I expect to answer
• Tutankamun	• Who was Tutankamun?
• Egypt	• What does his name mean in Egypt?
• treasure	
• death	
• curse	• How did he die?
• king	• What was his curse?
• prince	
• pyramid	• Where was his tomb?
• dry	
• people	• What were his treasures?
• prisoners	
• palace	• Why was Tutankamun named Tutankamun?
• (ici) ancient	
• lord	• When was Tutankamun born?
• tomb	
• pharaoh	• Who was his father?
	• Where did Tutankamun put his treasures?

Getting into the text: Stage 1

Only one strategy (modelled reading) has been mentioned for 'this stage. It is an extremely important stage. We do not throw non- or beginning swimmers into the deep end of a pool to find out if they will sink or swim. As our aim (as explained in Chapter 3) is to present students with challenging material, then the first reading should be modelled by an experienced reader who reads it with the students either in person, or on podcast or vodcast. But before reading, the teacher will often focus the students' attention to the main idea by posing a question or statement. For example, 'As I read this article on the events at Lambing Flat, think about what you might have felt if you were one of the miners from China'. (Refer to the Palmer Plan, pages 70–1 of Chapter 4.) There may be times where the students can manage the text independently (without this scaffold), in which case, this part is skipped, but more often than not it should be included.

The reader (usually the teacher) might pause for discussion about how some of their questions or predictions from the 'Getting ready for the text' category are being realised. Importantly though, too much interruption, especially on the first reading of a text, can be very confusing. Students may 'lose the gist' if there is too much pausing and talking. It is important therefore to initially read the paragraph, several paragraphs or chapter (depending on the text and the purpose), with minimal or no interruptions.

Getting into the text more: Stage 2

Having had the text modelled with minimal interruption to gain an overall 'feel', it is in this stage that the text is more carefully examined using some of the suggested strategies below.

Paraphrasing

The teacher re-reads the text but might paraphrase from time to time. For instance when reading *NIPS X1* the teacher might read, 'The principal paused, as if anticipating a round of applause or at least a surprised gasp or two *(which means he is thinking or anticipating that the students will give him a clap)*' (Stark, 2000: 5). Or 'Tutankhamun's tomb was discovered by the British Egyptologist Howard Carter who was excavating *(who was digging up)* …'

Think-alouds

Paraphrasing may well be part of a think-aloud, but a think-aloud also draws attention to other structural and linguistic features of a text. For example, when reading *How to heal a broken wing* (Graham, 2008), the teacher focused on the visual literacy grammar while reading (see Chapter 7 for a drama program on this book). Following is an excerpt of that think-aloud session:

> Teacher: *On this double page spread, we see Will finding the bird. I think Bob Graham may have deliberately used salience by colour to focus our attention to the contact between Will and the bird, but if we turn back a page (all turn back to the previous page) what do we see first?*
>
> Student: *Salience.*
>
> Teacher: *Yes and in this case it's salience by size.*

Then when reading the page where the bird is put into a box in the lounge room:

> Teacher: *Angle (which is an aspect of perspective) is an important feature here. When I look at this image, I'm not at the same level with the people, I'm at a high angle and so I think the author wants me to feel like an onlooker to this scene …* (Zammit, in progress)

Margin questions

This strategy (Gibbons, 2009) should not to be confused with a conventional set of comprehension questions 'because unlike traditional comprehension questions, margin questions focus not on the content of the text but on encouraging useful reading strategies … to use "clues" in the text to work out text meaning' (Gibbons, 2009: 94). Often students will work with a partner to discuss the margin questions as they read.

The example below is an excerpt of just some margin questions designed for students who were reading Nadia Wheatley's (2000) *A banner gold* during a unit of work on the Australian Gold Rush.

> *Saturday 26 August 1854*
>
> **Weather: Morning fine. Afternoon deluge!**
>
> This afternoon there was an enormous rain storm, when I was riding Tulip to the creek paddock. Just as I was sloshing back through the mud into the Gravel Pits, I heard a lot of shouting coming from behind the Ballarat Dining Room.
> (Wheatley, 2000: 73)

- After reading the first sentence how might you predict the meaning of this word?
- What do these words tell you about the rain?
- Imagine you had to mime 'sloshing back through the mud'. What would it look like? (visualising)

Coming back to the text (and getting into it more)

Making connections

This strategy helps students make a personal connection to the text. It is very useful in helping students understand how the writer of a text might be positioning them (text analyst).

Text	Me (the student)
'Mr Drummond likes multicultural days and he won't listen to anyone who disagrees with him.' (Stark, 2000: 4)	I don't like multicultural days because everybody just thinks that the only thing about Vietnamese culture is spring rolls.
An online factual article about how earthquakes happen	My cousin was in Christchurch during their earthquake and was really scared.
Schumann had to close his shoe shop because a shoe factory opened nearby. He lost his customers because the shoes were cheaper to buy from the factory. (Summary of one of the issues in the picture book *Schumann the Shoeman*, Danalis, 2010.)	That could happen to the shop where we buy our lollies after school if a supermarket opened nearby. I hope it doesn't because we like Mrs Pappas (the person who owns the corner store).

Focus on reading

True or false statements in combination with the 3H strategy

On page 86 in this chapter and with reference to the *Three little pigs* story, it was explained that questions about a text might be literal, interpretive or inferential. The 3H strategy paraphrases this for students using the terms 'here', 'hidden' and 'head'. The work sample in Figure 5.6 illustrates this.

The head category requires students to use their text analyst resources because they need to read critically to analyse the author's viewpoint. In the example below we can see that the student does understand the content, but at times does not recognise, for example, implied information.

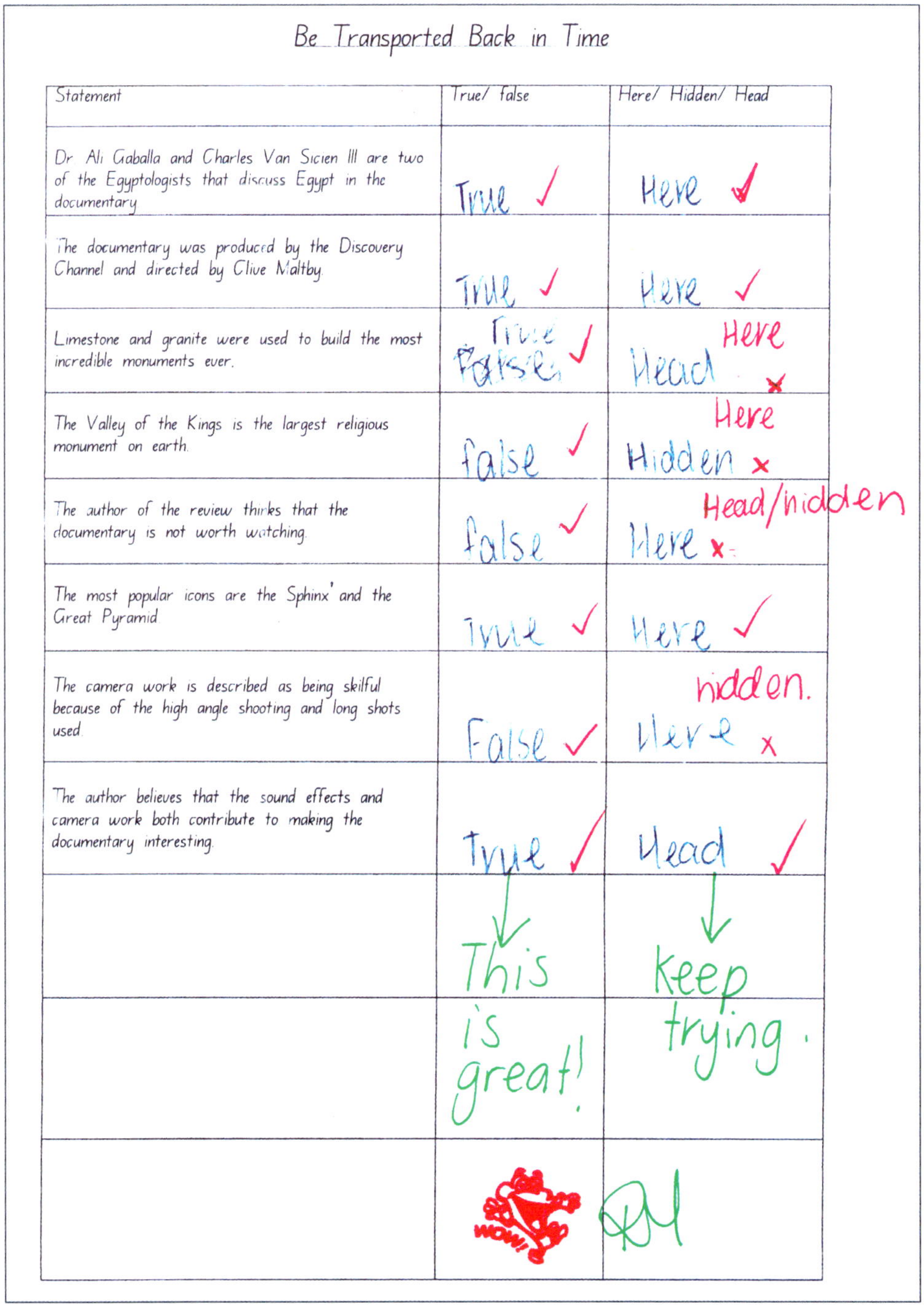

Figure 5.6
Here, hidden, head work sample

Be Transported Back in Time		
Statement	True/false	Here/Hidden/Head
Dr Ali Gaballa and Charles Van Sicien III are two of the Egyptologists that discuss Egypt in the documentary	True ✓	Here ✓
The documentary was produced by the Discovery Channel and directed by Clive Maltby	True ✓	Here ✓
Limestone and granite were used to build the most incredible monuments ever.	True / False ✓	Head ✗ (Here)
The Valley of the Kings is the largest religious monument on earth.	false ✓	Hidden ✗ (Here)
The author of the review thinks that the documentary is not worth watching.	false ✓	Here ✗ (Head/hidden)
The most popular icons are the Sphinx' and the Great Pyramid	True ✓	Here ✓
The camera work is described as being skilful because of the high angle shooting and long shots used	False ✓	Here ✗ (hidden)
The author believes that the sound effects and camera work both contribute to making the documentary interesting.	True ✓	Head ✓
	↓ This is great!	↓ keep trying.

Requiring students to make up their own 3H questions or statements can assist their understanding of how the author positions the reader. The example in Figure 5.6 was written by two eleven-year-old students in the late Developing English phase. Their teacher, Rebecca Hillis, had planned a comparative study of some of Shaun Tan's books and these 'head' questions and statements are for the short story 'Stick figures' in *Tales from outer suburbia* (2008). The students then gave them to another pair to answer.

- Do you think the author is asking the questions in the story to us or the characters in the book, or both?
- Shaun Tan is trying to say that people are afraid of what they don't know.
- Shaun Tan's message to the reader is that some people do not stick up for themselves even when they are bullied.

This sort of analysis requires students to examine the language carefully. For instance, to respond to the last statement, students examined and discussed the sentence 'the body remains passively upright until smashed to splinters between heels and asphalt' (Tan, 2008: 66).' In another class, students examined this sentence by constructing two sequential **still images** to depict the two scenes it contains.

> Refer to pages 151–52 of Chapter 7 for an explanation of the still image strategy. It is another useful strategy for coming back to the text.

Cloze activities

A cloze is a passage in which a word (or in some cases a phrase – see page 122) has been deleted. It is a useful strategy because it shows students that they do not rely on graphophonics alone to read. They will use their syntactic and semantic knowledge and, when applicable, visual or pictorial clues. In addition, a cloze demonstrates that competent readers often use backward and forward referencing to ascertain meaning. This knowledge need not be hidden from students. That is, when using this strategy, explain to students the strategies they should use to complete a cloze by modelling the process on an overhead projector or IWB.

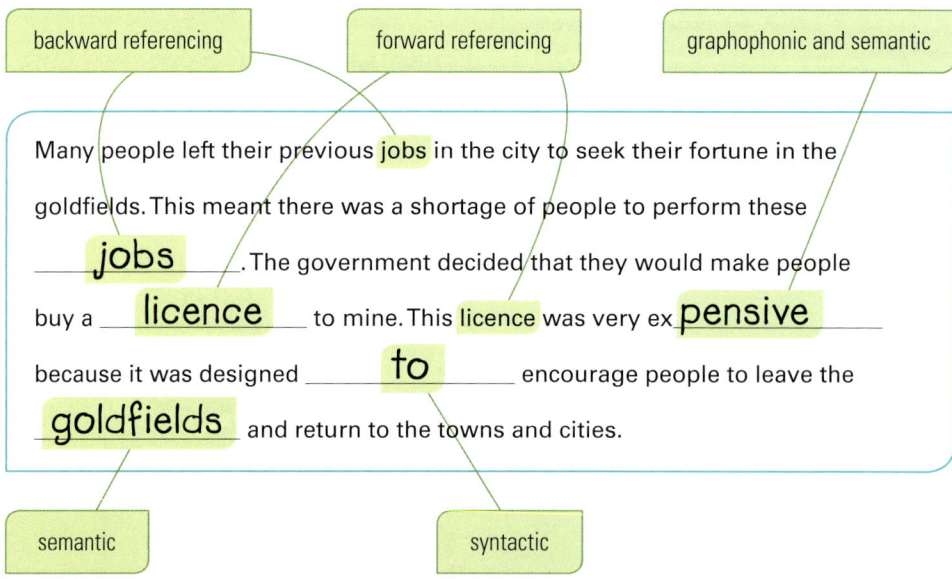

Cloze passages can be used for a variety of purposes and across all curriculum areas. Cloze passages are sometimes suggested for spelling instruction but the focus is then taken away from reading and this diminishes their usefulness for language learning. Similarly, there are commercially available cloze exercises but the best ones are made by the teacher to focus on particular language structures and specific to the text being read and/or the topic being studied.

Constructing a cloze

This will vary depending on the *purpose* but general principles include:
- Spacing of deletions: Deletions should usually be the same line length (see previous example). This avoids confusion as it does not limit students to using a word that is only three letters when maybe a word of seven letters is just as appropriate (eg sad or unhappy), noting however that with very technical or specific vocabulary this may not be as appropriate.
- Number of deletions: Usually the first sentence or two are left intact to give an initial impression of what the passage is about. From there on one can delete about every seventh word, as more frequent deletions can result in a loss of cohesion, but again this is dependent on the purpose.
- Proofreading: Ask another adult to proofread or trial the cloze, as deletions can sometimes make the activity inadvertently ambiguous.
- Answers in a box: This will depend on the purpose. If answers are at the bottom of the page, consider having more words than for the spaces in the cloze. The intention is not to trick; rather it promotes a lot of discussion about the most appropriate word.

How to implement a cloze

- Because we are using cloze as a learning strategy as opposed to a testing strategy, it should be completed in pairs as this promotes discussion about the meaning of the passage as students debate and negotiate likely answers.
- To ensure students do work together (rather than just sit together) only give one worksheet per pair, or if on a computer use only one computer per pair.
- Ensure students read the complete passage before attempting to write answers. A standard gag in one class is 'sit on your pencils the first time you read'.
- Remind students that they will be using all or some of the following strategies to assist them.
    - forward referencing
    - backward referencing
    - real world knowledge
    - graphophonic cues
    - syntactic cues
    - semantic cues
    - visual or pictorial cues, if applicable.

Example

The excerpt below is from a longer cloze for *Boy overboard* (Gleitzman, 2002). It was constructed to focus the students' attention to how Gleitzman uses action verbs to create an image of tension and urgency because the girl Bibi should not be playing soccer in public. Before doing the cloze the students had read this scene several times to construct a still image (refer to pages 151–52 in Chapter 7). The students also performed a Readers' Theatre to further develop their understanding of the figurative language (refer to Chapter 7 and the PETAA website: www.petaa.edu.au) and how it should be expressed.

> In this case the words have been placed in a box below but note that there are more words than needed to encourage the pairs to debate the best choice.

'Tackle her,' I say to the others.

They _____ at me confused.

'Get the ball off her,' I say.

Now they understand. We all _____ at Bibi. Without slowing down she sidesteps Aziz, _____ past Mussa, and _____ the ball between my legs.

I can't believe it. She's remembered every single ball skill I've taught her.

'That's not fair,' I yell as I _____ after her. You promised you'd only do soccer in your bedroom. You promised.

She ignores me and heads for goal. Yusuf, uncertain, _____ on the goal line, eyes on the ball.

> sidesteps, lunge, flicks, look, sprint, run, moves away from, kicks, weaves, crouches, squats, stare, criss-crosses

The intent of the cloze on page 101 is to focus on prepositions. Before the students did this cloze they had:
- jointly constructed the written instructions for an obstacle course with the teacher
- tested the obstacle course for themselves
- completed the obstacle course with their junior buddy class.

Other types of cloze include reverse cloze, cluster cloze, synonym cloze, read-around cloze, not needed cloze and prediction cloze, and readers are directed to Paul Dufficy's e:update *Cloze encounters* (2010) and *Designing learning for diverse classrooms* (2005) for a comprehensive explanation of each.

Focus on reading

1. Before you leave the classroom put on your hat. Quietly walk onto the veranda.
2. Walk to the Jacaranda tree.
3. Walk around the tree in a clockwise direction.
4. Run to the green garbage bin in front of the canteen door.
5. Walk around the garbage bin twice and then walk between this garbage bin and the canteen door.
6. Skip to the seats where 4H sits for lunch.
7. Jump over the green seat and run across to the handball court next to the Library.
8. Jump three times on top of Number 4.
9. Walk to the school administration building and crouch below the Principal's office window, so she can't see you, for 3 seconds.
10. Run around the corner and walk between the two bottlebrush trees behind the photocopy room's window.
11. Without too much noise skip to the bubblers and have a quick drink before returning to the classroom.

Before you leave the classroom put _____ your hat.

Quietly walk _____ the veranda.

Walk _____ the Jacaranda tree.

Walk _____ the tree in a clockwise direction.

Run to the green garbage bin _____ _____ _____ the canteen door.

Walk around the garbage bin twice and then walk _____ this garbage bin and the canteen door.

Skip _____ the seats where 4H sits _____ lunch.

Jump _____ the green seat and run across to the hand ball court _____ _____ the Library.

Jump three times on top of Number 4.

Walk to the school administration building and crouch _____ the Principal's Office window, so she can't see you, for 3 seconds.

Run _____ the corner and walk _____ the two bottlebrush trees _____ the photocopy room's window.

Without too much noise skip _____ the bubblers and have a quick drink before returning to the classroom.

Collecting and/or summarising information using visual outlines

There are many different visual outlines and the purpose or intent of the text will determine the best one to use to present information. Since the matrix strategy was explained in Chapter 4 it is not discussed here, but it is an important strategy to consider.

Venn diagrams

Venn diagrams are very useful when comparing and contrasting. Similarities are placed in the middle. Rebecca Hillis's ten- and eleven-year-old students in the Developing and Consolidating English phases read an article about the climatic conditions in Egypt and in pairs constructed Venn diagrams to identify differences and similarities.

The teacher then used these diagrams to teach connectives other than 'but':
- The sterile land is away from the Nile River, *whereas* the fertile land borders the river.
- The sterile land is away from the Nile River, *however* the fertile land borders the river.

Figure 5.7
Sample Venn diagram

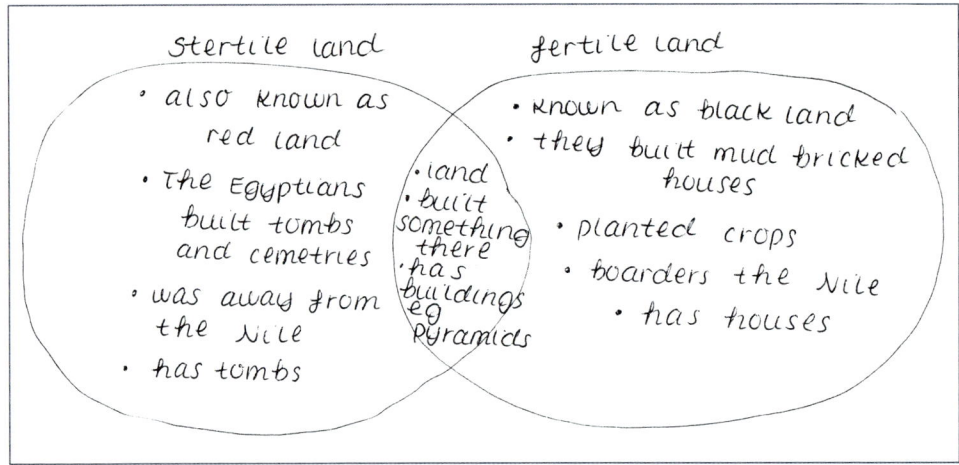

Flow charts

Flow charts are useful for summarising sequential information and the example below also illustrates cause and effect.

Key point: The miner's licence

| Shortage of workers in cities because so many people went to the gold fields (e.g. Ballarat). | **so** | The government decided to make miners pay for a licence because they hoped they could not afford it and would come back to the city. | **as a result** | The miners became very angry and held protests. |

Figure 5.8
Sample flow chart

Mind maps

A central key word or idea is placed in the middle of the page and key words or concepts are linked to it.

Students from Rebecca Hillis's class constructed mind maps in pairs after reading an article about Tutankhamun (Figure 5.9).

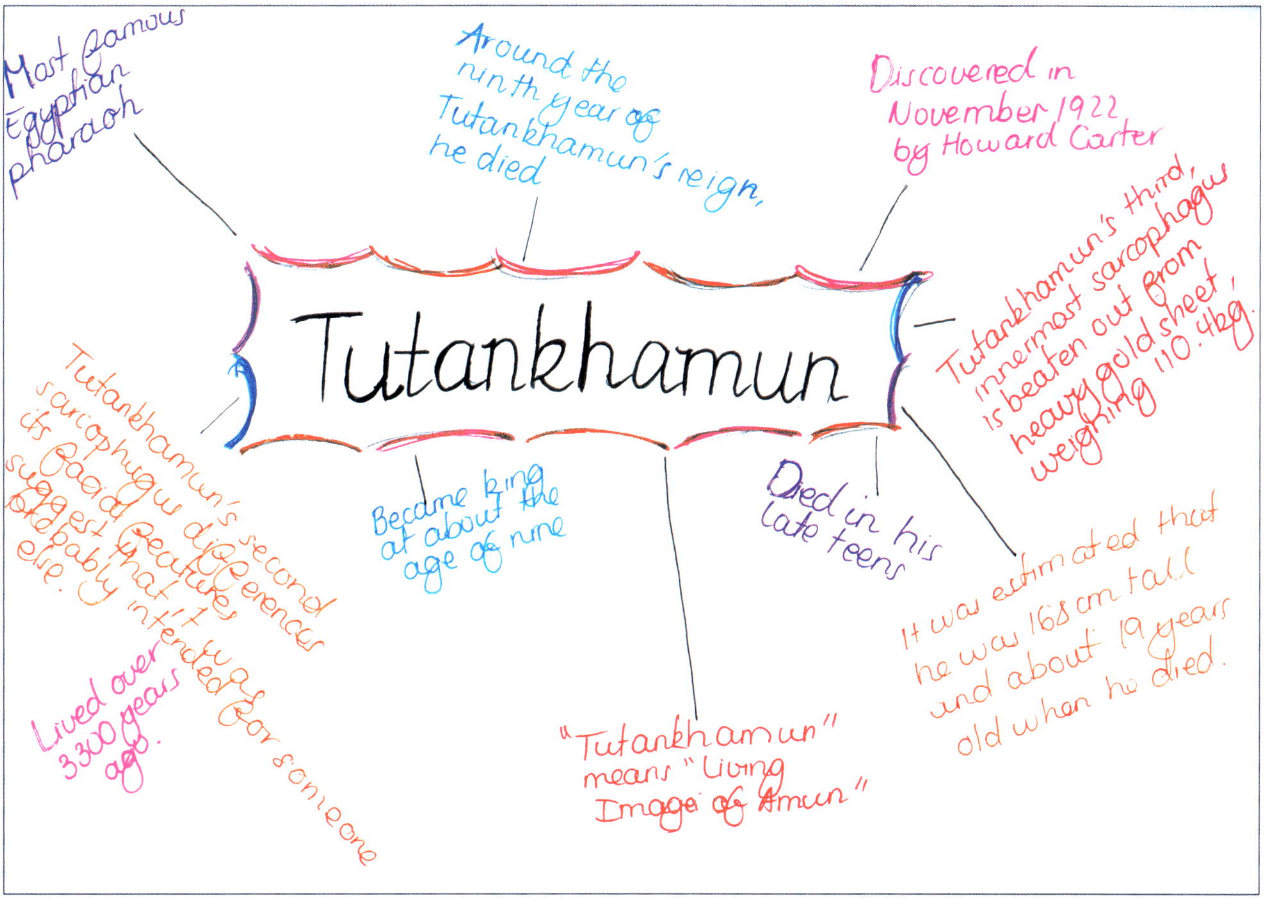

Focus on reading

Figure 5.9
Student mind map about Tutankhamun

Figure 5.10
This mind map illustrates a student's opinion about the themes and issues in the book Marianthe's story *(Aliki, 1998)*

Text reconstruction

Often these are designed by the teacher but you might consider asking students to make their own because this enables more in-depth textual analysis. The example below was written by an eleven-year-old student who cut it up and then gave it to another peer in Rebecca Hillis's class to reconstruct.

Figure 5.11
Student designed text reconstruction

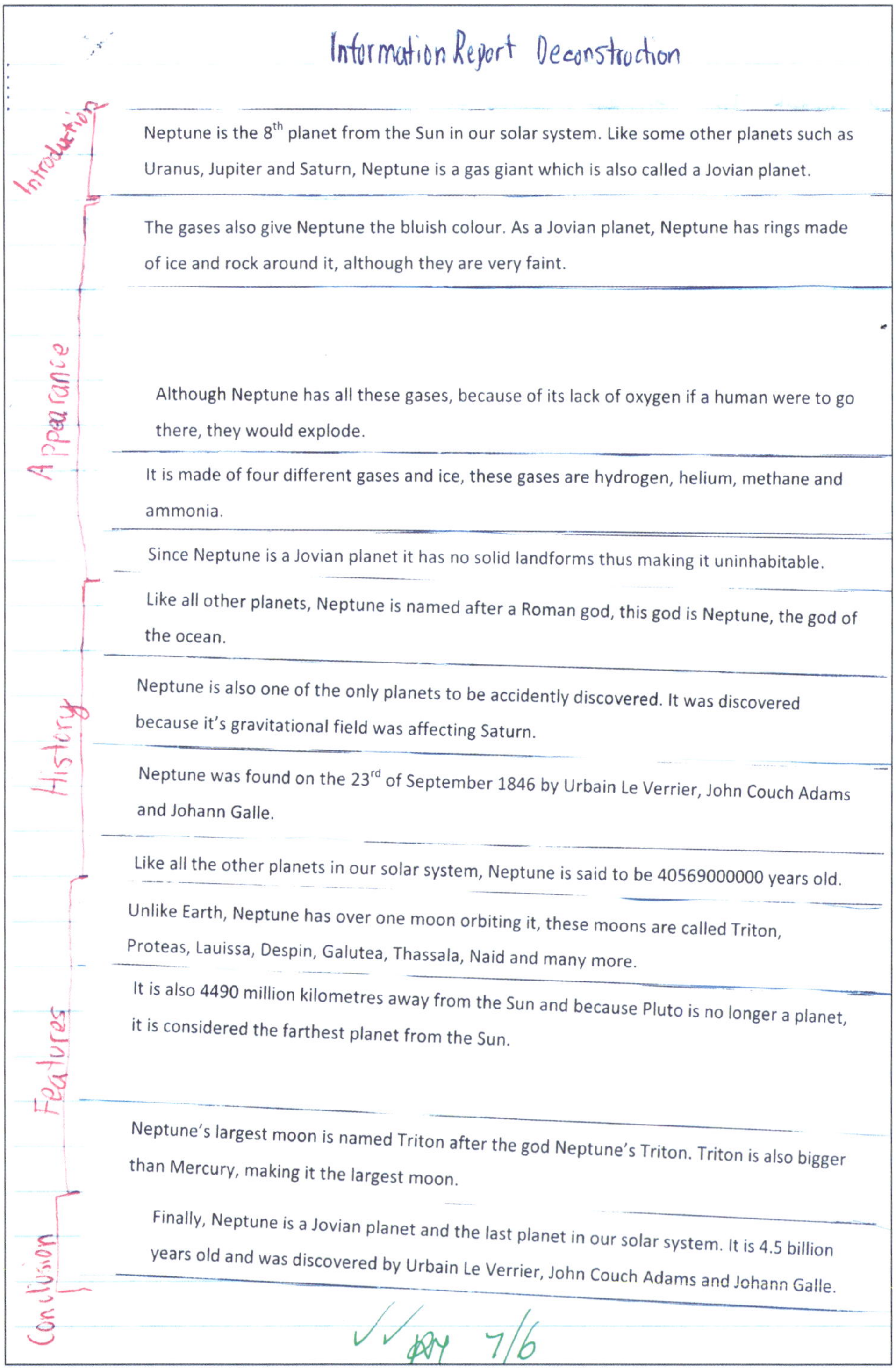

Information Report Deconstruction

Introduction

Neptune is the 8th planet from the Sun in our solar system. Like some other planets such as Uranus, Jupiter and Saturn, Neptune is a gas giant which is also called a Jovian planet.

The gases also give Neptune the bluish colour. As a Jovian planet, Neptune has rings made of ice and rock around it, although they are very faint.

Appearance

Although Neptune has all these gases, because of its lack of oxygen if a human were to go there, they would explode.

It is made of four different gases and ice, these gases are hydrogen, helium, methane and ammonia.

Since Neptune is a Jovian planet it has no solid landforms thus making it uninhabitable.

Like all other planets, Neptune is named after a Roman god, this god is Neptune, the god of the ocean.

History

Neptune is also one of the only planets to be accidently discovered. It was discovered because it's gravitational field was affecting Saturn.

Neptune was found on the 23rd of September 1846 by Urbain Le Verrier, John Couch Adams and Johann Galle.

Like all the other planets in our solar system, Neptune is said to be 40569000000 years old.

Unlike Earth, Neptune has over one moon orbiting it, these moons are called Triton, Proteas, Lauissa, Despin, Galutea, Thassala, Naid and many more.

It is also 4490 million kilometres away from the Sun and because Pluto is no longer a planet, it is considered the farthest planet from the Sun.

Features

Neptune's largest moon is named Triton after the god Neptune's Triton. Triton is also bigger than Mercury, making it the largest moon.

Conclusion

Finally, Neptune is a Jovian planet and the last planet in our solar system. It is 4.5 billion years old and was discovered by Urbain Le Verrier, John Couch Adams and Johann Galle.

✓✓ 7/6

Going beyond the text

Going beyond the text is important because it involves moving beyond the existing text in order to understand it better. This stage requires students to respond to the text, in order to analyse how it is positioning them as readers. Students often do this by making connections and drawing parallels with both other texts and/or their own experience of the world. To this end, it was argued earlier in this chapter that students need access to well written, authentic texts. Texts of literary merit not only serve a linguistic purpose (they are better written than many 'readers'), but for want of a better word they have some 'guts' and so have the potential to stimulate the reader to explore the themes, issues and concepts, and this applies to both fiction and factual texts. Below are some suggested strategies that make evident that imaginative and creative thinking is central to analysis.

> Note that as for the other categories, there may often be considerable overlap between this category and 'Coming back to the text'.

Drama

Refer to Chapter 7 as many of the activities in this chapter fulfil this function; for example:
- creating of a sequence of still images for *Marianthe's story* (Aliki, 1998) on pages 155–56
- questioning in role the grandson in *Nyuntu Ninti* (Randal, 2008) on pages 158–59
- questioning in role the mother or father in *How to heal a broken wing* (Graham, 2008) on page 162
- parallel improvisations for *How to heal a broken wing* (Graham, 2008) on pages 164–65.

Music

After reading online articles about the invention of penicillin, twelve-year-old students wrote scores to depict the feelings of people saved by this medication.

Turning a written text into a digital animation

For example, after reading the narrative *The selfish crocodile* by Charles Faustin (1998), some eight-year-old Emergent English phase students in Georgia Constanti's class made their own digital animation using 'Movie Maker'. To achieve this, they constructed the text with their teacher (refer to Chapter 6 for an explanation about joint construction). Their animation focused on the theme of sharing and was about sharing the handball courts in the playground.

Text innovation

This is different to writing a different ending to a story. Rather, the structure of the text remains very similar (it simulates the text) but the content or the details might be changed. The example in Figure 5.11 is an innovation six-year-old ELL students made using the same structure as in Mem Fox's book *Time for bed* (1994).

Not only were they attending to the structure of the text, it also indicated that they comprehended the story – if you get lots of rest you will be able to function better the next day.

It's time for bed, little duck, little duck, Tomorrow might bring you lots of luck.

It's time for bed, little possum, little possum, So dream tonight of eating lots of blossom.

It's time for bed, little pig, little pig, Get lots of rest so you'll grow up big!

Figure 5.12
Text innovation

Readers' Theatre

Although also suitable in the 'coming back' category, Readers' Theatre is included in the 'Going beyond' category because students when in role as a character, often make connections with their own experiences and circumstances and bring their unique interpretation to the reading. (Refer to Chapter 7; and for a comprehensive explanation of this activity go to the PETAA website: www.petaa.edu.au.)

Figure 5.13
Child's visual arts response to 'Stick figures'

Focus on reading

Debating

For example, after reading differing viewpoints in both the articles and the letters page from a local newspaper about building a better highway (which would destroy the local koala habitat), the class held a debate and used both material from the newspaper as well as their own opinions.

Visual arts

This might include painting, sculpting, collage and so forth in response to an article, story or poem. The examples in Figures 5.13 and 5.14 are from Rebecca Hillis's' class are personal responses to 'Stick figures' (Tan, 2009).

When asked what she meant by 'some answers are lost but will be found one day', this student in the Developing English phase replied that *the answers to world problems have not been solved yet, but they will one day.*

The strategies presented in this chapter not only highlight how learning to read and reading to learn are simultaneous acts, but also indicate that while the focus might be on reading, oracy remains integral. Furthermore, many of the activities include writing. The following chapter explores in more detail the teaching and learning of writing, taking into account the specific needs of EL learners.

Figure 5.14
Child's visual arts response to 'Stick figures'

CHAPTER SIX
FOCUS ON WRITING

We cannot opt out of the Western print world and still remain active participants in society (Gibbons, 2002: 50). Most people living in the world today are not just consumers of the print world but actively create it. Current technology involves people young and old in creating text via emails, tweets, SMS, blogs and so on. Many current events in countries such as Egypt and Libya have seen messages posted around the world using electronic print media in English. Why? To attract the widest possible audience: the English speaking west. Writing is a social process. It is a means of connecting with others in order to share ideas and information. Yet learning to write is a difficult process and those who struggle are potentially disadvantaged. Those learners who have poorly developed language and literacy skills (in any language) and those whose mother tongue is not English commonly fall into this group.

Our students are writing more, but while we see *quantity* of writing, there may not, in many cases, be an improvement in *quality*. This chapter explains why writing needs to be taught explicitly and, why it needs to be taught in the context of a unit of work based on real texts that link the students to real world situations. Learning to write well in English is all about understanding the role of language in the context in which it is used. Teachers need to understand what a successful writer does and break this down for their students.

> If the most significant influence on pupil attainment is the classroom teacher, then the key to genuine and lasting school improvement must be developing the quality of teaching. (Hughes, 1999)

What is a successful writer?

Using the analogy of the swimmer, some students seem to know how to write well with little or no direction; having been thrown in the deep end, they swim. Yet, other students, usually those with less knowledge of English or who are English language learners, flounder and drown!

So what does a successful writer have? Figure 6.1 illustrates this.

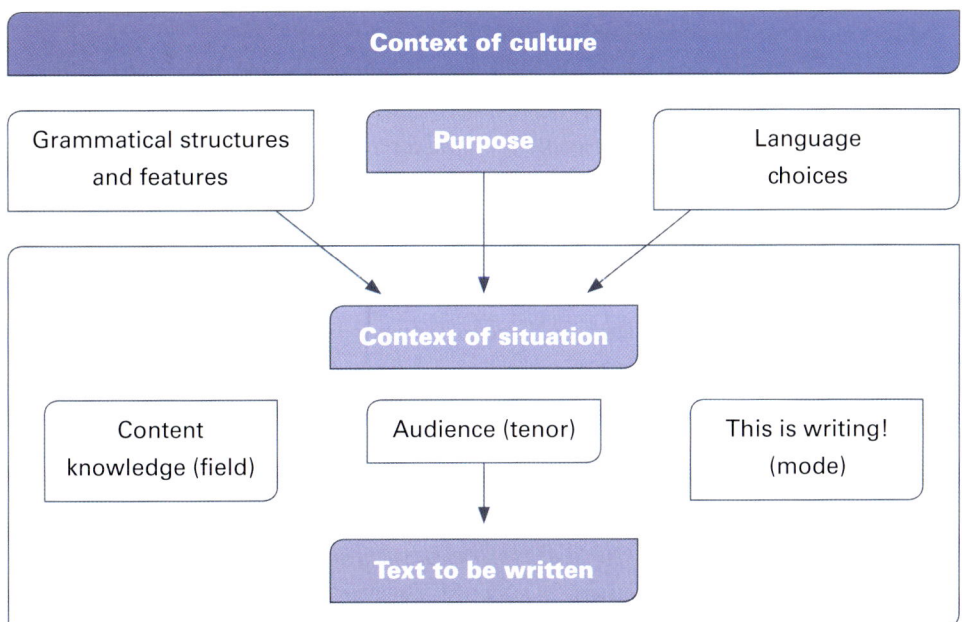

Figure 6.1
Attributes of a successful writer

Here is a more detailed list of the attributes of a successful writer:
- **An understanding of the context of situation and context of culture.** These things underpin all we say and write, and can provide the direction for the language choices we make if we understand the context.

Knowledge is transmitted in social contexts, through relationships, like those of parent and child, or teacher and pupil, or classmates, that are defined in the value systems and ideology of the culture. And the words that are exchanged in these contexts get their meaning from activities in which they are embedded, which again are social activities with social agencies and goals. (Halliday, 1985: 5)

Differences in age, gender, socio-economic status, generation, family history, country of birth, family background, interests and personality can potentially change the language used to write a text. What is valued may differ from culture to culture and person to person. The context of situation will also dictate the language choices a writer must make, including the audience and the subject as mentioned above and the channel of communication. Yet a written text can differ – if it is emailed, written in an exam, as an assignment, as a letter to the editor or a text message. The writer needs to very mindful of the considerable difficulties there are in writing a coherent text that conveys the message accurately with no misunderstandings.

- **A real purpose for writing.** By having a real purpose for writing the writer can make specific choices about the language they use. If a writer is persuading, they will make different language choices than if they were describing or recounting, though the topic may stay the same. It is essential for English language learners to know this. I will expand on this further in the chapter.
- **An understanding of the structure and grammatical features of the specific text type.** If the writer has sufficient topic knowledge but little information about the structure of the text type they are writing, they will also fail in the writing task. Each text type has a structure and specific grammatical features. Consider, for example, adjectives, which are commonly used in narrative texts to describe a character or a setting. They are also used in persuasive texts and explanations to describe, yet play a slightly different role. Many EL students have difficulty understanding the role grammar plays in different texts.
- **An understanding that English language choices can be made to suit the purpose and the audience.** You can and should manipulate language in order to suit both purpose and audience. This knowledge leads the writer to choose a *text type* suited to the purpose for which they are writing. By text type I mean the structured texts taught in Australian schools (see NSW Board of Studies, 1998 and NSW DET, 2005). Each text type has a particular language focus (see below).
- **An understanding of the difference between the written and spoken modes of communication.** A successful writer knows that in order be effective they must be well-organised, succinct and appropriate. They do not have the luxury of face-to-face contact to ensure meaning is clear, or to repair a breakdown. You can probably think of many throwaway lines people use in conversation such as '*what I mean is … to put that another way … in other words … you know … it's like … you know what I mean?*' but we would rarely use them in writing.
- **A good knowledge of the subject they are writing about (known as field).** Successful writers demonstrate an understanding of the topic. It is impossible to write knowledgeably about something you haven't learnt about. As a teacher this is where the balance between topic knowledge and text production is vital. If you provide students with all the support to write a specific text but limit the topic knowledge they will fail in the writing task because they lack depth in topic knowledge.
- **A clear idea of their audience (known as tenor).** It is not uncommon for students to be writing a text simply for the teacher to mark. Yet if the audience is not clear they will not be able to make accurate language choices. Knowing your audience will dictate the language choices you make in different ways:
  - The relationship you have with your audience changes the language choices you make. Consider for example the relationship between the writer and the reader in the emails on the next page.

Hi Marg,

Sorry I can't make the meeting. Something came up … You know what it's like out there! Can we make another time? Let me know ASAP.

J

Dear Ms Turnbull

I am sorry but I will unable to attend the consultation meeting planned for next Tuesday at 9:00 am. I have a previous engagement that I cannot avoid. If it is convenient to arrange to meet at another time I will make every effort to attend. Please let me know if this is possible.

Regards

Janet Freeman

- The difference in knowledge between the writer and the audience. Imagine you are explaining a cooking process. Consider the language choices you would make if you knew your audience was an experienced cook and how they would differ if they were a beginner.
- The relative power the writer has over their audience. Think of how you would write asking someone to do something if you were the boss to an employee, a wife to a husband, a teacher to his or her class, and consider how the language might change.

Talking to support writing

Research shows that many language focus areas are used in creating the vast array of spoken and written texts we use in our day-to-day interactions. I have chosen seven that link closely to the texts students are expected to write in schools:

- **Recounting**: recounting, retelling, narrating, describing.
- **Describing**: naming, describing, observing, defining, classifying, generalising, qualifying, referring, comparing, contrasting.
- **Instructing**: describing, ordering, commanding, listening, clarifying, noting, expressing conditions.
- **Explaining**: expressing causality, opinion, reasons or conditions; elaborating; exemplifying; referring; reiterating; emphasising.
- **Persuading**: previewing, expressing opinion, stating, reasoning, generalising, analysing, qualifying, arguing, refuting, explaining, referring, concluding, summarising, exemplifying, clarifying, hypothesising, extrapolating, justifying, evaluating, synthesising.
- **Responding**: recalling, recounting, revising, describing, defining, clarifying, comparing, contrasting, deciding, choosing, justifying, synthesising, speculating, hypothesising, evaluating, imagining.
- **Negotiating**: interacting, greeting, leave taking, requesting, inviting, apologising, suggesting, commanding, exclaiming, reiterating, emphasising, rephrasing, interrupting, turn taking, agreeing, disagreeing, confirming.

Each of these focus areas, with the exception of negotiating, link to text types commonly taught in Australian schools (NSW DET, 2005)

It is important to note that in the world outside school, most authentic texts would include a combination of these focus areas. They contain parts of many texts, especially when spoken. But there are significant differences between language competence in the playground and the academic language competence in writing across curriculum areas.

Writing is not the same as speaking or reading but, as Brian Gray (1990: 113) points out, 'it is doubtful if children can produce and understand written texts in any depth unless they can orally produce texts of that type themselves'.

We need to harness the capacity of our students' spoken language ability in order to support their writing in academic settings. Imagine a student telling you why they had not completed an assignment. They might begin with a recount of events. This leads to an explanation of why the assignment could not be completed, then this may quite possibly move into persuasive language in order to convince you that they should have an extension to complete the assignment. You may, of course, think the whole explanation is a narrative, but why not harness this ability?

There are many demands on the learner to write, which become increasingly complex in upper primary and secondary school. The expectations require the students to know an enormous amount about both the topic and language. In addition, they are also expected to marry the two in quite complicated ways. Below are some examples from different subject areas:

- English: Write the opening speech to a conference of dragons.
- Geography: Write a travel brochure describing an interesting site in Australia.
- History: Write a recount describing life in a medieval village.
- Science: Describe observations during an experiment and then draw a conclusion to explain the reaction.
- PDHE: Provide an explanation of a healthy diet and lifestyle.

Text types within language focus areas

As explained above, there are many text types taught in schools but in order to understand these different text types, students need to recognise both their social purpose and their structural and grammatical features. While it is rare for text types such as these appear in their 'pure' form in the world outside school, they are a place to begin when talking about the function and purpose of 'text' with students. As mentioned above, if students have a real purpose for writing they will choose an appropriate text type to meet the purpose, but they do need to understand the social purpose of each text in order to do so (see Table 6.1).

Consider the pieces of text in Table 6.2 and identify each text type from the definitions in Table 6.1. Think about how you know what each type is (you can cover the answers and try to guess first).

Focus on writing

Table 6.1 Different text types and their features

Literary description To describe, in literary terms, natural, physical, cultural and individual phenomena. May be part of a larger text such as a narrative.

Information report To present information and classify a general class of things whether artificial or natural.

Factual recount To document a series of events as they occurred and evaluate their significance in some way.

Observation To record events and respond to them in a personal way. There is no specific sequence. Used as a tool to develop recount and narrative.

Procedure How to do something. This may include instructions on how to carry out a task, rules of a game or directions on how to get somewhere.

Explanation To tell how and why things occur in scientific and technical fields.

Narrative A pattern of events, with a problem or unexpected outcomes that entertain and instruct the reader or listener. The behaviour patterns are often highly valued. The problems provide readers with opportunities to speculate on resolution.

Review A summary or analysis of a literary text with an assessment as to its appeal.

Exposition To argue a case for or against a particular point of view.

Poetry An aesthetic experience that works mainly through our emotions, sensory experiences and imaginative perceptions. Devices such as rhyme, rhythm, alliteration, assonance and onomatopoeia are emphasised.

Discussion To explore more than one side of an issue. To discover various perspectives before coming to an informed decision.

Literary recount To tell a sequence of events so that it entertains with expressions of attitude and feeling to build a relationship between the reader or speaker and writer.

Personal response To summarise and respond personally to a text.

Factual description To describe a particular living, non-living or natural phenomenon. Often part of a large text such as an information report.

Procedural recount A record, in sequential order, the steps taken to achieve a particular goal or outcome.

(NSW Board of Studies, 1998: 68–71)

Table 6.2 Text samples and types

Factual recount	First we went to the hamburger shop and then …
Procedural recount	We placed the hamburger buns under the grill to brown and then …
Procedure	Place the buns under the grill to brown
Information report	A hamburger is a sandwich consisting of a cooked patty of ground meat
Explanation	The term hamburger originally derives from Hamburg, Germany's second largest city, from where many immigrated to America.
Exposition	A hamburger is good for you to eat …
Discussion	Some hamburgers may be healthy however once you add…
Review	The best hamburger I ever ate …
Factual description	A hamburger has two buns and a patty of meat …
Literacy description	The burger sat on the plate glistening with juices and teaming with salad …
Observation	That hamburger is enormous!

The mode continuum

The mode continuum (see NSW Department of Education (1998): from Jones (1996: 21)) explained in Chapter 4 is repeated here and this time it plots texts using hamburgers as the topic on a continuum from texts which are informal and most spoken-like (language accompanying an activity) through to language that is crafted, edited and organised, and most written-like (spoken presentations). This is a useful tool for planning for teaching as you can plot the activities on the mode continuum and build the academic language through explicit language learning/teaching. Teachers can consider the language demands of both the topic (in this case, hamburgers) and the written text to be created and design activities to support both.

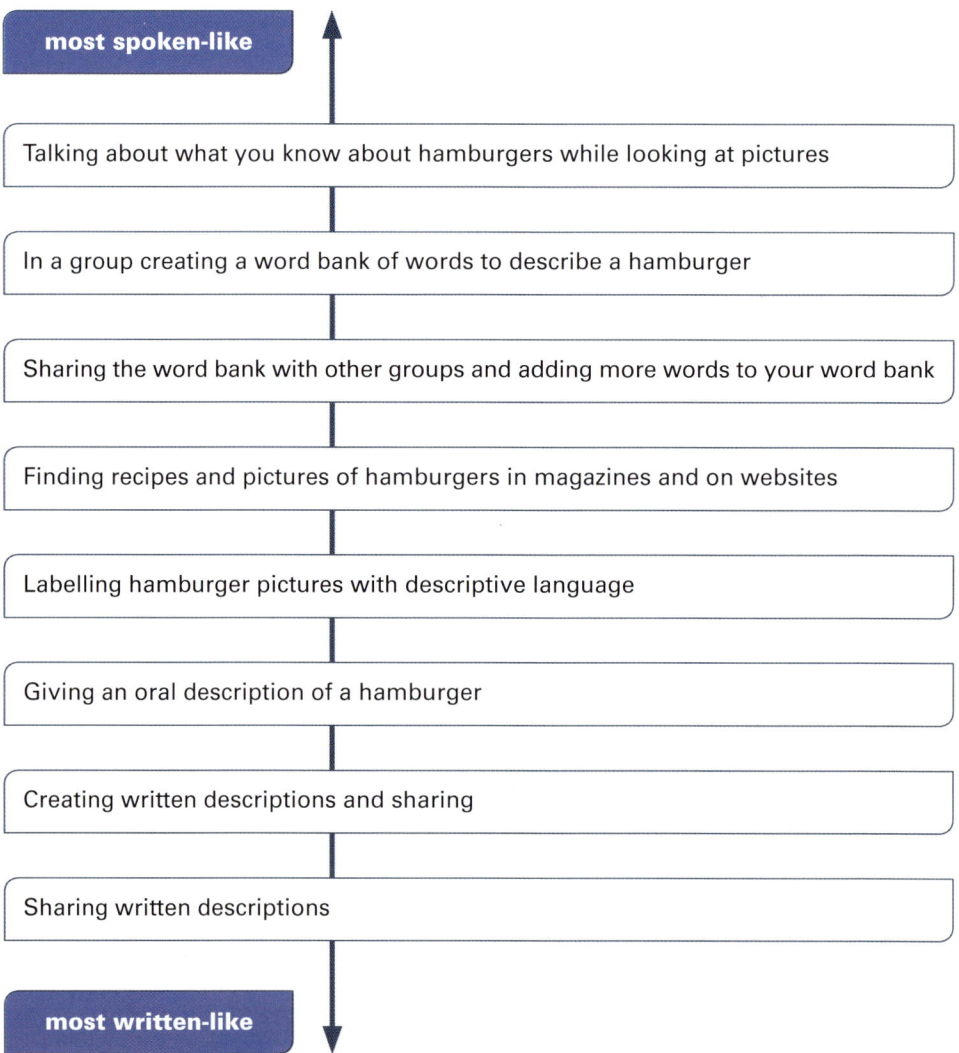

Figure 6.2
Continuum on texts describing hamburgers

The following suggested teaching sequence using the topic hamburgers uses the plan for writing as illustrated below. These same strategies can be used for a topic to suit any program. See the end of this chapter for an example of a scaffolded teaching and learning cycle. Others can be found on the PETAA website (www.petaa.edu.au/).

Focus on writing

Planning for writing

Figure 6.3 describes the steps a teacher needs to take in order to support student language development and ultimately writing. As noted above, it is unlikely that students can produce a coherent written text if they cannot first say it.

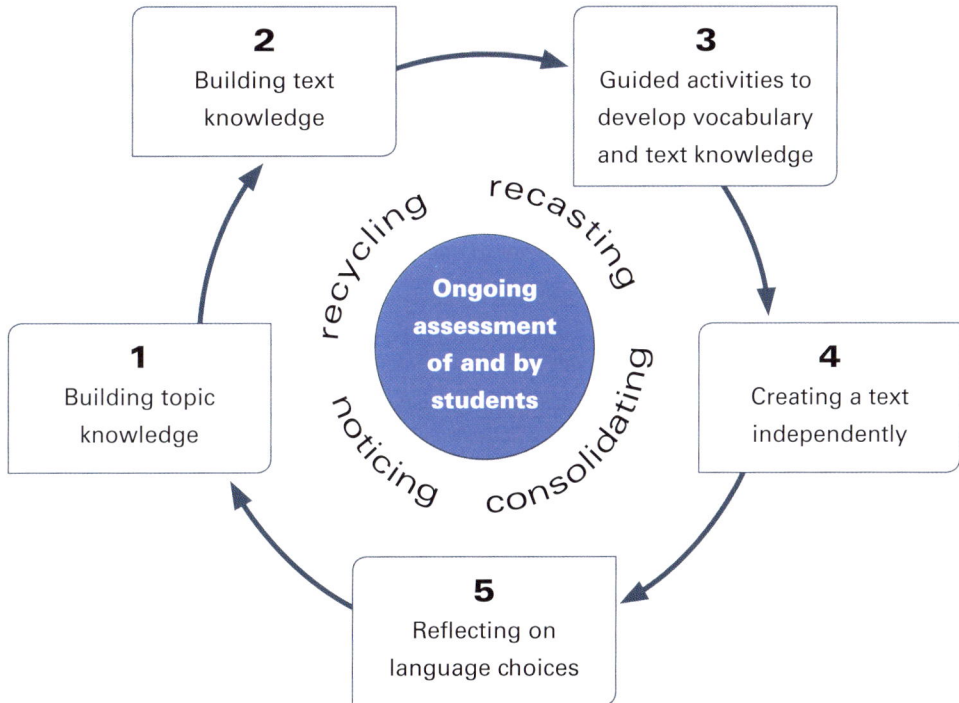

Figure 6.3
Building knowledge, skills and greater autonomy (adapted from Derewianka, 2007)

- In order for students to develop academic language they need to first be asked to 'notice' the target language. English language learners need substantial exposure to the target language in context.
- Students then need to 'recycle' the target language through a range of group and pair activities to that involve talking about the topic. This way, they hear it and say it in context.
- Once students have seen, heard, said, read and written the target language in the context of the topic, through a range of suitable activities, they may feel ready to 'recast' the target language in a less contextualised setting such as independent writing.
- Once students have completed an independent piece of writing, they need opportunities to reflect on their writing with peers and the teacher order to 'consolidate' this understanding.

What follows is a teaching and learning sequence to illustrate the above steps needed to teach your students firstly about the topic and secondly about the text and then to practise and consolidate their understanding. I have included a range of activities to give an illustration of the types of guided activities you can provide. In this case we are working towards constructing a procedural text. Refer to the end of this chapter for other abridged examples of this same teaching and learning sequence. Readers might like to use the strategies here for these other text types.

Building topic knowledge

Building knowledge on a topic begins with vocabulary (see Chapter 4 for more ideas on building vocabulary knowledge) and then moves to examining language structures, which is discussed in the cloze activity.

Before writing, brainstorm with students about the topic (hamburgers) and build up a vocabulary chart such as the one below. Ask them if they have eaten a hamburger (some may not have) or seen them made, and to discuss their experiences with the class.

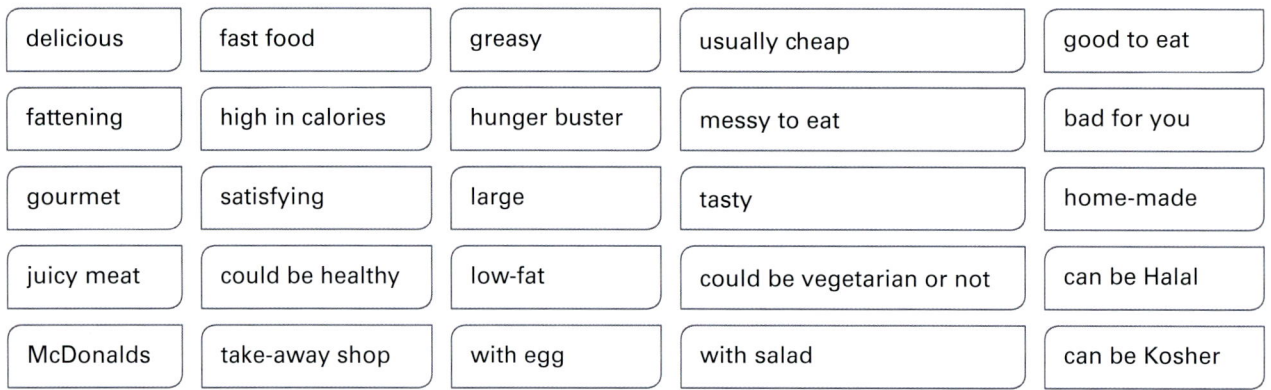

Figure 6.4
A vocabulary chart on the topic of hamburgers

Describing

The ability to describe, both orally and in the written form, is highly valued in English-speaking western culture. In order to use descriptive language students need to be able to understand how to expand the nominal group and then build in the *circumstances* (see Derewianka, 2011: 72). Beginning at the sentence level supports the students' understanding of the topic through description and vocabulary-building before developing the more complex structures of a whole text.

Create this sentence as I have done below:

Expand the nominal group for the 'burger' by asking some key questions. Each question will add adjectives that play particular roles (see Derewianka, 2011: 42)

Focus on writing

- What sort of burger is it?   *A beef burger*
- What kind of beef burger?   *A gourmet beef burger*
- What kind of gourmet, beef-burger?   *A delicious, gourmet, beef burger*
- How delicious?   *A really delicious, gourmet, beef burger*

Is there more information?
Now add some adverbials:

- Where from?   *From the fancy burger place near the beach*
- Why?   *For lunch*
- When?   *On Saturday*

Now ask the students to create their own sentence using Figure 6.5.

Figure 6.5
Expanding a sentence

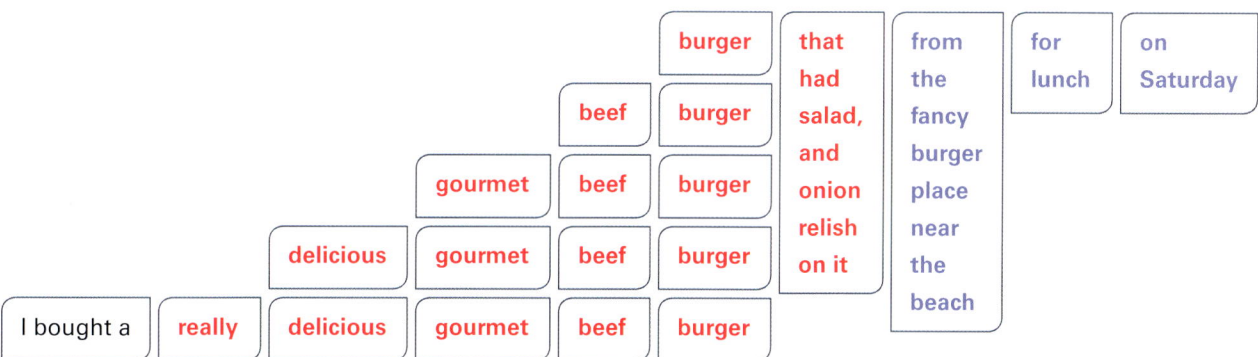

Building knowledge about the text

Now your students are ready to *read* about hamburgers in a more academic way. Consider the topic. What are the obvious choices? When teaching any unit of work where language and texts will be used, more than one text may be taught. It is best, however, to link the text with the topic. Avoid teaching a text type in a unit simply because it must be taught. The purpose may be incompatible with the topic. This is why a generic *scope and sequence* of text types taught in isolation over a period of weeks can be awkward. Isolated instruction on text types such as this is likely to be unsuccessful because the text type is being taught out of context and is unlikely to have a real purpose or a real audience (except the teacher who will mark it!). In addition, the connection to the topic may be tenuous for the students.

Topic and purpose

Look at the following two texts and decide which one suits the topic and purpose: **Why should minced beef patties always be cooked all the way through?**

> **Text 1**
> Ground beef safety standards are strict because ground meats have more exposed surface area, which gives bacteria more opportunities to contaminate the meat. Hamburgers should be cooked to a minimum internal temperature of 71°C all the way through to kill the bacteria E. coli.
>
> 'E. coli' is a type of bacteria that can cause food poisoning in humans. Sometimes referred to as 'hamburger disease' because it can be transmitted through undercooked ground beef.

> **Text 2**
> Once upon a time a bunch of ingredients got together to make beef burgers for a children's party. The minced beef, herbs and spices shaped themselves into patties and hopped onto the barbecue to cook while the buns lightly toasted themselves under the grill. Suddenly one of the patties left the grill undercooked. This was a disaster! If a human eats uncooked beef mince they risk food poisoning from E. coli bacteria. What were the other patties to do? Their reputations as party food were at stake!
>
> Through ruthless and devious means, the remaining patties contrived to force the miscreant off the side of the barbecue and into the mud, rendering it inedible. Luckily it was thrown into the garbage by a helpful human. The beef burgers' reputation survived and no humans were infected.

Text 1 is best, yes? Text 2 is about cooking beef burgers but it doesn't fulfil the cultural expectations of a scientific text the question calls for. These types of texts are fun to create for very capable writers but can cause great confusion for those learning to write in English for a science task. An explanation would always have been more appropriate. On the topic of hamburgers, an even more obvious choice is a procedure and in this case, a recipe.

Writing a procedure

In order to write a procedure, students should, if possible, follow the procedure and complete the task; in this case cooking a beef burger. A real experience shared by the students is best for creating language and engagement in context. If it is not possible to cook the burgers at school, organise an excursion or use a film to engage the students in the topic and develop that shared experience. I have used a YouTube film for this purpose (www.youtube.com/watch?v=J8uNiz7rBcs&feature=related).

Once you have built the topic knowledge with your students, you need to build text knowledge. Provide the students with an example of the text that you like and deconstruct it first. This means breaking the text up and showing the students its constituent parts. Talking about the text builds metacognitive awareness in students. When deconstructing a text you need to identify the both the grammatical structures and features on an exemplar for the students. For further information on the grammatical structures and features of text, see Derewianka (2011) and Droga and Humphrey (2003).

Label the text with the students as a class activity. It is messy but the students really need to identify all the parts of the text. It is beyond the scope of this chapter to discuss the grammar in detail and readers are referred to Derewianka (2011).

Focus on writing

> A list of ingredients is supplied.

> Each instruction follows the next, usually as a series of points of one or two sentences.

> The first word in each sentence is a verb telling the reader what to do.

> **Adverbs** may be used to describe **how** …

> Explanations are often embedded in the procedure. A circumstance of cause may be included.

> Highlighted purple are the circumstances of time. They tell the reader when or for how long …

> Highlighted blue are the circumstances of manner. They tell the reader how …

> Highlighted green are the circumstances of place. They tell the reader where …

A basic hamburger recipe

Ingredients

- 750 g beef mince (like topside)
- 1 large brown onion, grated
- 2 garlic cloves, crushed
- 1 tbs fruit chutney
- 1 tspn mixed herbs
- 70 g (1 cup) breadcrumbs
- 1 egg, lightly whisked
- Salt and ground black pepper, to taste
- 2 tbs olive oil
- 6 wholemeal hamburger buns, halved
- 3 medium ripe tomatoes, sliced
- Chutney or sauce, to serve
- 100 g mixed lettuce leaves or shredded lettuce
- Salt and ground black pepper, to taste

Method

- Place the beef mince, onion, garlic, chutney, herbs, breadcrumbs and egg into a large bowl. Season with salt and pepper. Combine **evenly** with your hands.

- Divide the mixture into 6 equal portions and shape each portion **carefully** with your hands into a patty about 10 cm in diameter and 1.5 cm thick.

- Place the patties onto a tray lined with greaseproof paper. Cover **securely** with plastic wrap and place in the fridge for at least 30 minutes, in order to help the ingredients bind and the flavours to intensify. If you chill the patties for more than 30 minutes, cook a little longer.

- Heat half the olive oil in a large, non-stick frying pan over medium-low heat and cook 3 patties for about 4 minutes on each side, or until browned and cooked through. It is important to cook mince right through to kill any bacteria present that may have been introduced during preparation.

- Put the patties on a plate, set aside and keep warm. Repeat with the remaining oil and patties.

- Preheat grill **on high**. Place the hamburger buns, cut-side up, under the preheated grill and toast for 1 minute or until golden. Leave the grill on.

- Lay the patties on the bottom halves of the toasted hamburger buns. Top each with the sliced tomato, tomato sauce and shredded lettuce, sprinkle **lightly** with salt and pepper to taste and then cover with the hamburger bun tops.

Guided practice of text

Once you have developed topic and text knowledge, the students need to be given a range of activities to consolidate the understandings they have just learnt. The suggestions made here are by no means exhaustive; they are just some I have used, that work. There are many cross references here with other chapters in this book. Please see Chapters 4, 5 and 7 as well.

The aim of these activities at this point of your unit of work is to provide English language learners opportunities to hear, see, say, read and even write the target language over and over again. Students prosper in an environment of *message abundance* (Gibbons, 2009: 156). That is, as many channels of communication as possible are used to support a variety of learning styles.

Barrier activity

Have students in two teams of three to four. Now give each team an identical set of (eight to ten) pictures. Ask them to look at each image carefully and note the similarities and differences in each image (in this case, hamburgers).

Figures 6.6 and 6.7
Two students doing a barrier activity

Focus on writing

> **Team A must:**
> 1 place their pictures in a line or array
> 2 describe their pictures in order for the other team to identify them.
>
> **Team B must:**
> 1 listen to the descriptions from Team A and, without looking at the other team's pictures, choose the picture
> 2 place the pictures as described in a line or array as directed by Team A (they may ask for clarification).

Word clines

A cline is a graded sequence of words whose meanings go across a continuum of meaning. A cline is usually shown on a sloping line. (The word derives from the Greek word *clino* – to slope.) The purpose of the activity is to have learners discuss and explore subtlety in meaning between similar words by arranging words in a continuum. This enables learners to reinforce their understanding of the meanings of words and also to add new words to their vocabularies. Here are some examples:

Verb	mix	combine, blend, fuse, amalgamate, toss, mingle, join, jumble, intersperse, mix-up, stir together
Adjective	hot	burning, scorching, blistering, sizzling, searing, broiling, warm, cool, tepid, cold, scalding, heated
Adverb	thoroughly	carefully, systematically, methodically, precisely, meticulously, painstakingly, conscientiously, assiduously

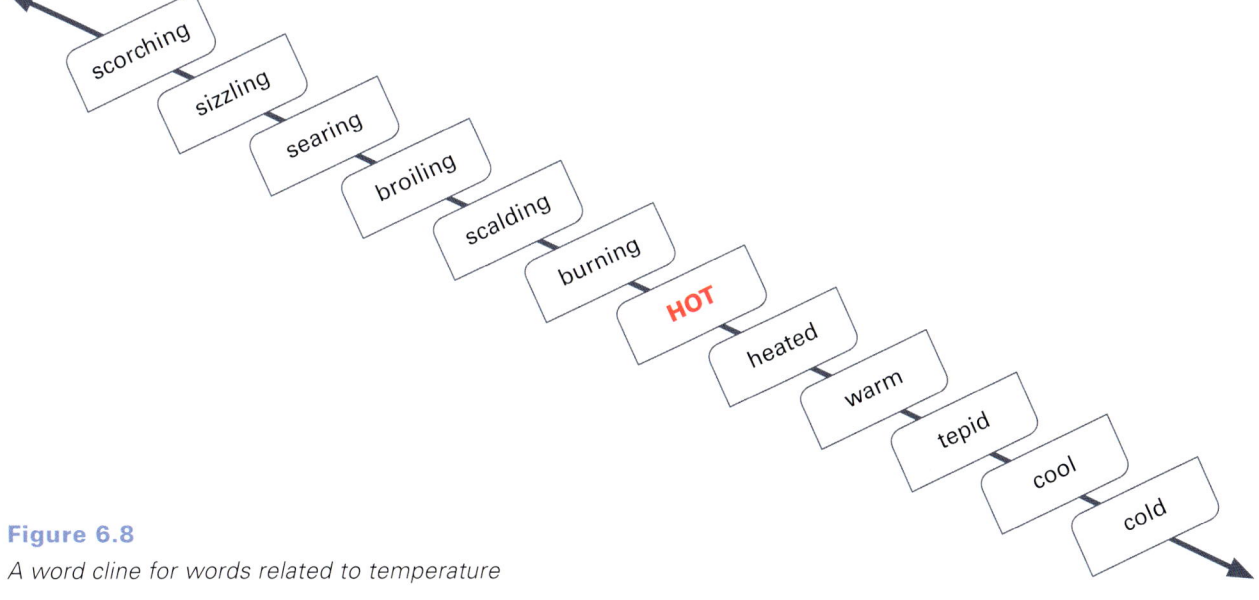

Figure 6.8
A word cline for words related to temperature

Text strips

Cut the procedural text into strips and ask the students in groups of two to three to put them into the correct order. This activity not only reinforces topic knowledge by getting the students to remember the steps but, importantly, attends to the language structures in procedures; in this case circumstance of manner, time and place.

- Place the beef mince, onion, garlic, chutney, herbs, breadcrumbs and egg into a large bowl. Season with salt and pepper. Combine evenly with your hands.

- Divide the mixture into 6 equal portions and shape each portion carefully with your hands into a patty about 10 cm in diameter and 1.5 cm thick.

- Place the patties onto a tray lined with greaseproof paper. Cover securely with plastic wrap and place in the fridge for at least 30 minutes, in order to help the ingredients bind and the flavours to intensify. If you chill the patties for more than 30 minutes, cook a little longer.

- Heat half the olive oil in a large, non-stick frying pan over medium-low heat and cook 3 patties for about 4 minutes on each side, or until browned and cooked through. It is important to cook mince right through to kill any bacteria present that may have been introduced during preparation.

- Put the patties on a plate, set aside and keep warm. Repeat with the remaining oil and patties.

- Preheat grill on high. Place the hamburger buns, cut-side up, under the preheated grill and toast for 1 minute or until golden. Leave the grill on.

- Lay the patties on the bottom halves of the toasted hamburger buns. Top each with the sliced tomato, tomato sauce and shredded lettuce, sprinkle lightly with salt and pepper to taste and then cover with the hamburger bun tops.

Cloze passage

To engage students further with the text, provide a cloze passage for them to complete in pairs. It is common to think of removing the verbs from a procedural text but in this one the verbs are very similar. Instead, take the circumstances (listed below) out of the text and ask the students to identify what each circumstance is telling you (usually where, how or for how long) the preposition (in turquoise) and the adverb, if present (in orange). Prepositions are often the most difficult words for English language learners to use appropriately. Here you will be teaching them in context. Circumstances are usually a combination of an adverb and a prepositional phrase or just a prepositional phrase providing essential details as to how, why, when and where.

Focus on writing

Circumstances from the cloze passage			
Place (where)	Time (for how long or when)	Manner (in what way)	Cause (why)
into a large bowl	for at least 30 minutes	evenly with your hands	in order to
onto a tray lined with greaseproof paper	for about 4 minutes	into 6 equal portions	
in the fridge	until browned and cooked through	carefully with your hands into a patty about 10 cm in diameter and 1.5 cm thick	
in a large, non-stick frying pan over medium-low heat		securely with plastic wrap	
		with the remaining oil and patties	
on each side	for 1 minute	on high	
on a plate	until golden	with the sliced tomato, tomato sauce and shredded lettuce	
under the preheated grill		lightly with salt and pepper to taste	
on the bottom halves of the toasted hamburger buns		with the hamburger bun tops	

How to make beef burgers cloze passage

- Place the beef mince, onion, garlic, chutney, herbs, breadcrumbs and egg _____ . Season with salt and pepper. Combine.

- Divide the mixture _____ and shape each portion _____ _____ .

- Place the patties _____ . Cover _____ and place _____ help the ingredients bind and the flavours to intensify.
  If you chill the patties for more than 30 minutes, cook a little longer.

- Heat half the olive oil _____ and cook 3 patties _____ _____ , or _____ . It is important to cook mince right through to kill any bacteria present that may have been introduced during preparation.

- Put the patties _____ , set aside and keep warm. Repeat _____ .

- Preheat grill on high. Place the hamburger buns, cut-side up, _____ and toast _____ or _____ . Leave the grill on.

- Lay the patties _____ . Top each _____ _____ , sprinkle l_____ and then cover _____ _____ .

This is a common cloze where words are omitted. There are many other kinds of cloze activities you can use: *reverse cloze*, *not needed cloze* and *read around cloze* for example (see Dufficy (2010) for more information).

You can see that much of the text is missing from the cloze and it will require considerable discussion for the students to reconstruct this text. This kind of talk is important to consolidate knowledge of text and content. As the students talk, they call upon their shared experiences with both the procedure they deconstructed with you and what they remember from cooking the hamburgers.

A cloze passage can be used as an assessment tool to see if the students understand the text and how it was constructed. As discussed in Chapter 5, cloze exercises should be done in groups of two or three to allow for discussion and negotiation. This is another strategy to ensure 'message abundancy' (Gibbons, 2002: 156).

Flow charts

Another way of developing student knowledge of the procedural text is a flow chart. Cut the instructions up and the students (in pairs or groups) must place them in order following the cues. They paste the steps on to paper and add the appropriate arrows (see example in Figure 6.9). Encourage the students to talk and discuss what goes where and why.

Place the beef mince, onion, garlic, chutney, herbs, breadcrumbs and egg into a large bowl. Season with salt and pepper. Combine evenly with your hands.	Lay the patties on the bottom halves of the toasted hamburger buns. Top each with the sliced tomato, tomato sauce and shredded lettuce, sprinkle lightly with salt and pepper to taste and then cover with the hamburger bun tops.	Divide the mixture into 6 equal portions and shape each portion carefully with your hands into a patty about 10 cm in diameter and 1.5 cm thick.
Place the patties onto a tray lined with greaseproof paper. Cover securely with plastic wrap and place in the fridge for at least 30 minutes.	Preheat grill on high. Place the hamburger buns, cut-side up, under the preheated grill and toast for 1 minute or until golden. Leave the grill on.	Heat half the olive oil in a large, non-stick frying pan over medium-low heat and cook 3 patties for about 4 minutes on each side, or until browned and cooked through.
Put the patties on a plate, set aside and keep warm. Repeat with the remaining oil and patties.	Are they cooked all the way through? **Yes** **No**	Continue cooking until cooked all the way through.

Focus on writing

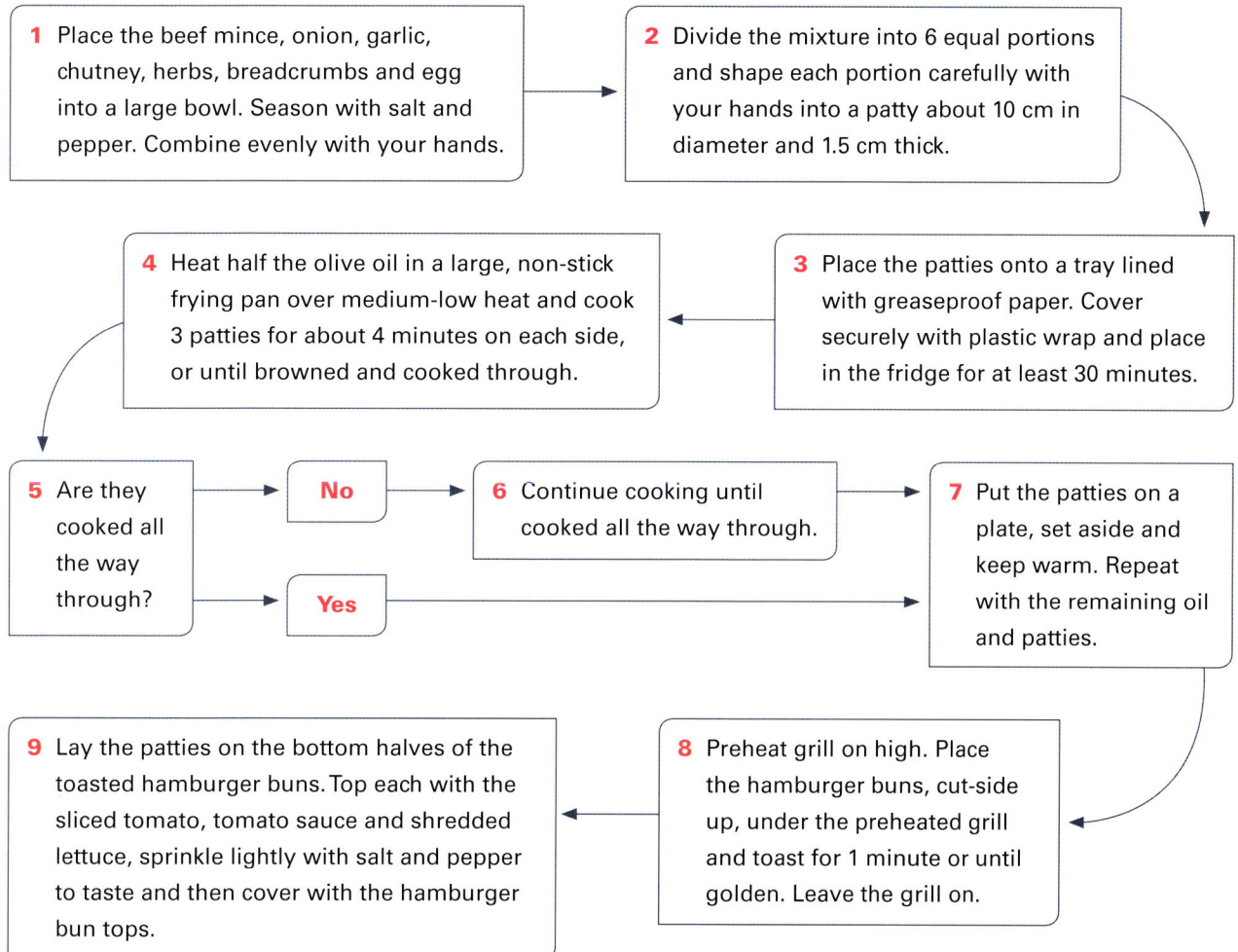

Figure 6.9
Construction of a flow chart

Independent practice of text

When the students have completed a range of tasks through group and pair work and have consolidated their understanding of both the topic and the text type, they are ready to write independently.

Provide a very explicit rubric for your students so they know what you want them to write and how well you want them to write it, as in the example below.

Write a recipe for your peers to make a hamburger.
Include all the ingredients that would make a healthy hamburger.
Use language that your peers will understand.
Use a procedure format as used in class.
Consider the use of verbs and adverbs at the beginning of each step and make certain to include all the necessary information needed to describe where, how and for how long.
Be clear and concise.

Encourage students to use all the resources collected up to this point and have them displayed around the room or readily available for consultation. Remind students that, as this is the first time they have written the text, it is a first draft. Some students are hesitant to take risks and need reminding that in drafts we cross out and rewrite, in order to make the message clear.

Figure 6.10
Students drafting their hamburger recipe

Reflection and self-assessment

Students need time to read their own writing aloud and reflect. Using a rubric like the one at the top of page 127 will help them to consolidate their understanding of the task.

Student reflection and self-assessment is important. You can talk with a student about a completed text but it is much more productive if they have read their own writing and thought about what they have written. Reflection takes time but it forces a student to actively connect with what they have written and to take seriously what they have spent time creating. By providing the time to reflect, you are conveying to the students that you value their writing and want them to do so too.

The next step to successful student writing is providing quality feedback. Providing feedback is part of effective teaching. The feedback we provide should be explicit, meaningful and aimed at improving student outcomes.

Focus on writing

Writing rubric	Student comments
Write a recipe for your peers to make a hamburger *(Have I achieved my purpose?)*	Yes, I have written to instruct someone in my class on how to make a hamburger.
Include all the ingredients that would make a healthy hamburger *(Have I covered the topic?)*	Yes, I was giving a procedure on cooking a healthy hamburger.
Use language that your peers will understand *(Have I aimed my writing at the right audience and made good language choices for my audience?)*	Yes, they will understand my language. I made it simple enough for them to follow. The audience was my friends.
Use a procedure format as used in class *(Have I used the correct text structure?)*	Yes, I wrote in short sentences providing a sentence for each step of the recipe.
Consider the use of verbs and adverbs at the beginning of each step and made certain to include all the necessary information needed to describe where, how and for how long *(Have I used the correct grammar structures?)*	Yes, I used a range of verbs, at the beginning of the sentence and I was clear in my use of prepositions and included the important information such as cooking time.
Be clear and concise *(Have I made sense of the writing?)*	Yes.

> If you focus on providing students with improved, quality feedback in individual classrooms, departments and schools you'll have an almost immediate positive effect …great teachers give great feedback, and every teacher is capable of giving more effective feedback. (Dinham, 2008b)

Throughout this chapter I have tried to provide the essential elements of good teaching practice in writing. It is a step-by-step process that involves you knowing:
- what you want your students to know (knowledge of topic)
- what you want you students to write (knowledge of text as related to topic)
- how the text is constructed (knowledge of text)
- how well you want them to write it (knowledge of what good writers do)
- reflection and feedback are important (using a rubric).

This is an inclusive practice that will support *all* your students; it is not just for English language learners. It is possible in the busy world of the twenty-first century that your English speaking background students will not have the necessary skills to write effectively unless they are explicitly taught. It is, however, very likely that your students with limited English experiences and knowledge will benefit greatly from this kind of explicit, systematic quality teaching.

Remember, all your students are *learning to write* in an academic way and will continue to build on what you teach them throughout their lives as they encounter situations where they are expected to write with increasing sophistication across a range of topics in many different genres. You are teaching your students the skills for successful writing.

Following is a sample of a scaffolded teaching and learning cycle. Others can be found on the PETAA website at: www.petaa.edu.au/.

Sample scaffolded and learning cycle

Unit	Science: Energy – Building balloon a hovercraft				
Language focus	Recounting				
Degree of scaffolding	**Teaching and learning activities**	**O**	**R**	**W**	**Target language**
Controlled	1 Teacher: Explain to the students the purpose of recounting something and ask them to think about when they would use a recount (record student input).	•	•		What is a recount? **Definition:** **To reconstruct past experiences by retelling events as they occurred.**
Controlled	2 Teacher: Explain that the purpose of the recount they will create is to remind you and others of something that has passed and is useful when you want to reconstruct a similar event such as a science experiment or a person's life or an experience. It is often used by reporters.	•			When would you use? **Questions to ask:** When – time
Guided	3 Teacher: Ask the students to recall the last experiment they did and recount it orally (scribe); jointly reconstruct the experiment with the class. 4 Teacher: Using the original or another recount identify each of the following parts (see Appendix A below) • When – a clause of time • Who – a person or people • Where – a place • What – an action, incident or occasion • Why – a reason for the action (begins with 'because') **Take each part and expand individually.** **When – a clause of time**	•	•	•	Who – people Where – places How – adverbs What – actions/incident Why – because *On Tuesday the 21st September, Mrs Cole (4B) in 4B's classroom, carefully constructed a balloon hovercraft for the science unit on energy.* Clauses of time
Guided	Teacher discusses the term **a clause of time**. Make a list of all the time phrases/clauses you and the students can think of.	•	•		
Independent	Give students in groups or pairs a range of texts and ask them to find the 'when' in each of them. These can be added to the list. **Who – a person or people**				People
Guided	Teacher discusses the people in the recount. Make a list of all the people who could be in a recount and students can copy into their books.	•	•	•	
Independent	Give students in groups or pairs a range of recounts and ask them to find the 'who'. These can be added to the list.				

Focus on writing

Degree of scaffolding	Teaching and learning activities	O	R	W	Target language
Guided	**Where – a place** Teacher discusses and makes a list of all the places one can go, which students refer to.	•	•		Places
Independent	Give students in groups or pairs a range of recounts to read and ask them to find the 'where' in them. These can be added to the list.	•	•		
Guided	**What – an action, incident or occasion** Teacher discusses all the occasions that could be in your recount. Make a list of all the occasions and students can copy into their books. Teacher should discuss the fact that recounts often have many actions in them. Using phrases such as 'and then' or 'after that' or 'later on' students can link actions within the recount.	•	•	•	Actions, incidents and occasions
Guided	**Why – reasons (because)** Teacher discusses and makes a list of all the reasons you could be going somewhere or doing something and students share their thoughts. Discuss the use of the words 'because' and 'for' when explaining. Give students in groups or pairs a range of recounts and ask them to find the 'what' and the 'why' in them. These can be added to the list.	•	• •		Use of the words 'because' and 'for'.
Independent Controlled Guided	**Verbs – actions** Teacher and students Identify and list verbs from any given recount . Teacher and students use a thesaurus to find other words that mean the same as each verb and could be used instead; for example: 'walked = ambled, strode.' OR groups could look up given verbs and report back the synonyms for each verb on paper. Verbs can be put onto cards and students can sort these into groups of synonyms. Encourage the groups to use a dictionary to help them if they are unsure. *(This is a communicative activity.)* * *Teachers should reinforce the importance of past tense here as many of the verbs will be irregular past tense.*	• •	• •	 • •	Verbs Synonyms **Thesaurus:** a dictionary of synonyms and antonyms

Degree of scaffolding	Teaching and learning activities	O	R	W	Target language

Controlled
 	
Guided
 	
Independent
	Adverbs – describing the actions
	Discuss the meaning of the term adverb – that it adds information to explain how the action was done (eg He ran quickly).
	
	Using an existing list of verbs, think of words that could describe how the action was done. Act it out and make a list with the students.
	
	Put verbs and adverbs onto cards and pairs or groups of students can put them together and create sentences that use a verb and an adverb to read to the class.
	
	Ask the students to listen for similarities and differences from their own sentences.
	
	(This is a communicative activity.)
	
	* *Some verbs lend themselves to certain adverbs and this is what you want the students to understand. This is why they will probably hear many sentences that are the same as their own.*
	
	Abstract nouns – feelings
	Discuss the feelings one may experience on certain occasions. Teacher makes a list. Use a thesaurus for common abstract noun synonyms (display).
	
	* *Students may wish to act the feelings; drama is a good way to express feelings.*
		•
		
		  •
		
		  •
			
			  •
					Past tense
					Irregular past tense
					
					Verbs
					Adverbs
					
					Same
					Different
					Making sense
					Abstract nouns

Controlled
 	
Guided
 	
Independent
	Writing a recount
	Teacher gives students a recount outline and explains the expectation that they must produce a recount with all the elements in order, in past tense and with a 'because' clause. (Use lists displayed in classroom.)
	
	Following their own construction attempt in science
	Students write a recount of their own (with teacher support if needed).
	
	Ask them to consider verb and adverb use and encourage the use of a thesaurus.
	
	Students should all produce a recount. They may, however, share ideas.
	
	Students present their recount orally and their peers listen for all the elements of a recount using a checklist.
	
	Students publish their recounts for display or a class book with illustrations.
	
	(This is still highly supported and guided.)
		•
		
		  •
		
		  •
			•
			
			  •
				
				  •
					
					All lists from room display
					
					Same
					Different

Degree of scaffolding	Teaching and learning activities	O	R	W	Target language
	Evaluation of the program				Making sense
	• In each section of the teaching learning cycle it is important to remember that the students will achieve at different levels depending on their level of English and their experience of recount in reading and writing. In accordance with this difference you will need to adapt support according to need. Some students will require more support 'scaffolding' than others. Some students will be ready to 'take risks' before others. It's a balancing act and you may find you need to revisit some aspect of the teaching sequence for some students for them to clarify their understanding.	•	•		
	• Ultimately, of course, the achievement of outcomes will provide evidence of a successful teaching sequence but it's the deep language knowledge gained that will support the ESL students as they move into other areas.				

© Janet Freeman 2011

Model of a recount (joint construction)

Constructing a balloon hovercraft

On Tuesday the 21st of September, Mrs Cole came to 4B's classroom and carefully constructed a balloon hovercraft for the science unit on energy.

Firstly, Mrs Cole got the equipment to make a balloon hovercraft. The equipment was an old CD (Compact Disc), a light brown wooden cotton reel with a hole in the middle, a hot glue gun, glue sticks and a big green balloon.

Two weeks ago Mrs Cole and some of 4B used the hot glue gun to glue the wooden cotton reels onto the CDs. We had to glue the reel onto the top of the CD so that the hole in the reel lined up with the hole at the centre of the CD.

Next, Mrs Cole waited for two weeks for the glue on the CD to dry.

Then, Mrs Cole came back to 3–4B classroom today and began the experiment. Firstly, Mrs Cole stretched the balloon so it would be easier to blow up. Then Mrs Cole blew up a small, green balloon.

After that, Mrs Cole twisted the neck of the balloon twice to stop the air from escaping out of the balloon.

Then, Mrs Cole stretched the neck of the green balloon over the light brown wooden cotton reel. Next Mrs Cole had to put the hovercraft on a classroom desk because we needed a flat, shiny, smooth surface. We decided that would be a suitable surface.

After that, Mrs Cole gently let go of the balloon and the air escaped slowly through the hole in the cotton reel and the CD.

Then, Mrs Cole gave the hovercraft a gentle push to make it hover in the right direction, so it could hover and slide across the desk.

Finally, when Mrs Cole let the hovercraft go it rotated and moved over the smooth table. The hovercraft hovered approximately 1 mm (millimetre) above the desk. When the air in the balloon had escaped, the hovercraft stopped rotating and spinning and the balloon fell down onto the table.

© Janet Freeman 2011

CHAPTER SEVEN
ROLE TO COMMUNICATE: LEARNING ENGLISH THROUGH DRAMA

When you have to use your imagination, you can think up better ideas … so when you think, you must be learning English. (ten-year-old EL learner)

It [drama] helps you communicate your thoughts because you can feel the situation, and you have more opinions because you take on that role. (eleven-year-old EL learner)

For some students, taking on the role of another person gives them the opportunity for sustained talk (and then often reading and writing) because it allows them to take a safe risk. If they make a mistake, it is the character who makes the mistake and not them; if they say something that really is from the heart, again it is the character and no-one else need know that it really is *their* thoughts, as explained by one eleven-year-old boy, who said, *I like drama 'cause you can say things that are you, but nobody has to know because you are acting someone else.* It is for this reason the chapter is titled 'role to communicate'.

Drama and language learning

To move beyond conversational language and acquire academic language proficiency ((Cummins, 2008) as discussed in previous chapters), students need to be exposed to and then practise a range of registers and language functions. Within a classroom program, providing authentic and believable situations for practising such a *range* is important. This is why 'role play' is often a suggested strategy. For example, in quite a few units of work on the 1850 Australian Gold Rush, role playing miners digging for gold is a suggested activity so that students can simulate (role play) the methods for extracting it.

Such activities may well be useful but they often remain at the level of what I term 'open ended simulations'. Open ended simulations differ from drama because they usually miss one of the most important components of drama. For drama to be drama, there needs to be a plot, a complication, some tension. When simulations become drama there is far more material to work with and *hence* talk about. So, for instance, the example of simulating miners digging for gold can become drama if the situation was that miners (without a licence because they could not afford it) were panning for gold when a trooper arrives asking for their licence. This provides some dramatic tension. The focus, and so the themes explored, would therefore be hardship, justice, and so forth. Nevertheless, assuming a role (as for example a miner or trooper) is difficult for many students and especially as students get older, some feel inhibited and embarrassed.

In this chapter we will explore how to set up structures for these students to take risks and feel safe and confident, because drama can enhance language and literacy development (Crumpler & Schneider, 2002; Fleming et al, 2004; Ewing, 2010; Kao & O'Neil, 1998; Stinson, 2008); but, as Stinson stresses, 'one of the main aims of a drama class is to give students something to talk about and a safe physical, cognitive and emotional space to figure out the best way to express their ideas' (Stinson, 2008: 194).

Readers' Theatre

Readers' Theatre (RT) is the oral reading of a narrative or poem. It is a drama form that supports students' reading comprehension, fluency and critical literacy. At the same time it helps students understand the elements of drama such as pace, tone, expression and gesture. Performance of RT connects talking and listening skills with reading and writing. The process of turning narrative prose into dramatic script gives students an insight into the technical choices authors make. When involved in RT, students are actively engaged in analysing a text, but they do so from *within* it. That is, by taking on the roles of the characters and enacting the author's choice of language, students become *text participants*. As well, students gain an insight into the author's point of view and hence analyse how this text positions them as the reader (*text analyst*). This can be a very powerful outcome. In one Year 5 class, for instance (Hertzberg et al, 2006), several groups of students in the Developing English phase, were preparing a Readers' Theatre for an excerpt from *I am Jack* (Gervay, 2000). The students debated the tone of voice the mother should use. Was she cross with Jack or was she just trying to appeal to him to be patient? There were varying opinions across the groups and these different interpretations were portrayed through their RTs. These variations were viewed and then discussed and debated (text analyst). Furthermore, because students needed to reread the script at least several times before presenting their interpretation, they were repeating and therefore practising a good model of English.

Making RT scripts

Texts with a lot of dialogue are best and the text is adapted to make it suitable for performing as an oral reading. For instance, indirect speech might be altered to direct speech (making it a good way to explore the concepts of first and third person) but the original meaning and the vocabulary used by the author is retained. For example, the text '"What great big ears you have!" said Little Red Riding Hood' in the narrative, would be altered so that 'said Little Red Riding Hood' is deleted because, when performing it, Little Red Riding Hood is speaking these words. At times the narrated text might be divided and allocated to different readers.

The excerpt of a RT script is demonstrated below.

Character	Script
Narrator 1	When Joseph was a baby, his grandfather made him a wonderful blanket.
Narrator 3	To keep him warm and cosy and to chase away bad dreams.
Narrator 2	But as Joseph grew older, the wonderful blanket grew older too.
Narrator 1	One day his mother said to him:
Mother	Joseph, look at your blanket. It's frazzled, it's worn, it's unsightly, it's torn. It is time to throw it out.
Joseph	Grandpa can fix it!
Narrator 2	Joseph's grandfather took the blanket and turned it round and round …
Grandpa	Hmm …
Narrator 4	And his scissors went snip, snip, snip and his needle flew in and out and in and out.
Grandpa	There's just enough material here to make … a wonderful jacket!
Narrator 3	Joseph put on the wonderful jacket and went outside to play.
Narrator 2	But as Joseph grew older, the wonderful jacket grew older too.
Narrator 1	One day his mother said to him …
Mother	Joseph, look at your jacket. It's shrunken and small, doesn't fit you at all. It is time to throw it out!
Joseph	Grandpa can fix it.
Narrator 2	Joseph's grandfather took the jacket and turned it round and round …
Grandpa	Hmm …
Narrator 4	And his scissors went snip, snip, snip and his needle flew in and out and in and out.
Grandpa	There's just enough material here to make … a wonderful vest!
(From P. Gilman (1992), *Something from nothing*, Ashton Scholastic, Sydney. Adapted for Readers' Theatre for classroom use only and not for performance.)	

Side notes:

This script was written by the teacher. Scripts can be written by students, but it is advisable to provide them with many teacher-made models first.

It is intentional that this is Narrator 3. I have divided up the narration so that some narrators have more difficult parts to read.

As you read further down this script, you will note how repetitive Narrator 2's part is and hence it might be suitable for a weaker reader. The same applies to the roles of Joseph and Grandpa, but Narrators 1 and 3 and the mother need to be better readers.

Each student highlights their role as shown here for the role of Grandpa.

Even though teachers are writing these scripts for reading instruction, copyright must be considered. After all we are manipulating the unique and creative work of the author. This is another important reason for retaining the exact vocabulary of the author and only making changes necessary for an oral telling. To comply with copyright, the referencing format shown here should always appear at the footer of each page in the script.

Staging Readers' Theatre

In RT, performers remain 'on stage' for the duration of the reading, and they read the script rather than memorise lines. In addition, there is minimal stage movement by performers, and they face the audience as they read the story, as can be seen in Figure 7.1.

While RT can be rehearsed and refined to include stage sets and costumes, I usually do not include these, or keep them to a minimum. The reason for this is twofold. First, costuming can detract from the purpose of RT, which is to use the drama skills of, in particular, voice, gesture, levels and space to tell the story. Second, and more importantly when using RT for English language learning, the organisation of costuming and props becomes an additional drain and strain on teachers' time. As a result, and understandably, RT might then not be used routinely for enhancing English language learning.

Figure 7.1
Readers' Theatre in progress

The Readers' Theatre instructions that students can use when preparing their RT are shown below.

> 1 Decide on your roles and highlight your part.
> 2 Practise reading the script together.
> 3 As you practise, think about the following aspects and as a group decide on:
>
> Verbal expression: How will you speak your part?
> - tone (eg happy/sad)
> - volume (eg loudly/softly)
> - pace (eg quickly/slowly)
>
> Body language: What sort of expressions will you have? What sort of gestures?
> - facial expressions
> - hand and other body gestures.
>
> Position: What position will you take when you read your part? (In Readers' Theatre you do not move very much, and you face the audience.)
> - Where will you stand or sit?
> - Will you alter your position at times?
>
> Sound effects: Do you need sound effects? If so, which?
> - Do you want to use some instruments for sound effects?
> - Do you want to use body percussion?
>
> © Margery Hertzberg, 2009.

Using RT as an oral reading strategy

As discussed in Chapter 5, oral reading is a difficult skill, but it is beneficial because students both articulate good models of English and practise pronunciation. However, reading aloud can be an intimidating experience for many students and also on a first reading many students just decode as opposed to comprehend.

These sentiments were confirmed by an eleven-year-old EL learner in the Developing English phase, who said:

> Well, the first time I'm not reading really good with people. The first time I mean I get embarrassed, but not when I've done it lots of times and with my friends. When we do Readers' Theatre, we read it [the script] heaps of times and so then I can read the words and understand what the story is about. Usually I just read the words but I don't know what I'm reading.

Another EL learner put it this way:

> You don't feel stupid if you make a mistake because they all know you're only practising and it's not like the whole world is going to see it.

For more information on how to make scripts and for examples of scripts, go to the PETAA website: www.petaa.edu.au.

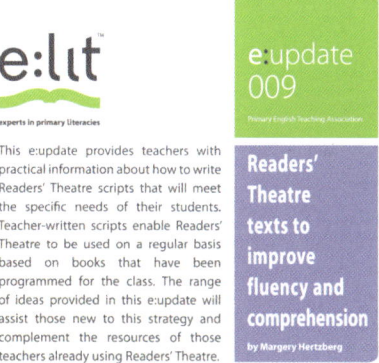

Figure 7.2

This article on the PETAA website, describes Readers' Theatre in more detail

Readers' Theatre is but one form of drama that encapsulates why drama is such an important part of a student's English language learning education. The emphasis in the rest of this chapter is on a type of drama termed educational drama.

Educational drama

At the core of 'educational drama' is *enactment*. The phrase 'walking in someone else's shoes' is often used to describe this feeling. The emphasis is not about *acting* someone else, it is about *being* someone else and explicitly attending to the drama elements of gesture and facial expression, space and levels, verbal expression, sound and silence. And as stated previously, for drama to be *drama* as opposed to simulation there needs to be a problem – some tension which addresses an underlying focus (theme) to be explored. Often an object, or repeated word or movement throughout the enactment will act as a symbol.

Educational drama is different to learning and then acting a published play script performed for an external audience. Although such play scripts may also be a part of the overall drama program or syllabus, in 'educational drama' the fictional context to explore an issue is developed *by the students* and they use their prior knowledge and experience to create a unique role for themselves within an imagined and fictional context. Creating this fictional context that parallels reality, and enrolling students so that enactment occurs, means that EL learners are using language during enactment that is meaningful and quite often in contexts that would not normally be part of a school's regular program. So no matter how fantastic the dramatic context may appear from the outside, within the drama at this time (here and now) the purpose for using language is realistic and authentic. This is possibly why one ten-year-old EL learner once said to me at the completion of a drama lesson, that she was *going to pretend to do drama* when being examined on the imaginative writing component of a national test, *because then I use my imagination and come up with some good ideas*. That is, if she imagined a fictional context and assumed a role within it while sitting the examination, she would have something to write about.

Bolton (1992) uses the term 'metaxis' to explain that drama enables a person to see two worlds at the same time (fictional and real), which is what young children do in dramatic play and from which educational drama emanates. (Heathcote & Bolton, 1995). Theorists such as Bruner (1986 and 1993) argue that dramatic play is fundamental to a child's language development (in any language) because the child uses language in new and untried ways and then practises this over and over again by re-enacting their favourite plays or scenarios.

Readers with experience with eighteen-month to eight-year-olds (approximately) will know that these children learn the vocabulary and language structures for mowing the lawn, baking a cake, taking orders in a restaurant or nursing a sick animal, because they enact these roles (with or without costumes or props) and often their carers will join in as well by taking on a role. If young children did not engage in this type of dramatic play, they would not talk the myriad of registers such play requires and thus their language use would be

> It is beyond the scope of this chapter to detail the aspects of drama in-depth, and readers are referred to Ewing et al (2004) for more information.

limited mainly to requesting and expressing everyday 'real time' needs, wants and events. However, during dramatic play they set up contexts that are authentic and believable because while engaged in the activity they really *do* believe that they are the cook, vet or teacher and so forth. That is, they use a range of registers, language functions and relevant vocabulary because they set up 'as if' situations to enable them to have these conversations.

Below is an excerpt from a four-year-old child who was being a waiter at an Italian restaurant.

Sarah: *Mummy! Mummy! Come and order your pizza!*

Mother: *Can I have one with anchovies and olives please?*

Sarah: *Yes, but don't you want tomatoes also?*

Mother: *Not today thanks.*

Sarah: *OK.* (And runs to the 'kitchen' – the coffee table in the lounge room.) *Oh no! We've run out of olives!*

Mother: *Well that's no good. I'll have to go to another pizza restaurant* (and starts to walk away).

Sarah: *NOOOOOOOOOO. Stay here! I'll find some.* (She rushes over to the sofa and looks under the cushions.)

The phone rings.

Mother: *Sarah we'll have to go. Daddy needs a lift home.*

Sarah: *NO! I'm not Sarah, I'm the waitress and I have to take the menu.*

And then what followed was a lot of cajoling to get her to stop the drama and get into the car. Furthermore, when Sarah was a waitress she also did a lot of writing, as can be seen in Figure 7.3.

Figure 7.3

Sarah's menu order

Dramatic play at school

Dramatic play is a feature in many early childhood classrooms for all the reasons discussed above, and is demonstrated in the photos below. These kindergarten students were in the Beginning and Emerging English phases and dramatic play was a regular and carefully planned part of the teacher's program.

Figure 7.4
Dramatic play in kindergarten

Figure 7.5
More dramatic play in kindergarten

At times it is useful if a good model of language enters the drama to expand the conversation and often this is the teacher (teacher-in-role). The teacher not only aids language development through recasting and reformulating, but can help build up the event so it becomes more 'dramatic'. This elaboration then provides opportunities for more extended communication.

Figure 7.6
Teacher-in-role recasting and reformulating language during dramatic play

In Figures 7.7 and 7.8, the students were deciding on their roles. They were taking time to make it believable for them in terms of deciding who was going to be the eldest brother.

Figures 7.7 and 7.8
Students deciding on their roles before playing going to the beach

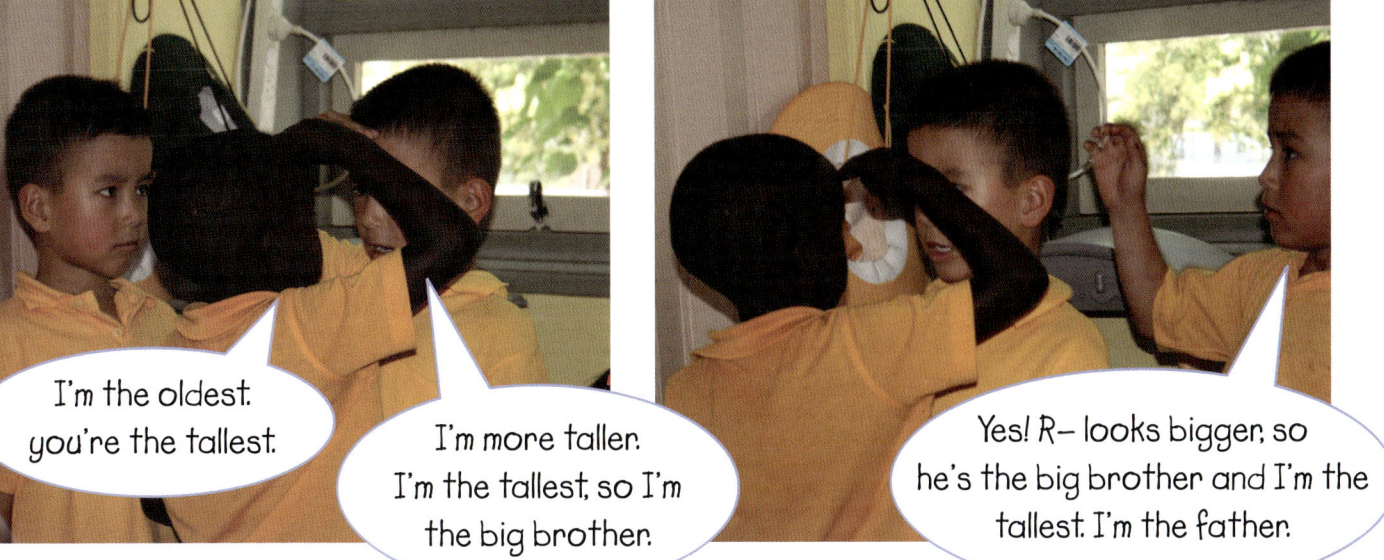

Communicating through drama

As discussed in Chapter 3, young children often learn English more quickly than their older counterparts because the *conditions* for language learning are often more suitable and the above examples of dramatic play demonstrate this. The students have many opportunities for extended conversation in different contexts and using varied language structures. Note for example the comparative language that was practised in Figures 7.7 and 7.8 (tall, taller, tallest, big, biggest, eldest). Furthermore, dramatic play can lead to writing as demonstrated in Figure 7.3 on page 139 (Sarah's menu writing).

Educational drama teaching and learning experiences also support other important conditions for language learning and these include:
- provision for talking and listening before and/or in conjunction with reading and writing
- practise in a range of higher order language functions and structures in sustained conversations – deducing, speculating, justifying and so forth
- opportunities to use a range of spoken registers – from most spoken-like to most written-like
- opportunities to use non-verbal language (facial expressions, body postures and sounds), which enables students to communicate their understanding even if they do not have the necessary English vocabulary yet
- connecting prior knowledge and experience to a new learning situation
- using outer speech (external dialogue) with others assists inner speech (abstract thinking) – essential for problem solving (Vygotsky, 1986).

More specifically though, when we examine how the process of enactment engages students, the use of drama for English language learning becomes even more compelling.

Drama and the Fair Go Project's student engagement framework

In Chapter 3 the Fair Go Project's (FGP) model of engagement was explained, and its alignment to many of the major theoretical principles of ELL teaching was described. Many of the teaching and learning experiences presented in this chapter come from my research with the FGP. Specifically, I analysed how educational drama can engage (as defined by the FGP, refer to page 43) EL learners and enhance language and literacy learning. It is beyond the scope of this chapter to report on all the findings and readers are referred to Hertzberg (2004b), Hertzberg et al (2006) and FGT (in progress). In summary though, the conclusions that support this position are:
- **Enactment:** When the content to be examined is both emotionally and academically challenging, students within the process of enactment are thinking hard (high cognitive), they are actively doing (high operative) and they are affected by what they are doing; that is, they have a committed feeling about the learning (high affective). The following comments typify what many students say:

Because you're actually being the person you have to work it out and see how it feels. (eleven-year-old EL learner)

I like it [drama] because I can think big ideas and plus I'm allowed to share them with my friends and I like how we work in groups and have to think for ourselves and I think Miss likes it because we are all good and we work more and then she is happy. (eight-year-old EL learner)

- **Content:** While the teacher may have determined the subject area and supporting resources, the ideas and materials for the drama are always negotiated and developed with students. This is possibly best explained by an eleven-year-old EL learner who said, *The teacher gives you the bones of it and we have to act the muscles.* Significantly, students receive engaging messages (refer to page 44); in particular about their ability (I am capable), control (we can do this together), place (being valued as a learner and ownership of learning) and voice (environment of discussion and reflection).
- **Metaxis and reflection:** The concept of metaxis (being able to see the two worlds – fiction and real – at the same time) enables students to make authentic connections (Bolton, 1992). These connections are contextualised within the fiction, and transferrable to the real world, giving students access to powerful knowledge about big ideas and concepts. Often this occurs during the reflection time, which is an integral part of educational drama. The following quotes are representative of comments made by EL learners:

    My Dad's a refugee and he always tells me how lucky I am and how great Australia is and like I sort of understood, but now I reckon I understand deeper because I had to really think about it (the issues) to do the drama. (thirteen-year-old EL learner)

    When I talk about it during drama I can think of heaps better ways of saying and I have more to say. (ten-year-old EL learner)

    The still images make me think harder because they make me imagine and explain things. (ten-year-old EL learner)

'Role to communicate' in the middle school years

It would be emotionally and socially ludicrous to incorporate dramatic play as described earlier in this chapter with older students, but we can replicate these opportunities using other drama strategies in the older years. The rest of this chapter will demonstrate some drama strategies to assist older EL learners. Reflecting on my data (Hertzberg, 1999, 2003, 2004b and Hertzberg et al, 2006) and specifically why students felt they were learning English through drama, I have coined the term 'role to communicate'. When students assume a role they are in a position to communicate using both verbal and non-verbal language suited to that situation, and as mentioned before, because it is a fictional situation they often use registers and spoken language that might not otherwise be common in a classroom situation. The following section of this chapter begins by demonstrating how some drama strategies have been used as just one of many activities during a lesson or sequence of lessons. That is, it explains how drama can be a 10-, 20- or 30-minute activity to address specific content and concepts in the same way as students might complete a cloze, a text reconstruction, a measurement activity or a science experiment as just part of a teaching and learning experience. Following this, is a more extended drama program developed to enhance students' understanding of a picture book (multimodal text).

Practicalities

Physical space

Drama is best done in the classroom, because it is argued that drama be prominent in ELL programs. Moving to another room is often tricky, making it less likely that drama will be used frequently. Usually the furniture does not need to be moved, as these drama strategies can be done in spaces between desks and at the back, front and sides of rooms as Figure 7.9 demonstrates.

Figure 7.9
Drama can be done without moving the furniture

Friendship grouping

I encourage students to form their own groups, which usually means they work with friends. One major aim of drama is for students to not only take risks with the production of language, but also take risks in terms of their imaginative and creative ideas. Because drama requires students to negotiate their ideas, I have found they are more likely to listen constructively and be co-operative with people they trust emotionally. The comment below from one student is representative of many students' opinions.

> Student: *Working in groups makes it more fun, but also it helps you think more because they have more ideas and you can put all those ideas together.*
>
> Margery: *What sorts of groups do you like working in?*
>
> Student: *My friends.*
>
> Margery: *Why?*
>
> Student: *'Cause you like them and they like you and then it's easier.*
>
> Margery: *In what way is it easier?*
>
> Student: *You don't worry about them laughing and all that [teasing] so you say things more.*

The reflection and debriefing (stepping out of role) component

This is mentioned before proceeding to the strategies because it is necessary for emotional reasons, as well as providing an important learning opportunity. Although there is a distinction between reflection (thinking about) and debriefing (stepping out of role), often the two are intertwined. That is, the students are reflecting on the issues or events raised and explored during the drama experience and at the same time coming out of their drama role and reflecting on the experience as themselves. I often say to very young students during either dramatic play or other drama forms, *Step out of your imaginary role because you are now you and no longer (role). Let's all stand up and shake the drama out* – they then shake their bodies and we talk about the experience. With older students I say, *You just took on the imaginary role of (character). That was the fictional 'you' and now you are the 'real you'. Let's talk about how we felt in our fictional roles.*

The above might be sufficient; however, in other circumstances, the drama could well explore issues that *are* tough and so there is more emotional investment. For example, if the student has played the role of an angry person or a person who is a thief, they need to be helped to make the distinction between reality and fiction. Just as for literature or movies, drama has a plot and there needs to be tension for it to be drama as opposed to simulation. This might be why drama is sometimes avoided but it is the very reason that I advocate it. It is a powerful tool to explore what it is like to be in another's shoes and view an issue from a different perspective. Morgan and Saxton explain the debriefing phase as 'students are taken *out* of the action of the plot and *into* the action of the theme' (Morgan & Saxton, 1987: 36). Or, as one twelve-year-old EL learner put it:

Like, isn't that the whole idea [for doing drama] because even though you're not really doing it because it's pretend, you can feel what other people are feeling and learn more.

The reflection and de-roling process regularly takes place in 'the drama circle' and it often begins with students talking to their partner and expressing how they felt about their role and the issues that arose. Then, within the circle, students share their thoughts with the whole group. This can be one of the most rewarding times in teaching because students often express very profound and philosophical thoughts that they may well not express in other subjects. Readers are reminded of the quote earlier in the chapter in which a boy stated: *I like drama 'cause you can say things that are you, but nobody has to know because you are acting someone else.* It could be that for many students the experience while *in role* protects them and sanctions them to express an opinion out of role and in front of their peers. For example, many older boys would not think it 'cool' to admit that when teased they go home to their bedroom and cry, but if the drama is about bullying, then they can express the real consequences of bullying for them, but distance it through their role in a drama about bullying. I suspect this was the case for many of the EL learners when we were discussing their enactments of a scene from the novel *I am Jack* (Gervay, 2000), which is about a boy who is bullied at school.

Reflecting and de-roling is important, regardless of the duration of the drama experience. The following suggestions demonstrate how drama can be just one 10- to 15-minute part of a teaching and learning sequence.

The quick drama teaching and learning experience to enhance understanding of a concept

Sculpting

This is a useful strategy to explore the emotions surrounding a significant event and can be used before and/or during and/or after reading a fictional or factual text. An example of this was suggested on pages 91–92 of Chapter 5.

One of the reasons it is such an effective tool is because students can demonstrate their understanding using non-verbal language and portray a very insightful and sophisticated perception of the issue(s), even if their productive language is not at the same level of sophistication. Many students are aware of this and it is often the reason given for liking this strategy. One EL learner reported that she liked sculpting because, *I can show what I understand by doing it. Sometimes I don't have the words.* But as will be illustrated in many of the examples, the doing does in fact lead to 'having the words'.

How to do it

Students work in pairs and A sculpts B. Explain to students that B is piece of 'clay'. A needs to direct and shape B to represent the significant moment using body language and position. Often within a 'formal' drama class, B is not

Role to communicate: Learning English through drama

expected to speak. That is, the onus is on A to use B (the clay) to interpret the situation as A sees fit. However, as this drama strategy is being used to develop language competence and understanding of content, encourage the students to negotiate their ideas.

Some teachers display the following on a poster:

> Communicate your message through:
> - body language or gesture
> - facial expression
> - position – levels (eg sitting, standing, lying, crouching).

Example 1: Using sculpting to make links with students' prior knowledge

Before reading an article about prejudice towards Chinese miners during the Australian Gold Rush, students were asked to sculpt their partner to show how they might feel when being emotionally abused because of their ethnicity. This readied all students to think about the article that described the circumstances at Lambing Flat.

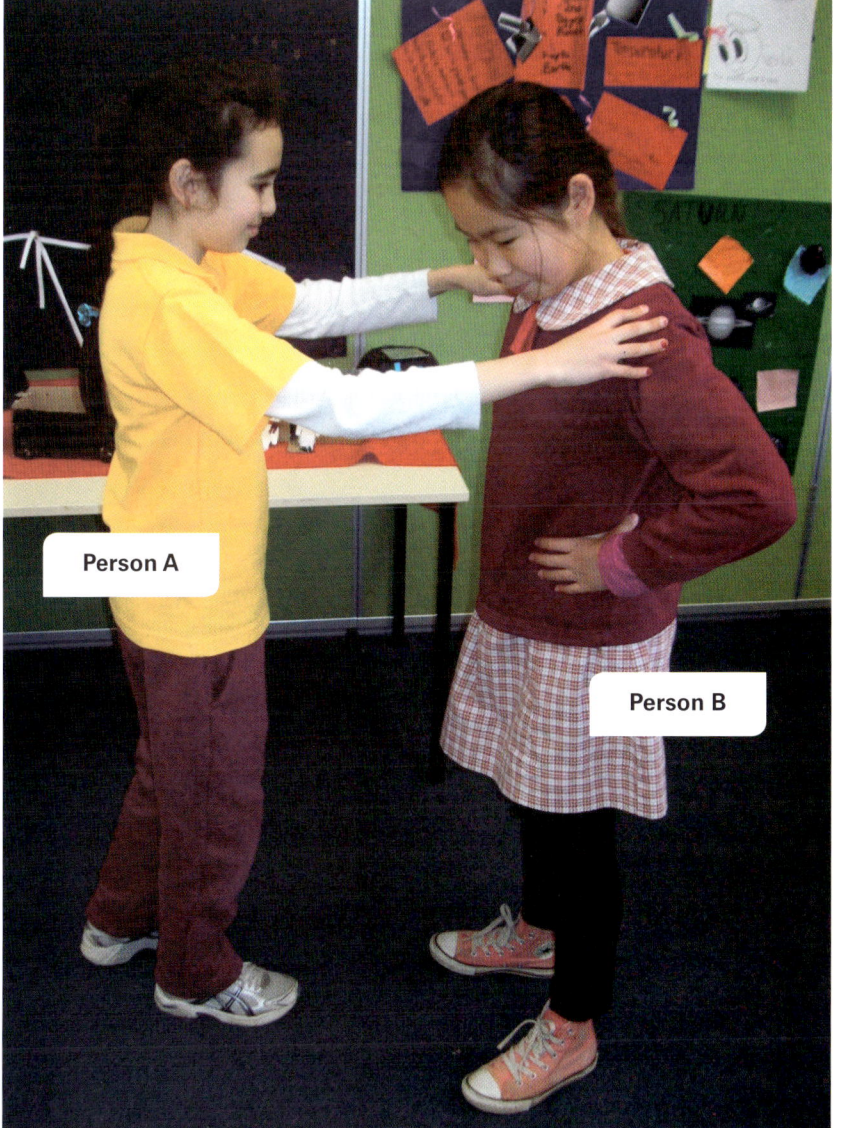

Figure 7.10

Students preparing their sculpture

> A: *What do we have to do?*
>
> B: *I have to look how it feels when someone is teasing me because I'm from a different country to them.*
>
> A: *Yeah Maria does that to Baseema. She says she's a terrorist because she's Muslim.*
>
> B: *Yeah I know* (and they talked about this for a while).
>
> A: *Stand up, but look down because you don't want to show them you're crying. Hands on hips. Here! because you're angry.*
>
> B: *And I'll make my face sad … no like I'm crying.*
>
> (Excerpt of dialogue recorded during one pair's preparation.)

Viewing the work

Many students do like to show their ideas and it can be a valuable part of the language learning component. Below is a suggested sequence:
- Explain that half the class will look at the other half of the class's interpretations and then swap.
- The audience close their eyes and the teacher or another student counts 3, 2, 1 slowly as the 'actors' prepare themselves.
- After saying 1, the counter then says 'curtains up'. The audience views the sculptures and the class discusses how their use of non-verbal language communicates the message. They will also note that each interpretation is different and hence it is a useful strategy for explaining multiple perspectives.

(It is strongly advised that only those who feel comfortable to do so, show their work to the rest of the class and especially when students are new to this strategy.) Much of the learning has already taken place in the preparation stage and a reflective discussion will still occur using those who have volunteered.

From sculpting to writing

Rebecca Hillis's students used the sculpting strategy to explore racial vilification in sport as there had been a lot of recent media attention given to this subject. After the sculpting activity, students were given a worksheet which defined the words discrimination and prejudice. In pairs, students wrote words or phrases to describe how a person might feel about discrimination. The words from all the groups have been combined below.

Discrimination

Unfair treatment of a person, racial group, minority, etc.
Action based on prejudice.

Prejudice

An unfavourable opinion or feeling formed beforehand or without knowledge, thought or reason.

Words to describe this feeling

Sad, upset, embarrassed, angry, cranky, start a fight, disappointed, scared, worried, full of rage, feel like punching someone, shy, silly, confused, embarrassed, awful, scared, full of danger, want revenge, unhappy, cross, frustrated, confused, upset, feels like doesn't have fair treatment, unforgivable, lonely, down, left out, bad, treated unfairly, ashamed, face turned red and angry, went blue and sad, annoyed, disappointed, uncomfortable, mad, discriminational (sic) comment, judgement, jealousy, emotional, physical, furious, strong, punchy, revenge, inappropriate movement.

Progressing from the above, work on modality and word clines would be appropriate (refer to pages 114 and 120–21 in Chapter 6). However, in this case the students responded on their class blog and the following is one post:

Ketura: *Doing the sculptures made me know what discrimination and prejudice mean. The words I would use to describe these feelings ... [include] mad, annoyed, disappointed and sad ... and angry, discouraged and upsetting.*

Michael: *Hi, Ketura I have seen discrimination before in public areas including at parks and in the city. I have seen a lot of racism in the city and at the park. People tease each other saying things like ... you're so black like chocolate or you're white like tissue.*

Example 2: Using sculpting during the reading of a book

During the shared reading of the class novel *Boy overboard* (Gleitzman, 2002), the teacher stopped reading just after the scene where the brother is terrified that his sister is running towards an area scattered with unexploded landmines. To heighten the students' awareness of narrative structure and specifically tension and complication, students sculpted their partner as the brother at this point in time. They photographed their sculptures and in PowerPoint added the text from the book to support their interpretations.

> Both of the examples in Figures 7.11 and 7.12 are correct. This is a good example of students using all four roles of the reader (see pages 86–88 in Chapter 5) and in particular the text user role as they skim and scan the chapter to justify their interpretation.

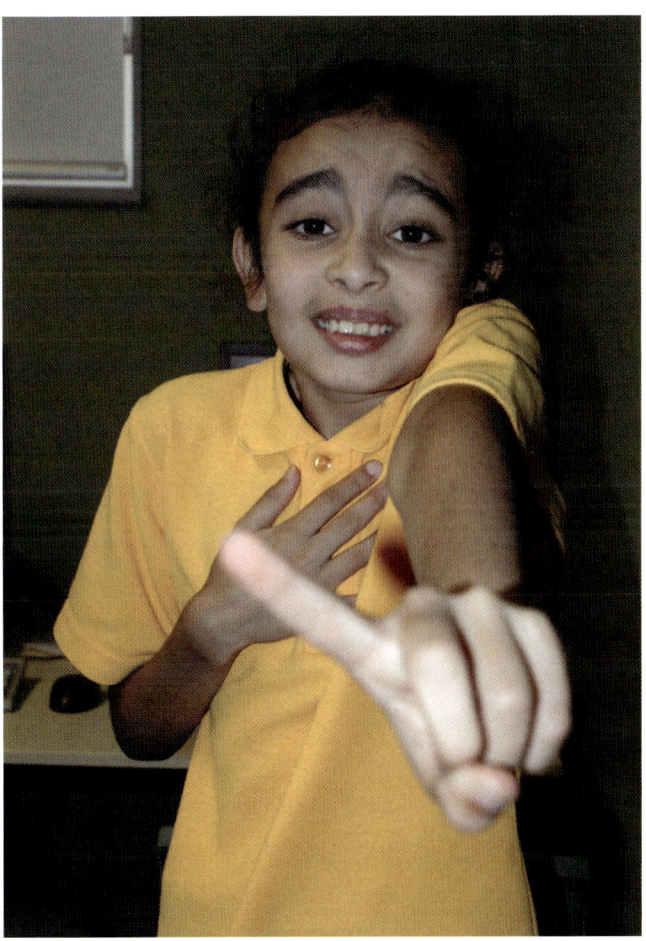

Figure 7.11
'Please, I beg the landmines silently. Don't let her tread on you. She's only nine. This is her first time out here. Be kind.' (Gleitzman, 2002: 7)

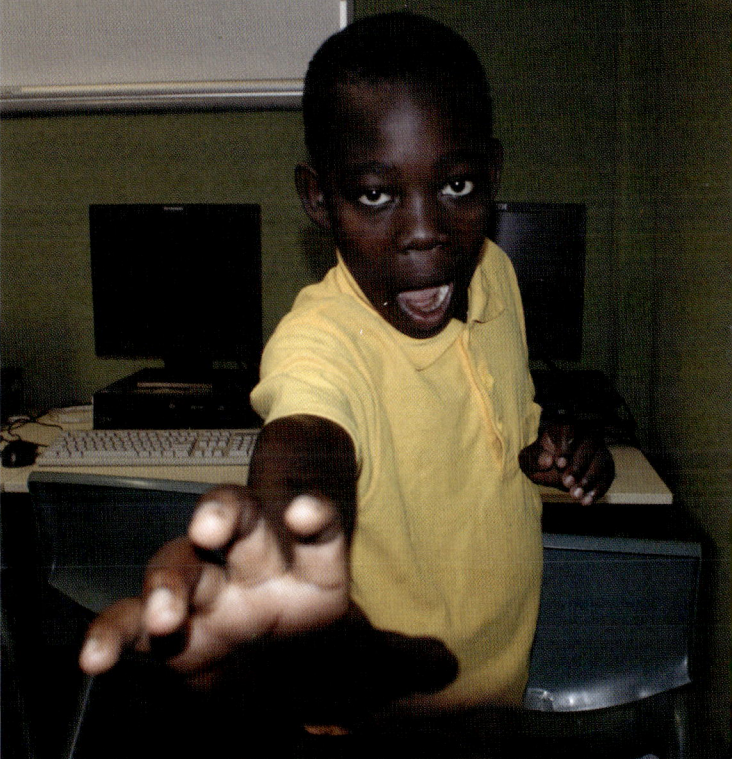

Figure 7.12
'I slither into the gully. Bibi isn't there. Neither is the ball. They can't be blown up or I'd have heard the bang ... I climb out of the gully and up onto a sand dune, peering into the wind. And see Bibi. She's down on the flat desert, running towards the ball. 'Bibi,' I scream. 'Watch where you're putting your feet.' (Gleitzman, 2002: 7)

Example 3: Using sculpting at the completion of a book to consolidate meaning

After reading the book *Six perfectly different pigs* (Geoghegan & Moseng, 1993), students were sculpted to show how they thought the bullied pig felt. Why might such sculpting experiences aid students? Earlier in the chapter it was stated that many students believe that sculpting allows them to demonstrate their understanding even without sufficient English. This conforms to the theory that receptive understanding precedes productive output. Eleven-year-old Tan, who had only been learning English for eight months, stated that she liked sculpting, *because I can tell you with my body*. Drama enables students like Tan to use non-verbal language to demonstrate their understanding. But, just as importantly, it enables these students to participate in the mainstream program and affirms their cognitive ability to their peers. Success breeds success is a maxim which needs careful consideration. But there are other significant advantages linked to the affective response. EL learners often say that drama helps them write because they can feel the situation and have more to say. As part of the FGP research (Hertzberg et al, 2006), we wanted to find out if this feeling of being in another's shoes did improve students' ability to write a more analytical response to a question. We did the following sequence with these eleven- and twelve-year-old EL students, and readers might like to conduct similar research with their students.

1. Shared reading of the book.
2. Students returned to their desks and wrote their answers to the following question: 'How do you think Paprika felt when he was being bullied?'
3. Students then did the sculpting exercise, followed by a discussion about the sculptures and brainstorming for vocabulary to describe their sculpture.
4. Students returned to their original answer to the question and added more information if they had it, referring to the discussion and using vocabulary from point 3 above.

Most students did have more information and furthermore were quick to do so. Josie's (a late Developing English phase student) example is representative:

Before sculpting: *Paprika must have felt like being the other person instead of the bullied one. She also must of felt alone.*

After sculpting: *She felt depressed and the other person is feeling guilty. She felt discriminated (against). When I did the activity I felt that I was Paprika and felt alone.*

Josie's sample demonstrates the use of more descriptive vocabulary after this six minute drama activity and her affective response of feeling like Paprika is interesting. Her response was not unique, as most other students' writing also improved. In interviews students frequently said that enactment helped clarify their opinions. As Manh said, *Because you're actually being the person you have to work it out and see how it feels*. Furthermore, every child interviewed thought drama helped them write their ideas. Ahmed's statement was typical:

Role to communicate: Learning English through drama

Like if you write it, you don't talk to anyone and you just think it out in your head … you don't get to give your opinions [like you do in drama] and then you can use them [opinions from the sculpting activity and subsequent discussion] in your writing.

For ELL teachers, Ahmed's statement is significant because he is confirming that 'doing' and talking about a concept *before* he writes helps him.

It should also be noted that many students in this class were disengaged with learning and school in general. Their teacher was selected for her expertise in working with such students. As my co-researcher, she kept a reflective journal and her comments about drama are summarised here:

Students are on task, excited about doing the activities … even the shy students are giving it a go. There is no avoidance behaviour on their part … there is increased student confidence and participation and increased inferential comprehension … perhaps it's because they have real ownership over their work and want to do their best.

Another drama strategy called 'still image' can also be used to precede and/or in conjunction with reading and writing.

Still image (sometimes termed depiction, tableau or frozen moment)

As for sculpting, still image is a good strategy to explore the emotions of an event and can be used across a range of subject areas. Figure 7.13 demonstrates what it looks like. I often explain to students that it is a 'real time' photograph.

Communicate your message through:
- body language – body gestures and facial expressions
- position – levels (eg sitting or standing, lying or crouching) and space and distance – near to or far from each other.

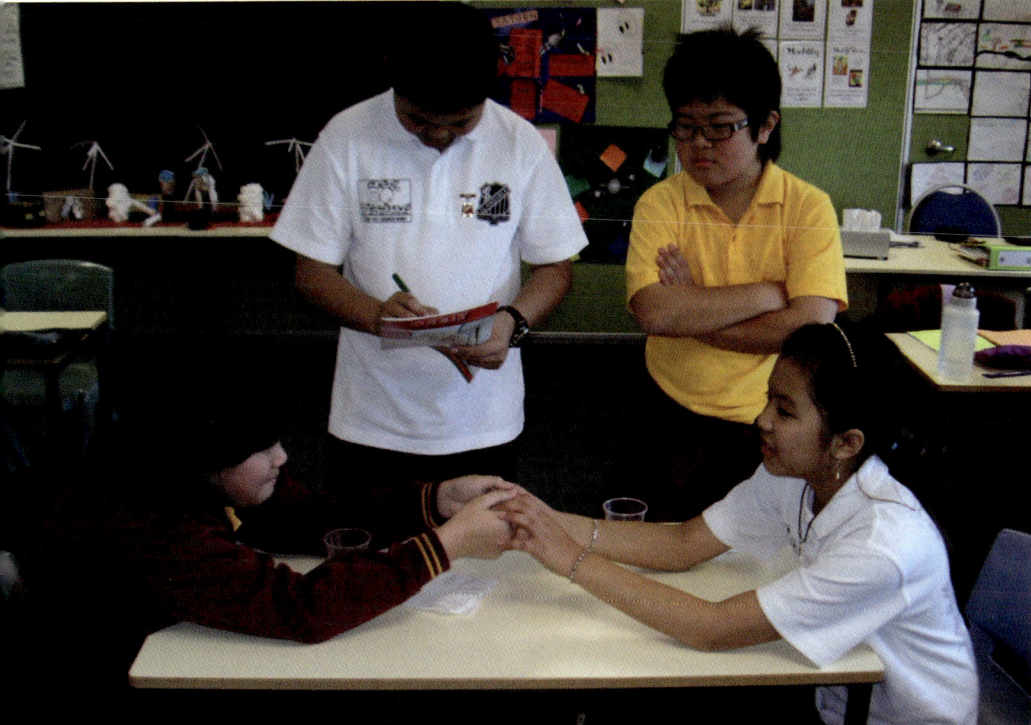

Figure 7.13
Preparing a still image

As well as explaining to students how to communicate their message, as shown above, each group is often provided with a laminated sheet with a set of 'planning your scene' questions which they use for preparing their still image. Refer to page 164 for a student work sample of this.

> ## Planning the scene
>
> - Who are we in this scene? (characters/roles)
> - Where are we in this scene? (setting/context) For example, are we at the beach or in the kitchen etc?
> - What is happening to make it dramatic? (problem/tension) For example, are we lost without water or is someone being unkind to someone?
> - What is the message we want to convey? (focus/theme/issue) For example, is it about friendship or hardship or jealousy or kindness?
> - How will we show this? (gesture/movement/levels etc) Note: You don't need to write your ideas down for this last point. Have a quick talk about it and then get up and work it out more as you practise.

Example 1: Creating a still image to critically interpret a scene from a book

The class novel was *Onion tears* (Kidd, 1989) and had been read in class up to page 14. The following excerpt was displayed. In this excerpt, the protagonist Nam-Huong is being asked what her name means, with varying degrees of hostility and aggression:

> Everyone at school keeps asking me what my name means.
>
> 'Does it mean princess?' Mary says.
>
> 'COCONUT!' Tessa shouts.
>
> 'Butterfly! Dragon!' They all try and guess.
>
> 'I know', says Danny. 'It means DIM SIM!'
>
> But I just shake my head. One day I'll tell them what it means. My Mum loved my name. She said it was very special. (Kidd, 1989: 9)

The students formed groups of four to make a still image of this scene, assuming the roles of Nam-Huong, Danny, Tessa and Mary. Examples of their still images are shown in Figures 7.14 and 7.15.

This activity highlights that some significant language and literacy learning concepts are being addressed:
- In order to construct their image, the students needed to re-read the excerpt and both reading fluency and comprehension were enhanced by multiple readings of the same text.
- To communicate this meaning they used verbal and non-verbal communication, including the use of space and levels helped to convey the meaning (variety of modes).

Figures 7.14 and 7.15
Different interpretations of the same excerpt from Onion tears

- Students needed to use interpretative and inferential thinking in order to construct the scene – they were using their text participant and text analyst resources. It is interesting to see how each group interprets the scene in slightly different ways.
- Students found that critically analysing this scene using drama was useful, for, as one student noted: *I really like watching everybody else … to see what interpretation they have of it.* As well, many students affirm the benefits of drama as an opportunity to discuss their ideas and interestingly the majority of EL learners I have interviewed prefer this type of discussion to more conventional book discussions. The following quote is representative:

> (It's) good to act out … so you just don't talk about it … Because when you're just talking about it you're just talking about it, you're not actually doing anything, you're just sitting there and talking. But when you're acting you're standing up and doing something so it gives you more opinion what you're doing. It's more interesting to do things like that. (ten-year-old student)

Thought tracking

In Figures 7.14 and 7.15, the students also added some dialogue. They said this dialogue when 'tapped in' on the shoulder. When the character is tapped, they say what their character is verbalising or thinking at this time. Note also that groups might also use this strategy during their own planning and rehearsal stages of extended verbal improvisations.

Figure 7.16
A pair's map of prominent themes in the book *Marianthe's story*

Role to communicate: Learning English through drama

Example 2: Using a series of still images to sequence key events in a story

The students (thirteen years old) had read the picture book *Marianthe's story* (Aliki, 1998). This is a good example of a sophisticated multimodal text, making it suitable for all age groups as it can be read on a variety of levels. An extended drama program for this book can be found in Hertzberg (2004a). After two readings, the students mapped the themes of the book (see Figure 7.16).

This book invites the reader to infer possibilities. Although the written text is lengthy, with further clues provided in the illustrations, readers are invited to explore the themes and elaborate on believable possibilities because explicit details are absent. In so doing, students need to critically reflect and analyse how the text has positioned them (the reader) to arrive at these possibilities. Accordingly and working in groups of four, each group designed a set of five still images to portray events that conformed to one of the prominent themes. One person from each group acted as a narrator and explained what each still image was portraying. Objects noted in the book were used as symbols.

The example on the following page demonstrates the narration for the first two of the five images. This group (Figure 7.17) used a newspaper within each still image and their focus was on migration. Other groups used either a paint brush, pencil and paper, soap, photo frame or ball.

Figure 7.17

One group's first still image in the sequence and using a narrator

> Narration: *This still image shows the family back in the old country. As you can see they are very happy. Uncle Theo has brought a newspaper and he's reading it to the family. He's reading the sports section about how their team won the soccer game.*

Another still image followed this, with the narration below.

> Narration: *In this still image Uncle Theo is reading the newspaper, but this time it is about the war that has started in their country. Now everyone is terrified about the violence that is occurring and there is a famine because there is a shortage of food.*

A further three images with narration then followed.

While observing the students it was interesting to note a progression of language choices made, from most spoken-like to most written-like (mode continuum), as they rehearsed and refined their work to get to this finished product.

Example 3: Using still image in history

A similar exercise was done with Year 5 EL learners who were studying the First Fleet. They developed a sequence of still images to portray the landing of the First Fleet from an Indigenous perspective, using the book *The rabbits* (Marsden & Tan, 1998) as their resource.

Role walk

This quick strategy encourages students to reflect on a situation in role. For example one class was learning about great inventions in science and watched a documentary. This led to further reading about some of these inventions. When learning about Alexander Fleming's chance discovery of penicillin which was then isolated and used as an antibiotic by Howard Florey, the teacher asked them to close their eyes and imagine they were a person whose life had been saved by this antibiotic. The class then stood up and in a large circle walked slowly around the room (see Figure 7.18) as the teacher talked about the implications for them: *You were very sick, but your life has been saved by this antibiotic … how do you feel?* and so forth. Then, as the students walked in this role, the teacher tapped students on the shoulder and they said what they were thinking.

Extension

This could lead into writing an article on the implications of this research from the point of view of a patient.

Questioning in role (hot seating)

More commonly called hot seating, the term questioning in role (Q in R) is preferred because it emphasises that this strategy has its focus on taking on a *role* in order to acquire information from the *perspective* of that person. Questioning in role can be used for a range of purposes. It can, for instance, be used to help students develop more insight about an existing factual or fictional topic or event, or it can be used to create an imaginative story. Using the term Q in R helps to distance it from the 'game like' approach used in some TV shows and

Figure 7.18
Students doing a 'role walk'

of equal importance it should not be confused with an ask and recall literal comprehension exercise. So if the person is a character from a narrative or from history they might conform to either the fictional or factual events, but the aim is for the person in role (with the help of questions from the rest of the group) elaborate and extend on the known to create a more in-depth account of the character's life and thoughts. When the character is well known this is very difficult to do without it turning into a literal comprehension exercise and for this reason it is best done with anonymous people. For example, to think more deeply about the conditions and circumstances on the *Endeavour* it would be best to question one of the unknown crew and not Captain Cook. In this way, specific likely events and feelings of this crew member can be made up and/or elaborated on but at the same time conform to historical facts. In contrast, if Captain Cook is questioned then the information needs to be historically accurate from his point of view, making it far more difficult to delve deeply into the situation.

The role is *created* by questions from the class. Questions should be asked to help build belief in, and knowledge about, the character. Encourage students to avoid questions that aim to trick the person being questioned. Working in pairs, students are given about 2 minutes to think of questions. Often these may be written down, but once the questioning begins and the story unfolds there will be further spontaneous questions relevant to how the person in role is responding. Should the person in role not have an immediate response for a particular question they just say, *I don't know yet* or *I haven't worked that out yet.*

Using Q in R to go beyond the written text in a narrative

This example illustrates how Q in R can be used to go beyond the story in order to understand the themes of the story (*Nyuntu Ninti* by Bob Randal, 2008) in more depth. In this book, the protagonist's grandson is only referred to briefly in the story and so the grandson was questioned to ascertain his likely experiences. This Q in R activity occurred within the following sequence:

1. Students were already familiar with the book from previous lessons.

2. Students re-read the song that is at the back of the book as they watched Bob Randall (the author) sing it on YouTube. NB Although there are twenty laptops that classes can book for sessions, Nicole usually has students working in pairs as, *two heads are better than one and they have to interact.*

3. Questioning in role of the grandson.

4. Review the song online and address the themes.

> Note that Q in R is not a literal recall comprehension exercise but rather a way to delve more deeply into the inferred events of the story.

Ninety per cent of the students in this class were in the Developing or Consolidating English phase. Their teacher, Nicole Wade, frequently uses Q in R because of this. The student in role was given time to think about who he was in more detail while the others thought of questions. When the student was ready, he put on the Q in R hat to indicate his readiness to answer questions. Although such a prop is not necessary it does help some students adopt their role. Note that there were a mixture of questions that involved evaluating, inferring and justifying (see Figure 7.19).

Following the Q in R, students went back online and reviewed the YouTube song again. This time they were asked to write down three themes this song addressed. One pair wrote:

> *By sharing Aboriginal culture with everyone, we can learn from each other and be joined together.*

When asked if the Q in R activity helped them understand the song better, one child replied:

> *Yes! The person comes alive and talks to me!*

Role to communicate: Learning English through drama

And Nicole added that she used Q in R on a regular basis because, *It makes the character more believable and the children become so engrossed in the story that they dig deeper and deeper and are really analysing and inferring at this deeper level – they move beyond the literal* (FGT, in progress).

Figure 7.19

The excerpt at left continues the Q in R to infer Jimbo's likely views and experiences

Q: *Do you have the same feeling about your country as your Grandfather?*

A: *Sure do and I'm going to look after it as well as he does.*

Q: *Why do you think that is important?*

A: *Because it is our responsibility to our ancestors and to our mob now.*

Q: *What sorts of games do you play?*

A: *We mostly swim in the billabong or play on our computers.*

Q: *Do you have computers?!*

A: *Yeah … we're the same as you guys!*

A longer drama program for *How to heal a broken wing*

This series of drama strategies was planned to read the picture book *How to heal a broken wing* (Graham, 2008). This multimodal text uses graphic novel and many other visual techniques so is a good example in terms of teaching EL learners visual grammar. It is another excellent example of a book that can be read on a variety of levels and appeals to children and adults of all ages.

Synopsis

The written text of *How to heal a broken wing* is about young boy, who, when walking with his mother in the city sees an injured pigeon. He asks his mother if they can take it home and somewhat reluctantly she agrees. They care for the bird and eventually it recovers and is set free. The text is minimal, but the illustrations tell a much more complex story, addressing the themes and values of apathy and empathy, war, hope, nature and conservation, tolerance of cultural and physical diversity, care and compassion, doing your best, respect and responsibility.

Walker books (publishers of this book) have a good program on their website (www.walkerbooks.com.au/Books/How-to-Heal-a-Broken-Wing-9781406307160) and this was used as the basis for planning this program, with alterations to some of the discussion activities to incorporate drama. Like any resources, teachers manipulate them to suit their class and their purpose. My purpose stemmed from my research data which indicates that many students prefer and even find it easier to understand an issue if they have done some drama activities related to it in conjunction with (or in lieu of) class or small group discussions.

This program would best suit students aged ten years and up and uses the same reading model referred to in Chapter 5: getting ready for the text; getting into the text; coming back to the text; going beyond the text (often in order to come back and get into the text again). Note that it is important that there are enough copies of the book for one copy per pair as a close examination of the visuals is crucial for understanding.

Getting ready for the text

- Explain the purpose of the shared reading to students – reading a picture book to examine how the visual text provides a more in-depth understanding of the multiple themes.
- Display Amnesty International's home page and discuss this organisation's purpose and ascertain students' understanding of the term 'human rights'. You might also discuss the logo and how students interpret this.
- Begin reading the back cover and end pages first as the text here explains that the book is endorsed by Amnesty International UK. This will help EL learners understand the focus of this book.

Role to communicate: Learning English through drama

Getting into the text

- Read the book with the students, with minimal discussion, but allowing enough time for students to read the visuals on each page.
- On the second reading conduct a think-aloud to include reference to the visual grammar (refer to page 95 in Chapter 5).
- In pairs, students re-read the book and discuss it using questions such as those that Monica Palmer has devised (refer to pages 70–71 in Chapter 4). Some suggestions are given below:
    - **Identifying main idea:** What are the main things the author wants us to think about?
    - **Identifying the author's purpose:** What is the author's point of view? How do you know?
    - **Inferring:** Choose one of the double page spreads to discuss: What do you think is really happening here? What did you have to do to make those inferences?
    - **Self questioning:** What were you wondering about as you were reading?
    - **Making connections:** How does this text remind you about other texts you have read?
- Pairs form quads and they report on their thoughts to date and discuss further.
- Following this, the class constructs a concept map to document the main themes or issues which is added to over the course of this book study.

Figure 7.20
Concept map of dominant themes

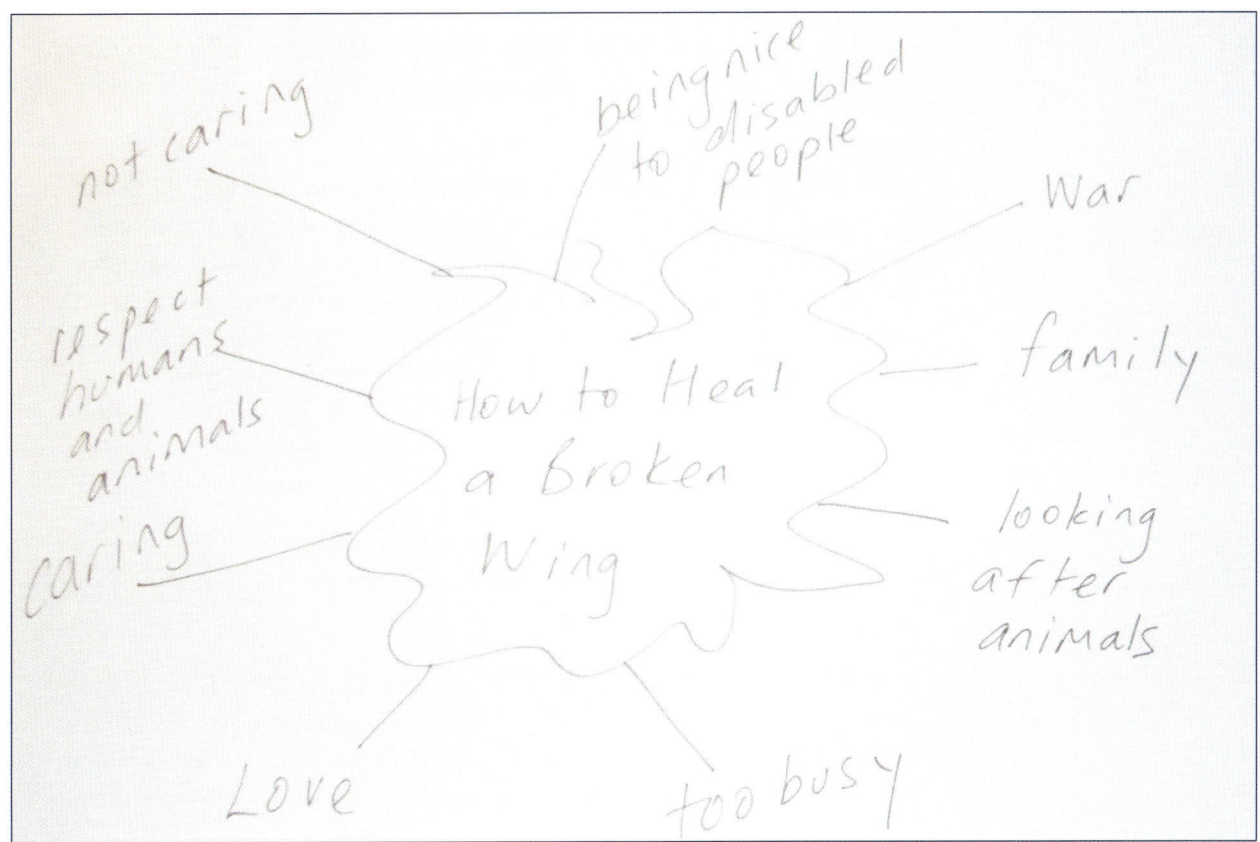

Coming back to the text

Point of view

One of the first activities suggested in the publisher's (Walker Books: www.walkerbooks.com.au) program for studying this book is:

- Look at the main characters in this story (the pigeon, the mother, the father).
- In groups, talk about how you would tell the story from the different perspective of each of these characters. Create a new story then present it to the class.

This is an important activity because it addresses the concept of point of view and the different points of view of the *many* characters in this book is a pivotal message. However, as discussed before, my research data suggests that for many students, discussion alone is not sufficient. To arrive at the same outcome, and using questioning in role:

- A student assumes the role of the mother or father. Although the concept that pigeons are sometimes referred to as 'rats of the sky' must be explored, assuming the role of an animal is difficult and I suggest be done once students are very familiar with this strategy.
- As the person in role is questioned, have a person (often the teacher) record the events and ideas (story) as they unfold. Rewrite this information in point form and display it on the IWB.
- Students use this summary to write a recount from the point of view of the mother or father.

Below is a recount from the mother's perspective written by a ten-year-old student in the late Developing English phase:

> I was walking with my son Will and suddenly Will saw the bird with the broken wing. I said to him in an angry way 'we're going to be late'. But then my son showed me the bird. At first I didn't care about the bird, but then I noticed the broken wing. I started to feel sorry for the bird. Will said to me 'can we keep it until it recovers'. Feeling proud of my son I said yes. So I wrapped the pigeon with my warm scarf to keep it warm. On the way home we stopped to buy some food for the poor little bird …
>
> I thought I could feel what the bird was feeling at that moment. The sadness in its eyes, then a tear went down my face. Everyone stood still for a moment.
>
> Time passed by and soon the bird could fly once more. I felt happy for it. I also felt sad when it left.

This student's teacher, Rebecca Hillis, sent me this recount as an example because: 'Wonderfully, it was written by one of my struggling writers!! I was very proud!' Rebecca was justifiably proud, as was the child, but this is not an unusual outcome. Booth and Neelands' important research about how drama can improve writing found that:

Role to communicate: Learning English through drama

The experience of taking on a character in drama also provided many students with enhanced empathy and understanding for a broad range of people ... [allowing] them to write sensitively and genuinely from a variety of different points of view ... Finding out about a character by asking questions and listening to and watching the responses the character makes ... will flesh out literally, the student's own ideas. (Booth & Neelands, 1998: 20–22).

Exploring the concepts of apathy and empathy through sculpting

Again, this idea has been adapted from the Walker Books program to use drama before class discussion. Definitions of apathy and empathy are displayed on the IWB and discussed.

- Pairs skim and scan the book and find an example of a person they believe Graham has used to portray empathy or apathy.
- Person A sculpts person B to illustrate this and explain to students that as an interpretation the sculpture does not need to replicate the illustration, but rather the intent.
- On a 'post-it' note, students then write what they think the person they sculpted might be either thinking or saying at this point of time and position it on the page.
- Extension: photograph the sculpture, insert it into PowerPoint and add the dialogue (refer to page 149).

Figures 7.21 and 7.22
Pages of the book with 'post-it' notes written by the students, saying what they think specific characters might be saying or thinking

Going beyond the text (often in order to come back to it again)

The activities in this section are working towards constructing a 'parallel improvisation'. That is, students make connections with the themes of the book and think of situations that are analogous.

- Display the following quote from the Walker Books program on the IWB:

  > I wanted to write a story of hope, putting empathy in the hands of a child – because children are our future and our hope for a more caring world to come. When all of the world's horrors and inhumanity appear daily on the television in our living rooms, I wanted to show a human counterbalance to these things enacted in ordinary, everyday and seemingly insignificant events … (Bob Graham in 'Classroom Ideas', www.walkerbooks.com.au/teachers)

Figure 7.23 Students brainstorming ideas using 'planning the scene' questions

- Who are we? *Billy, Braydon and Michael.*
- Where are we? (setting/context) *In the playground.*
- What are we doing? (problem/tension) *Braydon is teasing Billy because he can't play hand ball well and Michael sticks up for Billy but then Braydon says he won't be Michael's friend but Michael says he doesn't care.*
- Why are we doing it? (focus/theme/issue) *Kindness and unkindness.*

- Returning to the concept map, students review the themes connected to human rights (justice, fairness, care and compassion, empathy, respect, tolerance and so forth). In groups of three or four (and using the still image strategy), students plan an imaginary event (but very probably one connected to their experience) and depict this scene to illustrate one of these themes. Provide a variety of objects (refer to page 155 where this is explained). Groups can choose one of these objects or select one of their own. Often an object helps students think of an idea and it may become symbolic of the theme.
- In groups, students brainstorm ideas using the 'planning the scene' questions (refer to page 152), to assist and prepare the still image. From experience, I have found that the majority of groups will quite quickly think of an idea and it is important to give them this ownership. Conversely, there will often be one or two groups that cannot think of one. I always give them an idea; so they too can achieve the activity. Thinking of the idea is only one of the learning outcomes. Often they will adjust my suggestion in any case. Figure 7.23 on the previous page demonstrates this.

Showing and viewing the still images

The following procedure is useful:

> 1. One student explains what their group's still image is about before showing it.
> 2. Viewers close their eyes as a person counts '3, 2, 1, curtains up' and then view the image.
> 3. Discuss each image and it might be appropriate to tap in for dialogue to hear each person's thoughts.

Drama circle for reflection and debriefing

To begin, explain that the drama is now over as discussed on page 145. Invite students to discuss with their friends how they felt in their respective roles and then report back within the drama circle. Usually a discussion about the concept of human rights will feature in this discussion as well.

Stepping out

On the basis of the above discussion, students return to their respective groups. Stepping out is similar to tapping in but, as the name suggests, a character physically steps a short distance away from their group's still image and speaks for longer (usually about 15 seconds) but *in their role*. That is, they give a longer explanation or monologue on their feelings about the situation. They then step back into the frame. As they step out, the rest of the image remains frozen. Once this person has stepped back in, another steps out, and so forth. When all have finished, the original image is reformed and frozen for about 2 seconds as the ending. Often this strategy is done by pairing two groups. Group A watches group B doing the stepping out strategy and then vice versa.

Teaching English Language Learners in Mainstream Classes

Figures 7.24, 7.25, 7.26 and 7.27
An example of one group using the stepping out strategy

Role to communicate: Learning English through drama

Parallel improvisation

This still image become the basis for a short improvisation (a 30-second scene where the students use dialogue and movement).

- Ask students to improvise the scene up to the moment of their prepared still image so that the still image constructed previously will be the *end* of their improvisation. In this way they already have their ending planned. This is a useful technique because one of the most difficult things (as for writing a narrative) is to plan an ending. This could be why in some simulated role plays students end the play by shooting each other dead (logical finish) or just stand there and giggling saying, 'That's it – that's the end'.

Figure 7.28
One group's initial still image that was then used as the final moment in their parallel improvisation (see the sequence on page 169)

- Once students have worked out their improvisation provide a further instruction:

    Work out where you will all be at the *beginning* of this improvisation (your positions in your performing space). Place each person into position (still image). This is the *beginning* of your improvisation. To begin your improvisation, you need to freeze this still image (your positions) for 1 second and then move and talk the scene (ie improvise it) up to your ending still image, which you freeze for 2 seconds to indicate the finish.

Role to communicate: Learning English through drama

Figures 7.29, 7.30, 7.31 and 7.32
One group using parallel improvisation

Extension

At the time of writing this book, some students who were doing this drama program wanted to send Bob Graham a 'Movie Maker' presentation of their 'mini plays' to demonstrate that human rights begins within the immediate community.

Drama does take time

It is fair to say that adding drama to a teaching and learning sequence does take additional time. The drama activities and strategies demonstrated in this chapter will take more time than just a discussion. Drama will take more time than just writing an answer to a comprehension question, but the quality of learning will be enhanced, as demonstrated both in the student and teacher data that I have analysed over the years. Many students (though of course, not all) not only enjoy drama but believe it helps them learn, as demonstrated by one capable but very disengaged EL learner:

> Margery: *Well (student) I know you liked doing drama, but maybe it's because it takes longer and wastes time from other subjects.*

> Student: (with a vehement voice and stance) *It's [drama] NOT wasting time because wasting time means like you're out of it, like you're not doing anything, you're just sitting there bored but if you are in it, it's like it's fun and then you're learning … It's better, funner, teaching you more … [In other lessons] I just sit there pretending to do more but I don't. It's [drama] teaching more and having fun.*

CONCLUSION

The major purpose of this book is to assist mainstream teachers who may have minimal or no specialist assistance to cater for the needs of EL learners, and especially those students beyond the very beginning stages, by providing the strategies to both engage and enhance their proficiency in academic English. The theoretical underpinnings of ELL pedagogy are illustrated with suggestions of strategies to be viewed within a staged sequence of teaching/learning experiences. These practical strategies will also complement for example the Australian Curriculum's English as an Additional Language or Dialect: Teacher Resource materials to enable students to access the content and language demands of the Australian Curriculum learning areas.

The premise that oracy is a fundamental aspect in all teaching and learning sequences is exemplified and all the strategies presuppose a sequence with oracy as the 'glue'. For example, when reading a text or writing a text, talking and listening ebb and flow throughout each stage. The importance of oracy cannot be underestimated for all the reasons provided throughout this book.

It is not the intent of this section to summarise all the points of this book, but rather to consider just one overarching aspect. It was made clear in Chapters 1, 2 and 3 why older students who are reasonably proficient in their first language(s) or dialect(s) should, *with the appropriate pedagogical conditions*, learn English more quickly than children entering their first years of formal schooling. If these same older students are also literate in L1, then they have an even greater advantage. Nevertheless, many students in the early years of schooling may initially appear to learn English more quickly than their older counterparts. However, even for these younger students there is a risk of fossilisation (refer to page 10) without continued targeted and systematic English language learning support throughout their schooling years. In the later years of primary and middle schooling we need to emulate many aspects of early childhood pedagogy. Many early childhood educators explicitly plan for building knowledge of a topic and often this is done using a sequence that begins with oracy and then leads to reading and writing, but where oracy nevertheless remains a major focus. With the emphasis on 'play-based learning' (DEEWR, 2009) – which primary and secondary teachers refer to as active or participatory learning – students engage in authentic communication for a variety of purposes and across an array of registers. Furthermore, the emphasis is always based on building knowledge of a topic taking into account the child's cultural and linguistic background: 'the totality of the experiences that have shaped the learner's identity and cognitive functioning' (Cummins et al, 2006).

Considering the above and extending on it, perhaps the idea of 'quality versus quantity' is not so relevant when examining appropriate pedagogy for EL learners. Rather, *both* quality and quantity are important. It is what's *in* the *quantity* that is crucial. As educators, we aim for students to be engaged with their learning and the research literature demonstrates a high correlation between engagement and enhanced academic outcomes (for example, Fredricks et al, 2004). In Chapter 3 on pages 42–47, The Fair Go Project's definition of engagement (FGT, 2006; Munns, 2007) was described, since this project's research has taken place in schools with very high proportions of EL learners. The FGP proposes that a pedagogy that has high cognitive (thinking), high affective (feeling) and high operative (doing) learning experiences, with the appropriate language learning structures embedded within, improves learning outcomes and this involves a varied quantity of quality tasks in combination with engaging messages.

Slow cooking, slow teaching ... quality *and* quantity

Good English language learning pedagogy with a varied quantity of quality tasks will take longer and could be described as analogous to cooking roast lamb. Many gourmet cooks would suggest that a roast leg of lamb cooked on a low heat for 4 to 5 hours is more tender and tasty than the hurried roast on fan-forced high for one and half hours. Of course, the combination of herbs and spices added in the preparation of the lamb, combined with the basting throughout its cooking, enhances the flavour. But the flavour will only be good if the cook knows the appropriate herbs and spices to use and when and how often to baste because she or he has assessed prior cooking efforts. With the latest attempt, the cook again reassesses the result and these considerations will influence the culinary approach taken the next time.

In the same way the activities and strategies throughout this book (and positioned within the general theoretical principles described in Chapters 1, 2 and 3) will take more time than just a discussion. They will take more time than immediately reading or writing a text. English language learning calls for a quantity of quality experiences that do challenge students to think deeply. This necessitates carefully sequenced substantive and varied tasks, founded on appropriate English language learning theoretical principles to then inform programming. The table on page 173 illustrates many of the major principles that teachers need to apply in order to program for EL learners.

Conclusion

Some of the major overarching principles about teaching EL learners	
Knowing each student's existing English language ability	✔
Encouraging and endorsing students to maintain first language(s) and/or dialect(s), not only for social and emotional reasons but also as a support for English language learning.	✔
Knowledge and appreciation of the cultural and linguistic background of each student's family and community; thus providing culturally inclusive practices that account for each student's existing identity.	✔
Knowing when to provide support in terms of scaffolding and how to provide the scaffold.	✔
Teacher's knowledge of English grammar.	✔
Explicit and focused attention on integrating English language learning within the context of all subject-specific fields across the curriculum.	✔
Use of authentic and well constructed texts (written and/or oral and/or visual).	✔
Use of manipulative resources such as science and maths equipment, artefacts, other everyday objects and so forth.	✔
Continuous assessment, reflection and feedback throughout the teaching and learning process by both teachers and students.	✔

Considering these overarching principles, the next step is to plan the appropriate sequence of teaching and learning experiences. When planning these experiences, it is useful to first ask the following to ensure that all the boxes are ticked.

Based on prior and continuous assessment and reflection by both teachers and students, is the overall teaching and learning sequence:	
• responsive to the fact that the topic, and concepts within, may or may not be part of the student's cultural and/or linguistic familiarity (ie linked to their schematic knowledge) and thus accordingly, there is an emphasis on building knowledge of the topic?	✔
• extending the students within the zone of proximal development using a scaffolding support framework?	✔
• potentially engaging students because students will be involved in high cognitive, high affective and high operative activities and, by implication, there are authentic and purposeful opportunities for communicating (refer to pages 43–46)	✔
• conveying engaging messages to students that they have knowledge, ability, control, place and voice (refer to pages 44–46) in the learning environment, because the learning environment promotes inclusive conversations, where teacher feedback and student self-reflection about learning are central?	✔

Then, when considering a specific activity or task within the sequence, teachers may evaluate which distinctive English language learning feature(s) a particular task is attending to as demonstrated in the table below. This is useful when ascertaining which features are accounted for and/or their frequency within an *overall* teaching and learning sequence. This is not intended as a rigid recipe or formulaic checklist; rather, when considering the English language learning features of a task, one can reflect on what each task is explicitly achieving. If, within the overall teaching and learning sequence, there is an over-reliance on some features or absence of others, there may well be justifiable reasons for this. On the other hand, it might mean that some readjusting and replanning is required. Being able to justify, reflect and act accordingly is the essential component when reviewing.

Considering the distinctive language learning features of specific tasks within a teaching and learning sequence

Name of teaching and learning sequence (For example, just the following two tasks from the unit of work on the book *How to heal a broken wing* by Bob Graham (refer to pages 160–70) are evaluated below.)

Features/emphasis	Name of task: Sculpting empathic and apathetic characters on pp 13 and 14	Name of task: Writing dialogue for the selected character	Name of task	Name of task
Is it context embedded and cognitively demanding?	✔			
Is it context reduced and cognitively demanding?		✔		
Emphasis is within the controlled scaffolding support phase				
Emphasis is within the guided scaffolding support phase	✔	✔		
Emphasis is within the independent scaffolding support phase		✔		
Overall it involves collaborative small group work interaction	✔	✔		
Emphasis is on substantive active listening	✔			
Emphasis is on substantive purposeful talk	✔	✔		
Emphasis is on interpretative and/or inferential reading (as opposed to only literal)	✔			

Features/emphasis	Name of task Sculpting empathic and apathetic characters on pp 13 and 14	Name of task Writing dialogue for the selected character	Name of task	Name of task
Emphasis is on interpretative and/or inferential reading (as opposed to only literal)	✔			
Emphasis is on writing and/or designing and/or producing a text		✔		
Explicit attention to meta-language of content area		✔		
Promotes use of meta-language of content area		✔		
Task is open-ended and encourages risk taking	✔	✔		

To bring this book to a close, the final words are handed over to a class in one of the most disadvantaged areas in Australia. In their first year of high school, these thirteen-year-old EL learners' academic outcomes were improving (FGT, in progress). The snapshot below, from interviews with Sue Barrett (the teacher) and some of her students, demonstrates that enhancing the learning outcomes of EL learners in mainstream classes is a rewarding and achievable pursuit.

> Sue: *I plan for success so that students succeed. This does not mean it [the content] will be easy. I do not let students say it is 'too hard' – we say it is challenging. I would like to think students would see education as changing things, getting out of here … They deserve teachers who are dedicated and believe these kids can be successful.*
>
> Student 1: *We actually learn something [because] we have to work it out ourselves. She doesn't just tell us – she checks up, marks our books – she's like a stalker – she is our right hand when we need help.*
>
> Student 2: *She won't let us give up and we're not allowed to say it's hard, we have to say it's challenging.*
>
> Student 3: *[We work in groups] and that doubles the IQ, triples the IQ – we finish – we have friends in case you get lost in the question, instead of being alone, struggling.*
>
> Student 4: *Groups – you can choose your own. Everyone shares and combines good ideas. We don't have captains, we are all captains. … [We've learnt that] it's not about being 'the best'; it's about trying your best.*
>
> Student 5: *… work is challenging but it is easy to learn when we're having fun.*

REFERENCES

Aliki (1998), *Marianthe's story: Painted words, spoken memories*, Greenwillow Books, New York.

Allen, P. (2003), *Grandpa and Thomas*, Puffin, Melbourne.

Anderson, R. & Pearson, P. (1984), 'A schema theoretic view of basic processes in reading comprehension', in Pearson, P. (ed.), *Handbook of reading research*, Longman, New York, pp. 225–91).

Arthur, L., Beecher, B., Death, E., Dockett, S. & Farmer, S. (2011), *Programming and planning in early childhood settings* (5th edn), Cengage, Melbourne.

Australian Curriculum and Reporting Authority (2011), *English as an additional language or dialect: Teacher resource V 1.1*. (www.acara.edu.au/verve/_resources/EALD_teacher_resource.pdf, accessed 3 September 2011).

Baker, J. (2010), *Mirrors*, Walker Books, London.

Bernstein, B. (1996), *Pedagogy, symbolic control and identity: Theory, research, critique*, Taylor & Francis, London.

Board of Studies, NSW (1998), *English K-6 syllabus and modules*, Board of Studies, NSW, Sydney (http://k6.boardofstudies.nsw.edu.au/files/english/k6_english_syl.pdf).

Bolton, G. (1992), *New perspectives on classroom drama*, Simon & Schuster Education, London.

Booth, D. (1991), 'Drama talk', in Booth, D. & Thornely-Hall, C. (eds), *The talk curriculum*, Australian Reading Association, Melbourne, pp. 89–106.

Booth, D. & Neelands, J. (eds) (1998), *Writing in role: Classroom projects connecting writing and drama*, Caliburn Enterprises Inc, Canada.

Bruner, J. (1986), 'Play, thought and language', *Prospects: Quarterly Journal of Education*, 16, pp. 7683

—— (1993), *Actual minds, possible worlds*, Harvard University Press, Cambridge, MA.

Bryan, G. (2007), 'SSR (Sustained Silent Reading) or SSRE (Silence Stops Reading Engagement)?', in Dwyer, B. & Shiel, G. (eds), *Literacy at the crossroads: Moving forward, looking back*, Reading Association of Ireland, Dublin, pp. 182–98.

Callow, J. (2008), 'New literacies, New York & Web 2.0: A little knowledge is a helpful thing!', *SCAN*, 27(4), pp. 13–16.

Callow, J. & Hertzberg, M. (2006), 'Helping children learn to read', in Ewing, R. (ed.), *Beyond the reading wars: Towards a balanced approach to helping children learn to read*, PETAA, Sydney, pp. 41–54.

Carle, E. (1981), *The very hungry caterpillar*, Puffin Books, London.

References

Carnine, D., Silbert, J., Kameõenui, E. & Tarver, S. (2004), *Direct instruction reading* (4th edn), Pearson Lyon, Upper Saddle River, NJ.

Chambers, A. (1993), *Tell me,* PETAA, Sydney.

Clay, M. (1982), *Observing young readers*, Heinemann, Exeter, NH.

Coiro, J., Knobel, M., Lankshear, C. & Leu, D. (eds) (2008), *Handbook of research on new literacies*, Lawrence Erlbaum Associates, New York.

Collier, V. (1989), 'How long? A synthesis of research on academic achievement in a second language', *TESOL Quarterly*, 23, pp. 509–31.

—— (1995), 'National Clearing House for Bilingual Education', *Acquiring a second language for school*, (www.thomasandcollier.com/Downloads/, accessed September 2007).

Cruickshank, K. (2008), 'Oral language, literacy and EAL', paper presented at ESLIN Sharing Group, Sydney, November.

Crumple, T. & Schneider, J. (2002), 'Writing with their whole being: A cross study analysis of children's writing from five classrooms using process drama', *Research in Drama Education*, 7(1), pp. 61–79.

Cummins, J. (1979), 'Cognitive/academic language proficiency, linguistic interdependence, the optimum age question and some other matters', *Working Papers on Bilingualism*, 19, pp. 121–29.

—— (1981), *The role of primary language development in promoting educational success for language minority students*, in California State Department of Education (ed), *Schooling and language minority students: A theoretical framework*, Evaluation, Dissemination and Assessment Centre, California State University, Los Angeles.

—— (1984), *Bilingualism and special education,* Multilingual Matters, Clevedon, UK.

—— (1996), *Negotiating identities: Education for empowerment in a diverse society,* California Association for Bilingual Education, Ontario.

—— (2000), *Language, power and pedagogy*, Multilingual Matters, Clevedon, UK.

—— (2008), 'BICS and CALP: Empirical and theoretical status of the distinction', in B. Street & N. Hornberger (eds), *Encyclopaedia of language and education*, 2nd edn, *vol. 2: Literacy*, Springer Science + Business Media LLC, New York, pp. 71–83.

Cummins, J., Bismilla, V., Chow, P., Cohen, S., Giampapa, F., Leoni, L., Sandhu, P. & Sastri, P. (2006), *ELL students speak for themselves: Identity, texts and literacy engagement in multilingual classrooms* (www.curriculum.org/secretariat/files/ELLidentityTexts.pdf, accessed 19 November 2010).

Dahl, R. (1980), *The Twits,* Puffin, New York.

—— (1980), 'Little Red Riding Hood', in *Revolting rhymes*, Puffin Books, London, pp. 36–40.

Delpit, L. (2006), *Other people's children: Cultural conflict in the classroom*, 2nd edn, The New Press, New York.

Department of Education, Employment and Workplace Relations (DEEWR) (2009), *The early years learning framework for Australia* (www.deewr.gov.au/Earlychildhood/Policy_Agenda/Quality/Documents/Final%20EYLF%20Framework%20Report%20-%20WEB.pdf, accessed April 2011).

Derewianka, B. (1990), *Exploring how texts work,* PETAA, Sydney.

—— (2007), 'Cycle for teaching and learning in writing', unpublished paper presented at the University of Wollongong, 18 June 2007.

—— (2011), *A new grammar companion,* PETAA, Sydney.

Dinham, S. (2008a), 'Powerful teacher feedback', *Synergy*, 6(2), pp. 35–38 (www.slav.schools.net.au/synergy/vol6num2/dinham.pdf).

—— (2008b), 'Feedback on feedback', *Teacher,* May: pp. 20–23.

Droga, L. & Humphrey, S. (2003), *Grammar and meaning: An introduction for primary teachers,* Target Texts, Berry, NSW.

Dufficy, P. (2005), *Designing learning for diverse classrooms,* PETAA, Sydney.

—— (2010), *Cloze encounters. e:update 012,* PETAA, Sydney.

Dwyer, B. (2009), 'Scaffolding struggling readers from disadvantaged communities as they construct meaning in internet inquiry', paper presented at the National Reading Conference, Albuquerque, New Mexico, December.

Dwyer, B. & Harrison, C. (2008), 'There's no rabbits on the internet: Scaffolding the development of effective search strategies for struggling readers during internet inquiry', in Y. Kim & V. Risko (eds), *57th yearbook of the National Reading Conference,* National Reading Conference, Oak Creek, WI, pp. 187–202.

Ewing, R. (2010), 'Literacy and the arts', in Christie, F. & Simpson, A. (eds), *Literacy and social responsibility,* Equinox, New York, pp. 56–70.

Ewing, R. & Simons, J. with Hertzberg, M. (2004), *Beyond the script. Take two. Drama in the classroom,* PETAA, Sydney.

Fair Go Team (2006), *School is for me: Pathways to student engagement,* Priority Schools Funding Program, NSW Department of Education and Training, Sydney (www.psp.nsw.edu.au/resources/SchoolIsForMe_loRes.pdf, accessed 15 December 2006).

—— (in progress), '"Exemplary teachers" of students in poverty' [working title], Routledge, London.

Faustin, C. (1998), *The selfish crocodile,* Bloomsbury, London.

Fleming, M., Merrell, C. & Timms, P. (2004), 'The impact of drama on pupils' language, mathematics, and attitudes in two primary schools', *Research in Drama in Education,* 9(2), pp. 177–97.

Fox, M. (1994), *Time for bed,* Scholastic, Australia.

Fox, M. & Wilkinson, L. (1993), *English essentials,* Macmillan Education, Melbourne.

Fredricks, J.A., Blumenfield, P.C. & Paris, A.H. (2004), 'School engagement: Potential of the concept, state of the evidence', *Review of Educational Research,* 76(1), pp. 59–109.

Freebody, P. (2004), 'Hindsight and foresight: Putting the four roles model of reading to work in the daily business of teaching', in Healy, A. & Honan, E. (eds), *Text next: New resources for literacy learning,* PETAA, Sydney, pp. 3–17.

Freebody, P. & Luke, A. (1990), 'Literacies programs: Debates and demands in cultural context', *Prospect: Australian Journal of TESOL,* 5(7), pp. 7–16.

Geoghegan, A. & Moseng, E. (1993), *Six perfectly different pigs,* Hazar, London.

Gervay, S. (2000), *I am Jack,* Angus & Robertson, Sydney.

Gibbons, P. (2002), *Scaffolding language, scaffolding learning: Teaching second language learners in the mainstream classroom,* Heinemann, Portsmouth, NH.

—— (2009), *English learners' academic literacy and thinking: Learning in the challenge zone,* Heinemann, Portsmouth, NH.

Gilman, P. (1992), *Something from nothing,* Ashton Scholastic, Sydney.

Gleitzman, M. (2002), *Boy overboard,* Puffin, Melbourne.

Graham, B. (2008), *How to heal a broken wing,* Walker Books, London.

Gray, B. (1990), 'Natural language learning in Aboriginal classrooms: Reflections on teaching and learning style for empowerment in English', in Walton, C. & Eggington, W. (eds), *Language: Maintenance, power and education in Australian Aboriginal contexts,* NTU Press, Darwin, pp. 105–39.

References

Hakuta, K., Butler, Y. & Witt, D. (2000), *How long does it take English learners to attain proficiency? The University of California Linguistic Minority Research Institute Policy Report 2000–1*, (www.stanford.edu/~hakuta/www/research/publications.html 5_Acquiring-a-Second-Language-for-School_DLE4.pdf, accessed 17 August 2007).

Halliday, M.A.K. (1985), *Spoken and written language*, Deakin University Press, Geelong, Vic.

Halliday, M.A.K. & Hasan, R. (1985), *Language, context and text: Aspects of language in a social-semiotic perspective*, Deakin University Press, Geelong, Vic.

Hammond, J. & Gibbons, P. (2005), 'Putting scaffolding to work: The contribution of scaffolding in articulating ESL education', *Prospect* (20)3, pp. 6–30.

Hardy, B. (1975), *Tellers and listeners*, Athlone Press, London.

Hayes, D., Mills, M., Christie, P. & Lingard, B. (2006), *Teachers and schooling: Making a difference*, Allen & Unwin, Sydney.

Heathcote, D. & Bolton, G. (1995), *Drama for learning: Dorothy Heathcote's Mantle of the Expert approach to education*, Heinemann, Portsmouth, NH.

Hertzberg, M. (1999), 'How does Educational Drama Enhance Children's Language and Literacy Development?' Unpublished doctoral dissertation, University of Western Sydney, Australia.

—— (2003), 'Engaging critical reader response to literature through process drama', *Reading on line* [1/6/2003], (www.readingonline.org, accessed 1 June 2003).

—— (2004a), 'Drama when English is an additional language', in Ewing, R. & Simons, J. with Hertzberg, M., *Beyond the script. Take two. Drama in the classroom*, PETAA, Sydney, pp. 93–108.

—— (2004b), 'Unpacking the drama process as intellectually rigorous – "The teacher gives you the bone of it and we have to act the muscles"', *NJ (Drama Australia Journal)*, 28(2), pp. 41–53.

—— (2009), *Readers' theatre to improve fluency and comprehension. e:update 009*, PETAA, Sydney.

Hertzberg, M., Foord, K. & Manga, M. (2006), 'Dramatically 'e'ngaged', in Fair Go Team, *School is for me: Pathways to student engagement*, Priority Schools Funding Program, NSW Department of Education and Training, Sydney, (www.psp.nsw.edu.au/resources/SchoolIsForMe_loRes.pdf, accessed 15 December 2006), pp. 25–32.

Holdaway, D. (1979), *The foundations of literacy*, Ashton Scholastic, Gosford, NSW.

Hughes, M. (1999), *Closing the learning gap*, Network Educational Press, Edinburgh.

Jones, P. (1996), 'Planning an oral language program', in P. Jones (ed.) *Talking to learn*, PETAA, Sydney.

Kao, S.M. & O'Neill, C. (1998), *Words into worlds: Learning a second language through process drama*, Ablex, Stanford, CT.

Kidd, D. (1989), *Onion tears*, Angus & Robertson, Sydney.

Krashen, S. (1982), *Principles and practice in second language acquisition*, Pergamon, Oxford, UK.

Lester, A. (2004), *Are we there yet?* Penguin Books, Melbourne.

Lipson, M.Y. (1982), 'Learning new information from text: The role of prior knowledge and reading ability', *Journal of Reading Behaviour*, 14, pp. 243–61.

Liu, J. (2002), 'Process drama in second and foreign language classrooms', in G. Brauer (ed), *Body and language: Intercultural learning through drama*, Greenwood, Westport CT, pp. 51–70.

Mariani, L. (1997), 'Teacher support and teacher challenge in promoting learner autonomy', *Perspectives*, 23(2), Fall, Italy (www.learningpaths.org/papers/papersupport.htm, accessed 23 March 2001).

Marsden, J. & Tan, S. (1998), *The rabbits*, Lothian Books, Melbourne.

Maybin, J., Mercer, N. & Stierer, B. (1992), 'Scaffolding learning in the classroom', in K. Norman (ed), *Thinking voices: The work of the National Oracy Project*, Hodder & Stoughton, Sevenoaks, UK, pp. 186–95.

Mercer, N. (2000), *Words and minds: How we use language to think together*, Routledge, New York.

Morgan, N. & Saxton, J. (1987), *Teaching drama: A mind of many wonders* (4th edn), Hutchinson, London.

Moustafa, M. (2001), 'Foundations for universal literacy', a plenary address at Australian Association for the Teaching of English (AATE) and Australian Literacy Educators' Association (ALEA) joint national conference: 'Leading literate lives', Hobart, 2–5 July 2001, (www.education.tas.gov.au/curriculum/standards/english/english/teachers/discussion, accessed 6 April 2009).

Munns, G. (2007), 'A sense of wonder: Pedagogies to engage students who live in poverty', *International Journal of Inclusive Education*, 11(3), pp. 301–15.

Munns, G., Arthur, L., Hertzberg, M., Sawyer, W. & Zammit, K. (2011), 'A fair go for students in poverty: Australia', in T. Wrigley, R. Thomson & R. Lingard (eds), *Changing schools: Alternative ways to make a world of difference*, Routledge, London, pp. 167–80.

Newman, F. & Associates (1996), *Authentic achievement: Restructuring schools for intellectual quality*, Josey Bass, San Francisco.

Nicoll, V., Unsworth, L. & Parker, R. (1987), *Dimensions*, Thomas Nelson Australia, Melbourne.

NSW Department of Education (1998), *Focus on literacy: Talking and listening*, NSW Department of Education, Sydney (www.curriculumsupport.education.nsw.gov.au/primary/english/assets/pdf/talk_listen/fol_tandl.pdf).

NSW Department of Education and Training: Professional Support and Curriculum Directorate (2003), *Quality teaching in NSW public schools: A classroom practice guide*, NSW Department of Education and Training, Multicultural Programs Unit, Sydney.

NSW Department of Education and Training: Multicultural Programs Unit (2005), *ESL steps: ESL curriculum framework K–6 stage*, NSW Department of Education and Training, Multicultural Programs Unit, Sydney.

—— (no date), *English as a second language orientation: Professional development for teachers newly appointed to an ESL position*, NSW Department of Education and Training, Multicultural Programs Unit, Sydney.

Palinscar, A. & Brown, A. (1984), 'Reciprocal teaching of comprehension-fostering and comprehension-monitoring activities', *Cognition and Instruction*, 1, pp. 117–75.

Pica, T. (1992), 'Second language learning conditions', paper presented at the First Annual Pacific Second Language Research Forum (PacSLRF), Sydney, 14–17 July.

—— (1994), 'Research on negotiation: What does it reveal about second language learning conditions, processes and outcomes?', *Language Learning* (44), pp. 493–527.

Queensland School Reform Longitudinal Study (QSRLS) (2001), submitted to Education Queensland by the School of Education, University of Queensland, State of Queensland (Department of Education), Brisbane.

Randal, B. (2008), *Nyuntu Ninti*, ABC Books, Sydney.

Richards, J.C., Platt, J. & Platt, H. (1992), *Dictionary of language teaching and applied linguistics* (2nd edn), Longman, Harlow, UK.

Rossbridge, J. & Rushton, K. (2010), *Conversations about text: Teaching grammar using literary texts*, PETAA, Sydney.

References

Rowe, M. (1986), 'Wait-time: Slowing down may be a way of speeding up', *Journal of Teacher Education*, 37, pp. 43–50.

Jamal, N. (1998), 'It's green, spiky and too tough for some students', *Sydney Morning Herald*, 28 October, p. 1.

Starke, R. (2000), *NIPS X1*, Lothian Books, Melbourne.

Steffenson, M., Joag-Dev, C. & Anderson, R. (1979), 'A cross-cultural perspective on reading comprehension', *Reading Research Quarterly*, 15(1), pp. 10–29.

Stinson, M. (2008), 'Drama, process drama, and TESOL', in M. Anderson, J. Hughes & J. Manuel (eds), *Drama in English teaching: Imagination, action and engagement*, Oxford University Press, Oxford:, UK, pp. 193–212.

Swain, M. (1995), 'Three functions of output in second language learning', in G. Cook & B. Seidlehofer (eds), *Principle and practice in applied linguistics: Studies in honour of H.G. Widdowson*, Oxford University Press, Oxford, UK, pp. 125–44.

—— (2000), 'The output hypothesis and beyond: Mediating acquisition through collaborative dialogue', in L. Lantolf (ed.), *Sociocultural theory and second language learning*, Oxford University Press, Oxford, UK, pp. 97–114.

Tan, S. (2008), 'Stick figures', in *Tales from outer suburbia*, Allen & Unwin, Sydney, pp. 64–69.

Thomas, W.P. & Collier, V.P. (2002), *A national study of school effectiveness for language minority students' long-term academic achievement*, Centre for Research on Education, Diversity and Excellence, University of California-Santa Cruz, Santa Cruz, CA (http://crede.berkeley.edu/research/llaa/1.1_final.html, accessed 16 November 2010).

Unsworth, L. (1993), 'Evaluating reading materials', in B. Derewianka (ed.), *Language assessment in primary schools*, Harcourt Brace Jovanovich, Sydney, p. 229.

Vygotsky, L. (1986), *Thought and language*, MIT Press, Cambridge, MA.

Wallace, C. (1989), 'Learning to read in a second language: a window on the language acquisition process', *Reading in a Foreign Language*, 5(2), pp. 277–98.

Walsh, M. (2011). *Multimodal literacy: Researching classroom practice*, PETAA, Sydney.

Wajnryb, R. (1990), *Grammar dictation*, Oxford University Press, Oxford, UK.

Wheatley, N. (2000), *A banner bold: The diary of Rosa Aarons*, Scholastic Press, Sydney.

Winch, G., Johnston, R., March, P., Ljungdahl, L. & Halliday, M. (2010), *Literacy: Reading, writing and children's literature* (4th edn), Oxford University Press, Melbourne.

Zammit, K. (2008), 'Under construction: A world without walls', keynote paper presented at the ASLA Online III Virtual Conference: Digital literacy strand, 5–26 May.

—— (in progress), 'Reading multimodal texts: Using think alouds to develop visual literacy skills'.

The Authors and Publisher gratefully acknowledge the use of the following copyright material in this publication.

While every effort has been made to trace and acknowledge copyright and ownership of all included works, should any infringement have occurred, the publishers offer their apologies and invite copyright owners to contact them.

Australian Curriculum and Reporting Authority (2011), *English as an Additional Language or Dialect: Teacher Resource V.1.1*. Retrieved September 3, 2011, from http://www.acara.edu.au/verve/_resources/EALD_teacher_resource.pdf. Text copyright © Australian Curriculum and Reporting Authority August 2011. Reproduced by permission of the Australian Curriculum and Reporting Authority.

Cruickshank, K. (2008). *Oral language, literacy and EAL*. Paper presented at ESLIN Sharing Group, Sydney, Australia, Text copyright © Ken Cruickshank 2008, Reproduced by permission of Ken Cruickshank, Associate Professor in TESOL, Faculty of Education and Social Work, University of Sydney, Australia.

ESL learner diversity diagram © DET NSW

Morgan, N. & Saxton, J. (1987), *Teaching Drama: A mind of many wonders (4th edn)*. Hutchinson: London.

Taronga Zoo Interactive Zoo Map, viewed 3 September 2011, http://taronga.org.au/sites/all/modules/custom/taronga/taronga_map/taronga_map_print.html#zoom=18#lat=-33.84330818912546#lng=151.24134957790375#openmap=true. Image copyright © Taronga Zoo Sydney. Permission to reprint this image granted by Taronga Conservation Society Australia.

Unsworth, L. (1993), 'Evaluating Reading Materials' in B. Derewianka (ed) *Language Assessment in Primary Schools*, Sydney: Harcourt Brace Jovanovich.

Levesque, J.P. et al (2003), Disruption of the CXCR4/CXCL12 chemotactic interaction during hematopoietic stem cell mobilization induced by GCSF or cyclophosphamide, PubMed, 2003 Jan; 111(2); 187-96.

West, H. & Reid, K. (2011). *ESL Matters*, Catholic Education Office, Sydney. Text copyright © Kerrie Reid and Helen West 2011; Catholic Education Office, Sydney. Reproduced by permission of Kerrie Reid, Curriculum Adviser (ESL Primary), Catholic Education Office, Sydney.

Winch, G., Johnston, R., March, P., Ljungdahl, L. & Holliday, M. (2010), 'A Model of Reading', *Literacy: Reading, Writing and Children's Literature (4th edn)*. Oxford University Press, Melbourne.

INDEX

(Numbers in italics indicate figures or tables.)

Aboriginal and Torres Strait Islander students   21, 22, 31, 43
academic language   2, 112, 133
   proficiency   1, 2, 9, 10, 11, 15, 36
   registers   11
   writing and 115–27
ACARA: *English as Additional Language or Dialect: Teacher Resource V1.1*   6, 11, 12–14, 15, 31, 33, 39, 75, 171
active listening   48, 51
additional language learning   5
   for an authentic purpose   5
   and importance of good models   6, 53, 141
   and importance of first language maintenance   19–20
   and importance of reinforcement   6, 53
   and importance of risk-taking   52, 53, 126, 133, 134, 145
   and importance of teacher/student interactions   51–52
   and importance of supportive stress free environment   35
   integrating across all curriculum areas   51
   pedagogical conditions for   29–47, 142
   theories of   6–9, 34–35, 36, *37*, 49
   see also Beginning English phase, Consolidating English phase, Developing English phase, Emerging English phase
adverbs   122, *123*

assessment   4, 34, 38, 39, 57, 115
   cloze passages as assessment tools   124
   self-assessment   126–27
audience   110–11
Australia
   Australian Curriculum   *see* ACARA
   cultural and linguistic diversity within   30

back-to-back viewing   *63*
backward referencing   98
barrier games   54–60, *120*
basic interpersonal communication skills   9
Beginning English phase   12–13, 54, 140
beliefs and values   33
Bingo   *62*
brainstorming   92, 93, *164*, 165

carers   *see* parents and carers
Carnine Order   80
challenge/support patterns   *41, 42*
challenging work   39, 175
charting knowledge   93
circumstances   119, 122, *123*
classroom talk and initiation, response, feedback   51
clines   121, 148
cloze activities   66–67, 98–101, 122–24
   as assessment tools   124
   constructing   99
   example   100, *101*
   implementing   99

cognitive academic language proficiency   9
collaborative group work   *see* group work
communication, modes of   8, *50*, *114*, 110, 156
   communicative activities   53–60
comparison   65, 141, 142
comprehensible input   53
comprehensible output   53
Consolidating English phase   14, 35, 54, 86, 89, 158
context and language learning   36–37, *37*, 48, 49, 53, 109
contrived language   84–85
conversational English   2, 8, 9, 15, 36, 112, 133
counselling   24, 25
critical literacy   134
crosswords   57–60
cueing systems   81–82, 84
cultural diversity   30, 31, 33, 109, 127, 172
cultural misunderstandings   30, 33–34, 80
culturally inclusive practices   30–34, 47

debating   107, 134
debriefing   145–46, 165
decoding   20, 25, 79–80, 88, 137
deconstructing text   118
de-roling   146, *see also* debriefing
describing   111, 116–17
Developing English phase   13–14, 35, 54, 64, 78, 86, 89, 134, 137, 150, 158, 162

dictogloss 68–70
digital animation 105
digital texts 76, 78
dimensions of language proficiency 37, 49
discourse of power 44, 45
disengagement, academic 43, 44, 45, 87, 151, 170
disrupted schooling 9
drama 50, 105, 133–70
   communicating through 142
   emotional investment in 145
   and the FGP's student engagement framework 142–43
   and friendship groups 145
   and physical space 144
   program for *How to heal a broken wing* 160–70
   time needed for 170
   and writing 150
   see also dramatic play, educational drama, Readers' Theatre, role to communicate, sculpting, still images, questioning in role, role walk, thought tracking
dramatic play 35, 138
   at school 140–41
   and writing 139, 142
Drop Everything and Listen to Stories 78
Drop Everything and Read 78

EAL/D 2, 3, 11, *see also* EL learners
early childhood
   and drama 35, 138–9, 140–41
   and language learning 29, 142, 171
   learning contexts 29, 30
   learners 20
   and learning to read 84
educational drama 138–39, 142
electronic print media 108, 149
EL learners 3, 11, 127, 171–72
   diversity among 15–19, 22, 28, 30
   from minority backgrounds 30
   principles for teaching 173
   survey for 16–18, 19
ELL *see* EL learners
Emerging English phase 13, 54, 105, 140
empathy 145, 150, 156, 163
enactment 138, 142, 150
engagement, academic 42–46, 44, 45, 151, 172
   Fair Go Project's pedagogical framework for 42–46, 172
English
   academic 1, 2, 9, 112, 133
   conversational 2, 8, 9, 15, 36, 112, 133
   in electronic print media 108
   language learning in maths 65
   language learning progression 11
   teaching 2
   written literacy in 25
equality of speaker status 52
ESL 2, *see also* EL learners
excursions 28
explaining 111

face-to-face language 7
Fair Go Project
   definition of engagement 43–44, 46, 172
   and drama 142–43
   pedagogical framework for engagement 42–46, 44,
feedback 126
field 6, 7, 9, 11, 110
first language
   competence in 19–20, 171
   grammar of 22
   learning of 5, 48
   literacy in 12, 20, 25, 29, 79, 171
   maintenance of 20, 28, 32, 79
   teacher knowledge of 21–22, 28
   as a tool for learning a second language 48
floor storming 93
flow charts 102, 124, 125
forward referencing 98
fossilisation 9–10, 171
four roles of the reader 86–88
friendship groups 52, 145
frozen moment *see* still images

genres 6, 7, 79, 127
glogs 73, 74
grammar 64, 66, 70, 117–24, 100–01
   and EL learners 110
   grammatical cues 82
   visual literacy grammar 95
graphic organisers 66–74, 101–04
graphophonics 77, 79, 80, 82
group work 35–36, 52–53, 54, 64, 65, 66, 120, 124, 125, 145, 155, 175
   importance of for EL learners 75
   importance of using friendship groups in 52, 145

3H strategy 97, 98
high order thinking 10, 50
home language *see* first language
home/school connection 25–28
hot seating *see* questioning in role
How to heal a broken wing 95
   drama program for 160–70
   language learning features of tasks in the pedagogical sequence 174

imagination 133, 138, 143, 172
immigration experiences 22–28
Indigenous students 21, 22, 31, 43
inferential thinking 154
informal language 48–49
information gap activities 54–74
initiation, response, feedback pattern 51
inner speech 49, 50, 142
instructing 111
internet 76
interpreters, trained 26, 27
interviews with parents or carers 25–28
   conducting the interview 26–27
   considerations for arranging 26
   seating arrangements for 27
   using trained interpreters 26, 27
   what might be discussed 27–28

L1 *see* first language
L2 *see* additional language learning
language
   authentic 84–85, 133, 138, 172
   competence 112
   comprehensible input 38–39
   and cultural profile sample survey 16–18, 19, 25
   function 50
   intake 39
   productive 146
   receptive 48, 150
   situational context of 6, 7
   sociocultural context of 6
   uptake 39
   see also field, genre, mode, register, spoken language, tenor, text, written language

Index

language learning *see* additional language learning
LBOTE students *see* EL learners
learning in the challenge zone 39, 41
learning to read and reading to learn 77–107
 and importance of repetition 78
 and importance of using well-written texts 81, 82–85
 process of 79–90
 reading *with* students 78
lexical density 7
linguistic diversity 30, 33, 127, 172
listening skills 68–70
low SES students 29–33, 43, 46, 47, 108, 175
 and academic engagement 44, *45*

mainstream teachers 1
margin questions 96
matrix organisers 66–68, 101
 Australian animal information matrix 67–68
 junk mail matrix 68
 weather vocabulary matrix 66–67
message abundance 120, 124
metacognitive awareness 118
metaxis 138, 143
migrants 22
mind maps 102, *103*, *154*, *161*
modality 148
mode 6, 7
mode continuum 8, *50*, *114*, 156
modelled reading 78, 94–95
modelling language 49, 78, 134, 141
music 84, 105

names 20–21
narrative 89–90, 134
negotiating 111
NESB 2, *see also* EL learners
nominalisation 8
nonsense words 82, 84
non-verbal language 142, 143, 148, 150
noticing 38

onset and rime 83
open ended simulations 133–34
oracy 48–75, 171
 definition of 48
 and learning sequences 50
 posing questions to advance 70–74

 and reading 77, 80
 oral reading 88–90, 134, 137–38
ordering text 122
outer speech 49, 50, 142

pair work 52–54, 67, 121, 124, *see also* group work
Palmer Plan, the 70–74, 90, 161
paralinguistic language 7
parallel improvisation 164, 168, *169*
paraphrasing 95, *see also* reformulating language
parents and carers 25, 48
 and learning to read 78
 and educational drama 138
partner work *see* pair work
pedagogical conditions for language learning 29–47, 142
persuading 111
phases of English language learning *see* Beginning English phase, Consolidating English phase, Developing English phase, Emerging English phase
phonology 81–82
play-based learning 35, 171–72
playground English *see* conversational English
podcasts 78
poems 84, 134
point of view 162–63
positive self identity 31
prediction 35, 84, 90, 91, 93, *94*, 95
prepositions 122, *123*
print
 directionality of 21, 79
 print based texts 76, 78
 print literacy 12, 79
 Western print world 108
prior knowledge 34–35, 91
 ascertaining 29
 building on 29, 34–35, 38, 91–94, 142
 and sculpting 147–49
procedure writing 118, *119*, 122
productive language 48, 146, 150
progressive brainstorm *92*, 93
pronunciation 137

quality and quantity in teaching and learning 172–75
questioning in role 156–59
questions 90, 95

Readers' Theatre 84, 106, 134–38, *136*
 instructions for 137
 making scripts 134–35
 staging 136
 using as an oral reading strategy 137–38
reading 76–107, 171
 aloud 80, 88–90, 134, 137–38
 challenges 77
 and comprehension 86–90, 134, 137
 critical 88
 and decoding 20, 25, 79–80, 88, 137
 independent silent 78
 learning to 77–90
 modelled 78, 94–95
 model of 87
 and print directionality 21, 79
 repeated 84, 134
 roles of the reader 86–88
 sequence 91–107
 on screen 76–77
 and sculpting 149–51
 silent 88–90
 to learn 77–78, 90–107
 with students 78
reading sequence 91–107
 coming back to the text 96–104
 getting into the text 94–96
 getting ready for the text 91–94
 going beyond the text 105–07
recasting language *see* paraphrasing, reformulating language
receptive language 48, 150
recounts 111, *132*
reflecting on learning 126–27, 143, 145–46, 165
reformulating language 49, 51, 52, 141, *see also* paraphrasing
refugees 9, 22–28, 43, 143
 circumstances of refugee children 23–24
 previous educational experiences of refugee children 24–25
 refugee organisations 23, 24
register 6, 7, 138–39
religion 21, 29
repetition 120, 134
responding 111
right to remain silent 35
rime 81, 83

risk-taking, importance of in learning 52, 53, 126, 133, 134, 145
role play 133, 138
role walk 156, *157*
Roman script 21, 80
rubrics 125, 126
running record tests 89

scaffolding 36–42, 46, 52, 53, 58
    controlled support 38–39, 40
    cycle 39, 40, 127, *128–31*
    definition of 38
    guided support 39, 40
    independent support 39, 40
    reading sequence 91–107
schema
    definition of 33
    schema theory 33–34
    schematic knowledge 80, 88
school counsellors 25
scripts (Readers' Theatre) 134–36
sculpting 91, 146–51
    to consolidate meaning 150–51
    to explore empathy and apathy 163
    how to do it 146–47
    and linking to prior knowledge 147–49
    use while reading a book 149
    viewing 148
    and writing 148–49
self-assessment 126–27
semantic cues 82
semantic maps 66
sentence building 116–17
spoken language 8, 110, 146, *see also* informal language
Spot the Difference 60, 62, 64, *65*
still images 98, 151–59, 165
    planning 151–52, 168
    parallel improvisation 164, 168, *169*
    reflection and debriefing 165
    showing and viewing 165
    stepping out from 165, *166–67*
    use of in history lessons 156–59
    use of to interpret a scene from a book 152, *153*, 154
    use of to sequence key events in a story 155–56

stress free environments, importance of 35
student background information 16–18, 19–22, 77
summarising 90
Super Six Strategies 90
support
    affective 41, 46
    challenge/support patterns *41, 42*
    supported learning *see* scaffolding
    supportive environments, importance of 35, 38

tableau *see* still images
talk
    and drama 133, 143
    for learning 35, 49, 51
    importance of teacher/student talk 52
    to support writing 111–12
    talking buddies 51
Taronga zoo map and clue cards 60, *61*
tasks *41, 42,* 43
    authentic 30, 42, 80, 82, 133
teacher guidance 52
teaching and learning sequence 114–27, *128–31,* 172–75, *174, see also* scaffolding
technical language *see* academic language proficiency
tenor 6, 7, 110–11
texts 6, 7
    authentic 82–83, 84, 85–86, 105
    building knowledge about 117–24
    guided practice of 120–24
    independent practice of 125
    innovation on 36, 105, *106*
    linking to topic 117
    of literary merit 82–84, 105
    multilingual 32
    multimodal 155
    purpose of 112
    reconstruction of 104, 122, 123–24
    reflection on 126–27
    repetitive 84
    strips 122
    types of 110, 111–12, 112, *113*
theatre *see* drama, Readers' Theatre
think-alouds 95

think-pair-share strategy 51
think time 51
thought tracking 154
topic 114, 117–18, 127
    building topic knowledge 38, 87, 117–19, 116, 172
    and purpose 117–18
Torres Strait Islander students *see* Indigenous students
translation services *see* interpreters, trained
trauma 23–24, 25
true or false statements 97–98

Uninterrupted Sustained Silent Reading 78

Venn diagrams 66, *102*
verbal interaction *see* talk
visual arts response *106,* 107
vocabulary 10, 116, 121, 139
vodcasts 78
vowel sounds 81

words
    authentic 82–83
    word clines 121, 148
writing 108–132, 171
    academic 11527
    attributes of a successful writer *109,* 109–11
    and audience 110
    explicit teaching of 108
    learning to write 108
    a procedure 118, *119*
    purpose for 110
    from sculpting 148–49
    written language 8, 110, 114
writing sequence 115–27
    building knowledge about the text 117–19
    building topic knowledge 116
    guided practice of text 120–25
    independent practice of text 125–26
    reflection and self-assessment 126–27

Zone of Proximal Development 36, 42, 53